THE BIBLE
AND MODERN MAN

Erich Gompertz

Translated by Palmer Hilty

106445

FREDERICK UNGAR PUBLISHING CO.
NEW YORK

Translated from the German
Sagt die Bibel die Wahrheit?

Printed in the United States of America

Library of Congress Catalog Card No. 65-19170

FOREWORD

Since the day of the Greek nature speculators from about 400 B.C., two opposed views about the world have confronted mankind. According to one, nature is in control of a deity or deities concerned with human welfare; according to the other, it is a system operating by impersonal laws inherent in it, indifferent to man's hopes and fears. The first is espoused by supernaturalists, who believe in a god or gods more or less amenable to prayer and persuasion, the second by naturalists (humanists), who detect no evidence of any god or gods and find no cosmic car attentive to their pleas and petitions.

According to the first view, a divinity made and sustains the universe and may interfere in events to fulfill its plans or the wishes of the faithful. This deity, or trinitarian committee of them, just happened to exist. According to the second view, the stuff of the universe has always existed in some self-contained potentiality. It just happened to exist, being completely intelligible in itself (including the supernatural beliefs) and only in itself. No discernible consequences in nature attend belief in a deity; to baptize the integrating process of the universe and call it God is otiose.

In the naturalist tradition the world operating according to inexorable laws is not a set of bleak formulas but a vast encompassing life. Nature is not a congeries of small particles whirling in space. It is rather a yearly renewal of life, an immense fertility bringing forth life, including that of man with his infinite capacity for joy, beauty, happiness, but also for sorrow and wretchedness, especially when mismanaged. The most generous values and happy creations of man grow out of the same primal nature as do stone and planet, starfish and palm. The lowliest sea urchin and the most inspiring human hope and most awe-filled piety come out of the selfsame cradle of eternal nature.

Erich Gompertz is heart and soul a part of this naturalist tradition. He is one of those noble souls who have discarded ancestral myths and achieved a serene humanistic outlook. He has nothing in common·with those who moan about the alien world that science pictures or with those who proclaim that the soul is restless until it rests in a god. He holds that man is rooted in nature and that yearning for heavenly hyacinths beyond his home in nature is sentimental posturing or delusion. Man's deepest and highest commitments are rooted in nature and the human heart, ultimately one. The free spirit of man, so noble in reason and infinite in faculty, finds its divine possibilities only in nature.

Though Mr. Gompertz comes from a family noted for academic scholars, he himself has never held a university post. Instead, he has been a successful business man and manufacturer in Hannover, Germany, and a generous philanthropist. He is now in his mid-eighties and has only just given up his business.

It may not be amiss to add that Mr. Gompertz was a fugitive in Belgium during the Second World War, years he devoted exclusively to scholarly pursuits. After the war, many German Jews who had found asylum in Belgium were imprisoned as German nationals. Mr. Gompertz at once addressed himself to Belgian authorities and to the British occupation forces and was permitted to form a committee of fugitives composed chiefly of German Jews, who procured the release of these imprisoned Jews. He was also instrumental in getting support from the International Refugee Organization to help needy Jews get a new start in life in Belgium.

When asked for a succinct statement of his fundamental beliefs, Mr. Gompertz replied that he is a freethinker, has socialist leanings in his approach to political and economic problems, and is a humanist in his philosophy of life, motivated above all by pity for the suppressed and exploited. He said, "I find the noblest life in helping others."

Mr. Gompertz has been, as it were, a philosopher without portfolio, with a sustained interest in defining and promoting the good life and humane living. Though no starry-eyed romantic, he does hope that the effort to make a more enlightened culture prevail will give men a better understanding of their destiny in nature and more determination to live as brothers in truth and in peace.

The Greeks called a man a barbarian who was content to believe without reasons and live without freedom. Read with a bit of sympathy and good will, this book will help to rally men against surrendering to superstition and delusion, which destroy the stimulus of freedom and the life of reason. It will arouse reflective interest in the nature of the universe and man's lot in it. It is one more significant signpost pointing the way to a more humane and liberated future, an enlightened naturalism, the goal mature minds inevitably approach. The heart and mind build slow, but build they will.

PALMER HILTY

Washington State University
Pullman, Washington

CONTENTS

INTRODUCTION

The universe, without discoverable beginning or end in space or time, runs the cycle of all that happens according to impersonal principles inherent within it. In its infinitude the universe sloughs off the concepts of number and old age as meaningless; yet all things existing and embedded in the immeasurable cosmos are given to change, to growth and decay. These unending processes tossed up man as a by-product and endowed him with a mind that will not rest from searching and questing after knowledge about his nature and destiny in the universe. In every age he labors to gain new insights, groping forward over truth and error.

Though it is unlikely that we shall ever have more than a general knowledge of man's earliest intellectual life and religious systems, we are fortunate to have records giving us a fairly clear notion of some ideas and attitudes men evolved in bygone millennia. Ancient tomb paintings of Egypt are a precious record. On the walls and partitions of the burial chambers are incised hymns to the gods of death. Marvelous burial objects of four thousand years ago testify to high artistic taste and power. Glorious works of art were composed and carved in those ancient times. The Rosetta stone inscribed and set up about 200 B.C. in honor of the young Egyptian ruler, Ptolemy Epiphanes, renders us great service. It was discovered in 1799 during Napoleon's Egyptian campaign. Of the three different scripts chiseled on this stone, only Greek was known. The Frenchman Champollion had the good fortune to decipher the hieroglyphic script, which paralleled the Greek text. This feat has given an insight into the ancient Egyptian world unsurpassed for grandeur and beauty. The religion and culture of Assyria was opened to us by Georg Friedrich Grotefend, who deciphered cuneiform writing around 1815.

1

No richer or more precious body of information on any ancient religion has been handed down to us than that on the divine world of Egypt. No ancient people made a more impressive pictorial representation of the gods and, especially, of the afterworld. In the sun god, Aton, the sun enjoyed the highest veneration as the principle of life. Osiris was the all-powerful god of the kingdom of the dead, and with him were linked the Egyptian myths about resurrection and redemption.

Even two thousand years before the time of Jesus, Horus, son of Osiris and Isis, was sent to earth as a bringer of salvation, according to the Egyptian hieroglyphic texts. The goddess Isis appeared in different shapes, among others as a cow, as which she suckled the boy Messiah. In ancient Babylon, the son of god who brought redemption to man was called Isu. When he had fulfilled this task, he again became a god and ascended to heaven.

The history of comparative religion has other parallels between the content of old beliefs and still living faiths. The interconnection of old and new ways of belief becomes intelligible when they are traced back to their common root. New matter for creeds is always created by thinkers, but it is always based on nature, whose phenomena we must try to explain. The ancient questions "Whence come I and whither do I go?" imperatively demand a reply. Traditionally men have peopled the world with gods and have expected answers and help from them, sometimes even deliverance from death. If man feels no need for redemption, as in ancient Greece, he finds his fulfillment in the happiest life possible on earth. One expression of this ideal is that all men are brothers.

Even though veneration of the gods assumed an important place in the ancient world, yet sufficient freedom generally remained to regard the world in new ways. Intolerance and arrogance on behalf of one's own beliefs are not the hallmarks of the religions of antiquity; they first became prominent in the great revealed religions of later times.

The varieties of religion in India, above all, illustrate the concept of development. From the earliest times, Indian religions have occupied a most important position in the structure of human belief. Standing on a lofty ethical plane, ancient Indian thinkers and religious philosophers were conscious throughout of the limitations set upon them by time, even in religion. Their religious books and texts testify to this. Their greatest national epic, the *Mahabharata,* has this to say about the holy text of the old Indian Veda:

> The authority of the law rests upon what the scholars
> of the Veda draw from it, but the words of the Veda
> fade away in the course of the aging of the world, as
> the writings of the Veda themselves teach us.

The religion of this period is gone, but its great thoughts live on even today under new forms which are truly worthy of preservation by humanity.

Likewise, the lofty spiritual creations of ancient China have survived in part among the Chinese, thus preserving one of the oldest civilizations on earth. The revolution of 1928 struck a shattering blow at the old authoritarian thought of Confucius, on which China had perhaps too long relied in the rejection of any progress; but when the country's anachronistic political system fell, a legitimate sacrifice to progress, the moral good of old Chinese customs was not abandoned. If mankind in the not too distant future turns to the erection of the great edifices of security, peace, and happiness for all, then the foundations will be obtainable from the spiritual treasures of China, India, and Greece.

All the religions of the past contain germs of thought still valid today and worthy of application. The basis of all human institutions is and remains the desire for life lived in peace, freedom, and happiness. Thanks to the uniformity of human sense organs and perceptions, irrespective of space and time, this ethical base is essentially immutable. Even the religious communism of the Persian Sassanids in the third and fourth centuries of our era serves no other purpose. It appeared to them that the desired state of happiness lay in the common enjoyment of all available goods. The ideal of possessing all values in common has been a factor in shaping society throughout millennia right up to the present.

To the vanished religions which exerted an influence in the first century of our era belongs the veneration and cult of Mithras.

Mithras originated in India and was elevated to a sun god in Persia. His triumphal progress extended deep into European regions. Older than Christianity and eventually competing with it, Mithraism held to revelation and redemption, as did the earlier Egyptian religion of Osiris. It is the same cycle of myth that was found in Egypt and later in Christianity. The god Mithras sent his son to earth as a man and proclaimed through him the message of the road to salvation. Afterward he returned to god the father in heaven. Mithraism also believed in the Holy Spirit, which poured itself into the faithful, who then participated in the immortality of the god. Christianity later appropriated similar beliefs.

The ancient Egyptian gods, the Indo-Persian Mithras, and a myriad other deities with their temples, priests, and rituals have vanished. They served their time and changed into new forms. Out of the old the new takes shape. To this cycle of being, of dissolution and re-creation there is no exception—not even for the lofty cathedrals of faith conceived of the human spirit and expressed in holy scriptures.

No religion can escape these vicissitudes. The final chapter of all existing structures of supernatural faith draws ever nearer. Christianity, the chief representative of monotheism, is today of significant influence only in Western Europe and America. Modern science and Marxian socialism are destroying it. The cardinal belief in the divine birth of Jesus is found only among the dwindling ranks of orthodox believers; for the foundations of the New Testament have long been questionable. The recent discovery of what are called the Dead Sea Scrolls will probably only contribute to the erosion of this belief.

In 1947 a young Bedouin goatherd accidentally stumbled upon some vases containing rolls of papyrus in a hitherto unknown cave in a cliff. Technical experts recognize the writing on these scrolls as an old pre-Christian Hebrew script. The first discovery led to the systematic exploration of unknown caves and shattered ruins and brought to light a whole library of such documents from the Jericho district. This library lay hidden in these caves, preserved for almost two thousand years in stone jars. The scrolls contain texts of Isaiah and, above all, the commentary on

Habakkuk. They found their way by devious routes from the chief center of discovery at Qumran to the Jewish university at Jerusalum and elsewhere.

The scrolls show that the life of Jesus parallels that of a Jewish sectary who lived about a century before Jesus. He is referred to in the texts as the "Teacher of Righteousness." He is said to have been tortured as a prophet. He is called "the servant of God." He preaches the duty of "living for virtue" and regards himself as the Messiah who is to free the world from sin. At the "End of the Ages" he will come to be the supreme judge. He was in conflict with the priests and was condemned and executed in 63 B.C. His death occurred in the reign of the Jewish king and high priest Aristobulus II (67–63 B.C.).

Christianity owes its origin to neither Bethlehem nor to Nazareth. Its spiritual content is partially the work of a Jewish prototype who lived before the birth of the Jew called Jesus. The latter apparently chose this "Teacher of Righteousness" as his model. The texts from the ruins of Qumran are unambiguous in this respect.

It was not to be expected that theologians would come to terms with this interpretation supported chiefly by a learned Frenchman with the concurrence of other scholars. Learned spokesmen of the Christian faith will understandably do everything possible to prove the untenability of this conception. And nobody will blame a believing Christian for still regarding Jesus as the sole representative of the doctrine of redemption. Practicing Jews must also be allowed to think that Christian teaching is of Jewish origin in some essential points. In any event, the controversy about the elucidation of these finds is not yet concluded. Only objective examination such as one can hardly expect from the public champions of Christianity must have the last word.

As ever in the creation of new forms, so here the lofty ideas of a noble and virtuous man are later adopted in shaping a new system. The true origin and its author are concealed. The "imitator" is regarded as the originator.

Such is the Jesus myth of the Gospels in which a noble Jew long dead, the "Teacher of Righteousness," again takes shape in the Christian savior.

1. RELIGION AND GEOGRAPHY

Out of the mists of the past, out of the sandy deserts of Meso--potamia and Palestine and the ruined mounds of a once blooming life, the Jewish religion projects right into our own time. It is far and away the oldest and therefore the most venerable form of religion to survive out of the meditation and reflection of the past three thousand years. Furthermore it is not only a patriarch among the great forms of creed but it is also bursting with youth.

Millions of people still carry with them a text derived from the early days of their history. They use this and have their prayerbooks written (and since Gutenberg, printed) in a form which has stayed unchanged for over a thousand years. To them the right-angled Hebrew letters seem sanctified, not only because their religious texts are published and read in it, but even more because the book declares visibly and audibly that the living are linked with an ancient line of predecessors.

Moreover, the two latest living religions are rooted in Judaism. Jesus, the awaited Messiah of his earliest Jewish followers, was turned into the savior-cult God of the Christians, and the Old Testament constitutes the bulk of their holy book. The Bible and Judaism were the chief source of the faith and theology of Islam, created by Mohammed in the seventh century. There is hardly another example in human history of such a vital tradition.

For three thousand years pious Jewish fathers have taught their sons and daughters this tradition of their ancient people, even if it does not tally with historical events. For these men of the ancient faith historical truth is not essential. These men have come down to us, almost unchanged, right out of Biblical times. Without entertaining any doubt about the words of Scripture they are intellectual contemporaries of the Egyptian Pharaohs, their oppressors, and likewise of the vanished world empires of Babylon, Assyria, Persia, Greece, and Rome. That is unique and magnificent, but it is also the root of the tragedy of Jewry.

The memory of empires that have faded from history lives on in the great figures they brought forth. They are portraits of mighty peoples and thus preserve them in memory. How striking therefore is the fact that Israel continued as a human community for thousands of years and remained united through a common faith, while history practically passed it by.

If one is to credit the ancient world surrounding and contemporary with these people, they produced scarcely anything worthy of report. That this small kingdom, like others, suffered destruction as a political entity accords with natural historical processes; but even during its political independence it never attained any importance in its own narrow geographical setting to distinguish it from neighboring states. From a historical point of view, Israel never emerged prominently from its surroundings. It was only occasionally and briefly capable of preserving its political independence. Only after losing their political freedom did the Jews accomplish their great inner religious revolution and produce the monotheism which its supporters carried forth in the Diaspora and preserved until the present. The significance of Judaism lies in this and in the value of its effects as worked on Christianity and Islam.

The three revealed religions follow one another at comparatively brief intervals. The Yahweh religion of the Jews in its essential and broad outlines had not begun in the time of the patriarchs and of Moses, but arose after the fall of the kingdom in the sixth century B.C., during the captivity in Babylon. All three creeds, therefore, took their essential form during a period of about one thousand years. The cradles of all three lie in the orbit of the Near East. From the fact that Moses, Jesus, and Mohammed were Semites, some conclude that the Semites have a special talent for evolving ideas of salvation and notions about human happiness; but that is an invalid inference.

The fates of people can be understood in terms of the potentialities for life offered to them by their environment. Convulsive revolutionary events in the life of a people over long periods of history produce internal structural changes, and these precipitate themselves in a change of the object of religious worship. How unsettled, therefore, the population of the region of Palestine and Arabia must have been, since it produced at brief intervals three savior figures from whom three world religions are derived. This shows that people undergo a natural reaction when their countries are exposed to heavy blows by their location and climate. Nothing mitigates their hard lot; neither rulers nor gods can avert disaster. All other help being denied, only a new savior can bring salvation. Thus religions arise. Moses springs out of Egyptian oppression; the God Yahweh out of the sufferings inflicted by Assyrian, Babylonian, and Seleucid tyranny; the "Teacher of Righteousness," the prototype of Jesus, out of the cruelties of war and revolution in his country; and Mohammed out of the civil wars of polytheistic Arab tribes.

The home of these founders of religions is the small area forming the junction of three continents—Asia, Africa, and Europe —between the Mediterranean and the Persian Gulf; its center of gravity, Palestine, is a north-south link between Europe and Africa and at the same time an isthmus for Asiatic aggression. In this unique geographical position of Palestine and of the Near East lies the key to its historical and spiritual nature. It is the eagerly coveted plot of land for the possession and control of which the peoples have struggled from early historical times up to the present.

The Palestinian land-link never knew long periods of calm. Here the Egyptians were already fighting five thousand years ago with the native population in order to keep open the communications with Lebanon, which they wanted securely under their control for the sake of exploiting and removing its cedars, the best building material for palaces and temple buildings.

About 2550 B.C. the Semitic prince Sargon I, king of Babylonia and Akkadian founder of the empire, founded the first world empire. He conquered the entire Near East and ruled everywhere from the Mediterranean Sea in the west to the Persian Gulf in the east and from Armenia in the north to Arabia in the south. In repeated campaigns, accompanied by every kind of atrocity against the innocent inhabitants, Egypt tried to establish dominion over the Hittites and the Assyrians. In the course of their long history, Assyrians fought Babylonians for the possession of Palestine. Small kingdoms united into a league, to which Israel and Judah belonged, and waged war against their common foes. Both these Jewish states succumbed in a struggle against the Assyrians and Babylonians. Palestinians were deported from their homes to foreign lands and were abandoned to the whims of their conquerors, without prospect of deliverance.

The Persians approached out of Asia, thrusting over the bridge that linked the world, in an attempt to conquer Europe and North Africa. Persian world empire gave place to Greek. In 334 B.C. Alexander the Great began his mighty march of conquest, after bursting out of Macedonia with his army. This march led him over the land-links toward Persia and India. Roman imperialism, which relieved the Greeks of world empire, had the most dire consequences for Jewish Palestine. The long suffering endured by the Jews neared its climax under Aristobulus II and the half-Jewish King Herod, installed by the grace of Rome. War, fear, and hunger were the whips with which the population, accustomed to trouble for many generations, was scourged by its new tormentors. Finally the time was fulfilled.

In the last lap of the century-long oppression of all human rights, there sprang from the blood-soaked soil the ideas of salvation and redemption which crystallized in Jesus of Nazareth. So this terrible period of a classical land of affliction ended in a healing act for suffering humanity, through the creation of a new faith which aims forever to remove injustice and violence from the relationship of man to man. The newly created Christianity founded its morality for mankind on Leviticus 19:18, "You shall love your neighbor as yourself."

A people that spends its days in assured well-being does not produce savior figures or new religions. Its concern is to maintain the *status quo.* It guards itself against changes in spiritual values and the content of its creed. An example of this is the ancient Rome of the *Pax Romana,* the Roman peace, under the shelter of which the golden age that began with Emperor Augustus and the beloved heathen gods unrolled for the first two centuries of our era. This brilliant period of antiquity is crowned by the

names of three poets—Vergil, Ovid, and Horace. The people
were so happy that they accorded the emperor divine honors.

In times of welfare no upheavals occur. A new faith is created
out of spiritual revolution born of hardship and despair from
which men find no other deliverance. New spiritual movements
and programs for improving human relations always spring from
such a background. This demonstrates an unwritten law of mankind that displays itself whenever the sufferings of a great community reach their peak. The creation of new forms of faith by
men is always an act of revolution.

2. THE DOCUMENTATION

One who visits the British Museum in London or the museum in Cairo and other collections is ever astonished at the number and beauty of the productions of the earliest past known to history. In our twentieth century, the ground of Egypt has restored to the light of day part of the treasures which the makers had determined should forever be delivered into the lap of the earth.

The mortal remains of the mighty history of Egypt, of Rameses II and Tutankhamen and other pharaohs, stand forth before the gaping crowd, taken impiously from their coffins, wholly unconscious of the sublimity of the moment. When buried, these rulers were so skillfully embalmed that their external bodily forms are still preserved. They were concealed as mummies under the all-covering sand shroud of the desert, equipped in their burial chambers with an amazing wealth of accessories such as thrones, jewelry, trunks, beds, chariots, and other objects, all executed with the consummate artistry which popular belief deemed essential for the use of the dead in their kingdom. Written papyrus scrolls, funerary inscriptions on tomb walls, and coffins were added, telling of the life of the departed and giving information about their religion, their prayers, and about the world of the old Egyptian Gods.

The distant past of the great Nile kingdom lies open to gazers moved more by idle curiosity than by a craving for knowledge. Thanks to "free admission on Sundays and holidays," the crowd jostles past these venerable potentates and passes by the statue of Pharaoh Amenhotep IV, the first man to proclaim the sun to be the one and only omnipotent sovereign of the world, although Userkaf had eight centuries previously introduced the sun cult. His wife arouses more wonder than he. Her alabaster bust has been taken out of its grave. It is painted with realistic colors and almost looks alive. It leaves an indelible impression. It is the charming Queen Nefertiti of whom her husband, Amenhotep IV, said in the obituary which has been discovered: "Nefertiti who remains living, healthy, and fresh with youth unto all eternity." The phrase is still valid today, after 3,500 years.

A wealth of monuments preserves the period of the Assyrian and Babylonian world empires, as well as their princes, peoples, and opinions. Among them the great Babylonian king, Hammurabi (ca. 1800 B.C.), is the most prominent. From him is derived the obelisk with a cuneiform inscription which a French archaeologist discovered in the Persian town of Susa in 1902. This monument, now in the Louvre in Paris, displays the symbol of fertility, a phallus, and portrays a scene in which Hammurabi stands before the sun god and receives from him the laws for mankind. On the stone these laws are published verbatim. This unique codification of wise and righteous thoughts, called the "Code of Hammurabi," remained in force for over a thousand years in its native Assyria and Babylonia and regulated with an ideal sense of justice the relation of man to man.

Later generations built legal systems on these foundations. Most important, the legislation promulgated in the continuation of the "Ten Commandments" (Exodus, chapters 21-23) displays striking parallels with the considerably older Code of Hammurabi. The scene represented on the obelisk, showing a god handing the laws to Hammurabi, was imitated much later by the writers of the Bible in representing God giving the tables of the law to Moses on Mount Sinai.

Other extensive cuneiform inscriptions of the Near East have recently been recovered in Tell-el-Amarna, the residence of Amenhotep IV, King of Egypt (ca. 1375–1358), He is also known to history as Akhenaten or Ikhnaton. Letters and memoranda in the form of clay tablets and cylinders recount the history of those old days of the fifteenth and fourteenth centuries B.C. A further library of some ten thousand clay cuneiform tablets has been dug up in our time out of the ruins of the old Hittite capital, the modern Boghaskoi, near the Turkish capital Ankara.

It provides new and valuable historical material for the oldest Mesopotamian and Palestinian period.

These magnificent records are amplified by the cuneiform library of the highly gifted Assyrian king Assurbanipal (ca. 669–626 B.C.). Recently this library, of the utmost importance for research into antiquity, was recovered from the ruins of ancient Nineveh on the east bank of the Tigris. It contains over twenty thousand clay tablets on which Assurbanipal assembled and had recorded the data available to him about the history, civilization, life, and activity of the two world empires, Babylonia and Assyria. The history thereby unfolded for those old days is immeasurably valuable for archaeology.

A wealth of well-preserved original monuments establishes the historical dates of the chief Mesopotamian rulers, including the great Assyrian king, Shalmaneser III. Excellently preserved bronze tablets recording his acts were discovered in his palace portals. Stone reliefs of Sargon II survive, as do those of other kings of the land of the two rivers, and all this comes from a pre-Biblical past dating back more than 2,500 years.

Where are comparable proofs for the existence of the three patriarchs of the Israelites, Abraham, Isaac, and Jacob, or of Joseph, Moses, and Aaron, or of the Kings Saul, David, and Solomon, or of the many kings of Israel and Judah down to the last king, Zedekiah, somewhere in the sixth century B.C.? All these are more recent than the majority of the historically attested rulers of Egypt—as, for example, Pharaoh Cheops, whose burial place, the Great Pyramid, testifies even today to his life.

Stone, bronze, papyrus scrolls, and cuneiform inscriptions on clay tablets are available in vast quantities for the peoples who flourished elsewhere; but no such media preserve particulars about the notables of Israel or their ancestors. No archeological trace of their existence is known. No autobiographical document gives any information about them. Did they not want it? So far as they existed, they would have shared the wish of their neighboring contemporaries to transmit their works and history to posterity. Were they not able to do it? If not in their own land, there was at all events in neighboring kingdoms an available supply of

materials of all types, and sculptors, masons, and artists. There
was enough money at hand to have enabled them to buy and
pay for whatever was needed. Trade routes made traffic and
transport simple. Were there no achievements important enough
to preserve in monuments for future generations?

The picture in the Bible certainly does not suggest this, for the
alleged acts of Moses, David, and Solomon alone would fill whole
archives. Was it against their principles? In the view of the
Biblical editors, God had dictated to Moses among other commandments "Thou shalt not make unto thee any graven image,
or any likeness of any thing, that is in heaven above, or that
is in the earth beneath, or that is in the water under the earth."
This meant that the production of busts, statues, or paintings
depicting the great personages of Israel was forbidden. Of course
this law may have been an interpolation of later Biblical editors
compelled to provide a reason for the lack of any documentation.
It was Moses who first published this commandment, according
to Holy Writ. So why did not Abraham, Isaac, Jacob, and Joseph,
who lived before the time of Moses, perpetuate themselves and
their period in monuments? Or did Moses establish his law with
retroactive force and destroy their statues and inscriptions? That
is unlikely, for how should Moses know about their sculpturing
when he lived far away from the Biblical habitat of the patriarchs?

There are no satisfactory answers to these questions. The
Bible, however, makes this certain: neither God nor Moses forbade
the writing and preservation of history. Why did the Jewish
Biblical characters not compose and carve in stone any report
of their history in old Hebrew, Aramaic, or cuneiform, the usual
scripts of the time? The great contemporary world around them
transmitted itself in these forms; so it would not have been
strange if such a prominent people as the Biblical Israelites had
left a similar record of itself. On the contrary, it is strange that
this people is wholly silent about itself.

The primitive alphabet, from which the scripts of modern world
cultures are derived, is of Semitic origin; so one cannot postulate
ignorance of writing among the Semitic Hebrews, especially since
it is not customary to regard Israel as being culturally beneath
its neighbors. Only a single meager written document is known

from the time of the Israelite Bible. The so-called Siloah inscription dating from the time of King Hezekiah of Judah (ca. 700 B.C.) makes a statement about the tunneling of an aqueduct in Jerusalem. This is the only direct information from an Israelite source about any contemporary event mentioned in the Old Testament.

Bearing in mind the legendary character of the Old Testament accounts, one is either forced to assume that the existence of the great Biblical characters is doubtful; or, if in the total absence of inscriptional evidence one is still willing to ascribe historicity to them, one must assume that their lives and times did not tally with the Biblical picture, which finally recorded mostly tales and legends circulated among many generations in the Near East. To verify historical accounts given in the Bible one is thus driven to non-Jewish sources. These, however, are pretty scaice.

The whole problem of the Jewish nation is made much easier to interpret when one observes that other little, insignificant neighboring peoples, like the Edomites, Amelekites, Midianites, Moabites, Ammonites, and others, have likewise left practically no inscriptional material. The most important sources of historical information about the small nations of the Near East, a group to which the kingdoms of Israel and Judah belong, are the cuneiform inscriptions and monuments of Assyria and Babylon. Subjugated and dominated by these two great empires, these little nations of only parochial importance were subject to the amoral law of might makes right.

In this fact lies the key to the riddle of why these small powers, involved as they were in continual fighting for survival, left no historical records. Warring among themselves with varying results these countries on the coastal strip of Palestine were ever a strategic objective of the big countries. One or another of the small nations constantly dominated the others. Under the leadership of the dominant power, this league of little states defended itself against the great conquerors and succumbed. The only result was maybe a change in the destination of the yearly tribute that had to be paid in gold and kind. The lot of these small nations was ever the same: subjection, captivity, and the loss of goods and chattels.

Peaceful periods of reflection and creative activity are not

possible for peoples like those on the Palestinian crossroads, whose
history is enacted in such tragic forms as far back as memory
reaches. Their life is a continual run of war, misery, starvation,
terror, and slavery. They are bereft of any possibility of peaceful
constructive labor, the prerequisite for creating cultural riches.
The lives of these generations are governed by war and want,
not peace and happiness. This is the seed bed for a messianic
redeemer.

Consequently, the last thing one could expect is an indigenous
historical documentation of these wretched times, lacking, as they
do, all the necessary raw material: deeds of glory, an era of peace
and happiness, intellectual giants to make the repute of the
nation worldwide, and men so keenly aware of the importance
of the times as to record the history of the people. The classical
cockpit of Palestine did not allow any such development for
these small states. When in the quiet of a royal palace, nevertheless, a wise man sets to work to write the tragic story of his king
and kingdom, a conqueror straightway comes out of the East
and destroys the historical records together with the palace and
the kingdom.

Scholarly research has largely discredited the authorial and
historical claims made for the Hebrew and Christian scriptures,
although every effort is made to shield the believing masses from
the result of this research and the doubts it might engender. It
is now known that the five books of the Pentateuch, the foundation of the belief in the God of the Old and New Testaments,
could not have been written in the time of Moses, that in fact
they are made up of three or four layers of material.

The same applies more or less to the rest of the books in the
Old Testament; none of them is a reliable transcript of history.
The original writers had very little bent for accuracy, and nearly
all of their works suffer from later interpolation and redaction in
the interest of Yahweh cult propagation. For example, Judges, the
Samuel books, and Kings present one history from Joshua to
the exile; Chronicles, Ezra, and Nehemiah another from the death
of Saul to Nehemiah's reign. The two histories disagree in many
things: Kings gives special prominence to the laws of Moses in
the reign of Josiah (639–609 B.C.), while Nehemiah is more

concerned with the laws of Ezra (ca. 425–400 B.C.). In Kings, however, we probably have the highest relative historical accuracy found anywhere in Scripture, though some dates in them are discrepant and the perspective sometimes warped.

It is impossible to ascertain the course of events in the composition of the Old Testament because its entire content rests upon tradition, oral transmission, sporadic records made in royal courts, and prophetic and other writings however and whenever compiled.

Consider the caution we must exercise in our own time in accepting the accounts nations give of their contemporary heroic achievements. This caution provides a yardstick for determining the reliability of historical material in the Bible, stemming out of a thousand year-old past, passing from mouth to mouth in the legend-loving East, and finally given their permanent written form many generations later. How easily, especially in days of anguish and distress, the composer of an Old Testament book can be tempted to glorify the distant past lying beyond accurate recall.

A suffering people needs the example of heroic ancestors, even if they never actually existed, in order that it may realize in them the ideal of its own development and so bolster up its own ego. Furthermore, every people has a period of history in which there is a clear call to national greatness. The less this greatness and grandeur is justified by history, the stronger it becomes as a dream in popular emotion and the more likely it is to be realized in a national literature at a given time. Thus the Bible came into being partly as the memory of old wishful thinking and as the spiritual inheritance of a long series of generations of the Israelites.

Consequently the worldwide task and significance assigned to Jewry in the Bible differ sharply from the indifference with which the Israel of the Old Testament was treated by neighboring peoples. As a small nation among other small nations, it did not excel its neighbors historically or spiritually. Its faith lay, from the remotest times, in the religions of Baal, Astarte, and other local gods of the land of Canaan. It was only in a small layer of society that intellectuals gradually formulated for themselves the later monotheism. By a logical build-up, they succeeded on a grand scale in exalting Israel as the chosen people of the only

God. Thenceforth the pride and glory of Israel would be to proclaim its God to mankind.

What is the nature of the available authentic material for Israel's history? Whence does it come? What does it contain? In the thirteenth century B.C., Pharaoh Merneptah II had a triumphal monument erected in which he tells of his campaigns. Among other things written in hieroglyphics on this stone occurs the following passage: "Despoiled Canaan and all its evil with it. . . . Israel, its people, are desolate, and its offspring exists no more." This presumably deals with one of the many campaigns of the pharaohs to insure communications with Lebanon across the coast of Palestine.

This earliest mention of Israel in history does not, therefore, relate to people of Israel established in Egypt itself, such as those led out of Egypt under Moses according to the Biblical account. The connection with Merneptah II becomes ever more difficult if he should be the Pharoah of the Exodus as scholarship pretty generally assumes, for then he would not need to undertake a campaign to Canaan, which lay far away in the north, in order to achieve the annihilation of Israel. Furthermore the Bible says that he was drowned in the Red Sea with his army, though his mummy today stands in the Cairo museum. So this so-called "Israel-stele" of Merneptah II cannot be adduced as vouching for the authenticity of the Biblical version of the history of the people of Israel.

A few genuine evidences for the historicity of the Israelites are found in the cuneiform inscriptions of the great realms of their Mesopotamian neighbors. The range of history ostensibly portrayed in the Old Testament begins with Abraham, ca. 1800 B.C., and ends with Ezra and Nehemiah in the fifth century B.C.

Out of these 1,500 years or so of Bible history, the cuneiform inscriptions give accounts of only some two centuries; thus there are almost no inscriptional records to cover a stretch of 1,300 years of history in the Old Testament. The oldest document stems from Israel's old hereditary enemy, the people of the Moabites; for their king, Mesha, who lived about 850 B.C., left an account of his military actions in what is called the Mesha stone. This stone now rests in the Louvre in Paris, and among its statements the following are of interest:

> Omri, King of Israel, oppressed Moab for a long time. . . .And his son [Ahab] followed him, and he also said, "I shall oppress Moab." In my time he spoke thus, but I have triumphed over him and over his house. And Israel has perished forever.

As a remarkable event, worthy of perpetuation in stone, the Moabite king reports that he conquered an Israelite city of 7,000 inhabitants. To see this in perspective one may cite the statement of the English archaeologist Woolley, who estimated that there was a population of about half a million in the town of Ur in Mesopotamia, the supposed home of Abraham. The observation on the Mesha stone that Israel has perished forever is an announcement of the victor. Correspondence between the announcement of the victor and the real facts is lacking in this case, as in many others in history. This little Israelite kingdom did not collapse until 125 years later.

Another country which gave the Israelites a lot of trouble was Syria, which played a considerable part in ancient trade because of its location. Surviving Assyrian chronicles indicate that Syria dominated Israel for a time, and this tells us something about the size of Israel. Both little kingdoms, along with other states, were conquered by the great Assyrian king Shalmaneser III.

In this campaign King Jehu of Israel had to perform military service for the ruler of Damascus, the capital of Syria. The Assyrian cuneiform inscription on this point runs:

> In the eighteenth year of my reign I crossed the Euphrates for the sixteenth time. Hazael of Damascus put his trust in his numerous army and called up his troops in great number, making the cone-shaped mountain [of Hermon] over against Lebanon his stronghold. I fought with him and overthrew him, killing with the sword sixteen thousand of his warriors. I took away from him 1121 of his chariots and 470 of his war

horses as well as his camp. He made his getaway to
save his life. I pursued him and besieged him in Damascus, his chief city. . . . At that time I received the
tribute of the inhabitants of Tyre, Sidon, and also of
Jehu, the son of Omri.

This Jehu was the King of Israel who supposably reigned from
842 to 815 B.C. The above cuneiform inscription is supplemented
by the famous black obelisk; the Assyrian King Shalmaneser III
had it set up to commemorate the victory. A strip of reliefs portrays various scenes of the campaign. One such relief represents
King Jehu of Israel, or an envoy of his, kneeling in obeisance
before Shalmaneser III. While he thus humbles himself before
the conqueror, his people deliver the tribute. For this there is
the following caption:

Tribute of Jehu, son of Omri: silver, gold bars, a golden
bowl, golden tumblers, golden buckets, a golden vase,
and tin.

The Old Testament does not vouchsafe us any information
about this defeat and gift of tribute.

Shortly afterward the cuneiform inscriptions have something
to report of the Assyrian King Adadnirari. He laid the Israelite
King Joahaz, son of Jehu, under tribute. Modern Biblical scholars
see in this Assyrian the "savior" mentioned in II Kings 13:5.
They relate this expression to the circumstance that now the
great Assyrian King instead of Damascus exercised suzerainty
over Israel. The opposite opinion is possible, that the designation
"savior" is little suitable for a new oppressor substituted for an
old one.

Important material about the kingdoms of Judah and Israel
comes from the cuneiform inscriptions of the most important of
all the Assyrian rulers, Tiglath-pileser III (ca. 745–727 B.C.).
He was on the throne at the time when the small states were
hoping to shake off the Assyrian yoke. Fear of him was so great,
however, that the campaign was over before it had really begun.
Among the princes who thereafter had to pay the Great King

tribute, there again occurs a King of Israel—Menahem. The Bible reports this in II Kings 15:19.

In the year 733 B.C. Tiglath-pileser III annexed all the Israelite towns under King Pekah of Israel except Samaria. The inhabitants were led away to Assyria into captivity. The Old Testament makes no mention of this decisive event. Samaria was now the only town in his kingdom left to King Pekah, and Tiglath-pileser deposed him from the throne, setting up Hoshea as king in his place. The cuneiform inscription about this runs:

> They overthrew their king Pekah and I placed Hoshea
> as king over them. I received ten talents of gold . . .
> talents of silver as a tribute.

Under Sargon II of Assyria came the dissolution of the kingdom of Israel when the small surviving fragment of the population was likewise deported to Assyria. The Old Testament yields only a garbled account of this fall of the kingdom. Documents cited above show that the deportation to Assyria took place at the hands of Tiglath-pileser III in 733 in the time of King Pekah of Israel, with the exception of Samaria, which, under Hoshea, was not forced to travel this path of sorrow until 722 by Sargon II.

A comparison between the Old Testament account and the cuneiform records about the fall of the kingdom of Israel shows how even the most important historical facts are distorted by the Biblical editors because of their dependence on oral tradition. We still have the cuneiform inscription of Sargon II to consult for precise details about the destruction of Israel. It runs in its principal part as follows:

> At the beginning of my royal rule and in the first year
> of my reign I besieged and conquered Samaria. I led
> away 27,290 inhabitants and levied 50 chariots for
> my royal corps. . . . I rebuilt the town and settled
> therein more people than had been there from lands
> which I had conquered. I placed an officer of mine as
> governor over them. I imposed tribute upon them as
> [is customary] for Assyrian citizens.

After the fall of the kingdom of Israel, the little sister kingdom of Judah, according to the reports of Sargon II, took part in a revolt against Assyria, without being called to account for it. Rebellious Judah, however, soon had to submit to Assyrian overlordship under Sargon's son, Sennacherib. In the so-called "Taylor Prism," Sennacherib makes the following report about it:

And I laid siege to forty-six strong towns, girt with walls, and to countless smaller towns around them, belonging to Hezekiah of Judah, who had not bowed under my yoke. And I conquered them by means of well-stamped [earth-] ramps and battering rams [wooden beaks for making breaches in town walls] brought near the walls and an attack by foot soldiers [using] mines, breaches, and sapper work. I led forth from them and counted as booty 200,150 men, young and old, male and female, horses, mules, asses, camels, oxen, and small cattle beyond counting. I shut him up like a bird in a cage in Jerusalem, his royal residence. I raised strong earth-works against him and molested those who issued forth from his town.

I took from his country the towns which I had plundered and gave them [here follow the names of various petty non-Jewish princes], and I reduced the size of his country. To the former tribute and tax I added tribute and gifts to my lordship and laid these upon him. Terror from the splendor of my rule overcame him, even Hezekiah, and the Urbi [homeless rabble] and his regular warriors, whom he had brought for the defense of Jerusalem, his dwelling place, deserted him.

Then Hezekiah sent to Nineveh, my chief city, thirty talents of gold, eight hundred talents of silver, precious stones, antimony, genuine Uknu stones, couches inlaid with ivory, thrones inlaid with ivory, elephant hides, ivory, all kinds of valuable treasures, his own daughters, his concubines, male and female musicians. To pay his tribute and to do me homage he sent his envoys.

This event is briefly touched on in the Bible in II Kings 18:13–16, but concludes (II Kings 19:9–36) with a pious legend about a victory over the Assyrians thanks to the slaughter of 185,000 men by an angel of the Lord. This transfigured description provides an excellent gauge of the mentality of the authors of the scriptures who could in a relatively short time transform a signal defeat into a victory wrought by a miracle of the god. It also raises questions about the accuracy of other historical material which the Old Testament adduces for still remoter periods.

The last available cuneiform inscriptions with statements about the Jews deal with King Manasseh of Judah, ca. 673 B.C. He had to pay tribute to the Assyrian king, Esarhaddon, and to provide him with auxiliaries for the campaign against Egypt. Esarhaddon used subject people as forced labor in constructing Assyrian public buildings. Manasseh also had to put troops at the disposal of Esarhaddon's successor, King Assurbanipal, for his wars.

Only the inscriptional records cited above have so far been discovered for the events mentioned in the seventeen books of the Old Testament from the time of Abraham to that of Nehemiah. It is obviously a very barren harvest.

This much is established, but it does not imply that only inscriptional records are valid in assessing the historical value of Holy Writ. Doubtless it contains extensive information about the past happenings of the people of Israel, even though it will never be possible to isolate the kernel of truth from the husk of oriental fancy and religious zeal. But we must recognize how untrustworthy are the accounts of historical events given in the Bible unless supported by other evidence. The result has been a historically false picture of the people of Israel, its faith, and its importance in ancient history, which has hurt nobody more than the Jews themselves.

Precise chronological tables are drawn up by modern writers

on the history of Israel. These chronological statements deal with
people about whom the most that can be said is that perhaps
they once lived, though little or nothing is known of their lives
and acts other than what has come down to us by way of ancient
legends from a long past age whose dates are calculated from
assumed figures by orthodox scholars in order to shore up their
religion. These dates, established somewhat arbitrarily, at best
are put on a level with such assured dates as, for example, Alexander the Great conquered Palestine 332 B.C., or Palestine fell
under Roman sovereignty in 63 B.C.

The result of this confusion of genuine historical chronology
with conjectural dates is that people of the Jewish and Christian
faiths picture the origin and development of the biblical religion
as a continuous panorama and come to assume that the historical
content of the Old Testament presents literal truth. But the
Old Testament does not give an objective history of the Judeo-
Christian development; instead, it is a tendentious creation and
interpretation.

3. ABRAHAM, JOSEPH, MOSES, AND SUN WORSHIP

The first book of Moses (Genesis) tells us that Abraham and his family migrated from Ur of the Chaldees to Canaan. God promises to make him the father of a great people and, for no particular apparent reason, makes a covenant with him, whereby God promises to give the land between the Nile and the Euphrates to the descendants of Abraham as their possession. To this was added a guarantee that all the people of the earth should forever be blessed through Abraham.*

Thus Abraham becomes the founder of a covenant between God and Israel and a herald of the Jewish mission to the world. Everyone who belongs to Jewry is a partaker in this covenant. This likewise raises Abraham to the position of racial ancestor of all the Jews, a conception still held today. Even today when a non-Jew marries a Jewess and is converted to the Jewish religion, he sometimes acquires the given name Abraham to show that he belongs to the covenant with God and is to be regarded as a descendant of Abraham. Such loyalty to a tradition is astounding.

It is not known who Abraham was. In what way he came to his new god, whether he brought him with him as a ready-made idea out of his god-fearing home of Ur, or whether he adopted him

* Islam also recognizes in the covenant of Abraham with his God the foundation of its own faith. In the Koran, the holy scripture of the Mohammedans, we read in sura 4, verse 125:

> Who has a better religion than he who submits himself entirely to God? He is the doer of good [to others] and follows the faith of Abraham, the upright one. And God took Abraham as a friend.

25

from other folk on his nomadic treks, or whether he developed him out of himself in some foreign land, or whether he really is the founder of the Jewish religion as he is regarded by the present world—all these are unanswered questions. The discovery of the primeval remains of Abraham's town of Ur on the Euphrates in the year 1854 by the English consul at Basrah has led archaeologists to form extensive associations of Ur with Abraham, especially since a British-American expedition in the first three decades of the twentieth century undertook systematic excavations and established that Ur had already been destroyed about 1730 B.C.

There is no definite proof that a man or a family or a tribe called Abraham lived at Ur. Even though the English scholar Woolley, to whom we largely owe these excavations, comes to the conclusion that Abraham might have existed, this does not bring us any nearer to the solution of the puzzle. It would be most desirable if the finds at this ancient place were to yield some form of proof for the existence of Abraham, since this would be significant for Old Testament history.

Apart from Biblical statements about him, there is a reference to Abraham dating from the second century B.C. in the Hellenistic writer Eupolemos of Alexandria. He reports that in the thirteenth generation there was born at the town of Kamarina, also called Urie, Abraham, one who "in descent and wisdom surpassed all others." The Greek's authority for this is not known. It in no way helps to make the Biblical history of Abraham clearer, for the author's mention of high ancestry leads one to expect that the great finds at Abraham's alleged home, Ur, could yield information about him. In connection with the information of Eupolemos it is also worth considering that he first composed his text some 1,700 years after the presumed time of Abraham. That is practically the same as if a historian living today were to produce new biographical facts about the apostle Paul.

How uncertain the problem of Abraham remains for the scholarship concerned with this area is made plain by the utterances of leading spokesmen. Besides Woolley, the Englishman already quoted, the Protestant scholar Alfred Jeremias makes a further illuminating remark:

If Abraham existed he could only have lived in the surroundings and under the conditions described in the
Bible. This must suffice historical research.

That simply says that nothing is known about the man who
allegedly founded the Jewish religion.

Abraham's son is Isaac, and his son is Jacob. There is no
evidence to show that either of these ever lived. Jacob struggled
with God according to the Biblical legend and got his hip dislo-
cated. Jewish ritual uses this injury of Jacob to explain a food
taboo, namely, why pious Jews still refrain from eating the sciatic
nerve portion in hind quarters of beeves. The origin of the name
"Israel" is also derived in the Bible from the wrestling of Jacob
with his God, for then the God gave him the name Israel, meaning
"he strives with God."

In the Biblical legend, Abraham, Isaac, and Jacob, the three
patriarchs, are described as the ancestors in the flesh of the Jewish
people. In this connection, it is helpful to bear in mind that the
invention of a flattering genealogy and noble ancestry by people
fancying themselves superior is by no means limited to the Old
Testament. The Gospel of Matthew has one genealogy tracing the
descent of Jesus through David back to Abraham, and the Gospel
of Luke another carrying it still further back all the way to Adam.

The three patriarchs, together with Jacob's son Joseph, are the
heralds of faith in the Jewish God, Yahweh. Joseph is an especially sympathetic figure in the Old Testament, though there is
no evidence that he ever lived. Egypt is the scene of his life.
Consequently he falls out of the geographical area occupied by
other Old Testament heroes. The extent to which facts and fiction
are woven into his life will never be untangled.

If we assume that the man Joseph was real and that the Biblical
legends regarding him have a kernel of truth, then the information
in Genesis, chapters 41–45, becomes important. It tells how
Pharaoh gave him in marriage the daughter of the priest at On.
Near Cairo, On is the Egyptian Heliopolis famous as the center
for the cult of sun worship. We may readily imagine the life of a
foreigner who has attained to high honors at the Egyptian royal

court. His master, a court official, must have already been connected with the priesthood of the temple of the sun, for his name, Potiphar, probably means "gift of the sun-God Re." When, according to Genesis 45:8, Joseph says of himself, perhaps with some characteristic oriental exaggeration, that he is a father to Pharaoh, lord over all his house, and ruler of all the land of Egypt, it can only mean that Joseph belonged to the sun cult at Heliopolis.

Whatever foreign beliefs he may have entertained as a 17-year-old youth, he must have changed not only his customs, dress, and language, but also his religion in order to advance and become the king's most trusted minister. This is all the more certain if his sovereign conferred upon him as a wife the daughter of an important religious dignitary.

Such reasoning is quite foreign to the unknown editor of the Biblical chronicle of Joseph. He represents Joseph as praising the God of Israel who had directed everything for the best for himself and his brothers. Joseph continually remembers this God, for when Potiphar's wife daily asks him to sleep with her, he, "a goodly person and well favored" refuses to accede to her wish. Indeed, he flees from her to avoid abusing the confidence placed in him by his absent master and hence sinning against the God of Israel, even *his* God.

In this story we do not doubt that Joseph was a genteel and noble character who would not allow his lord's wife to seduce him. The only question is whether a man like Joseph would have remembered in such a situation a god who was foreign to himself and to all his environment, especially when for many years he himself had no longer retained any association with his tribe and god, both of whom had mistreated him very badly. Moreover, if Joseph, as an influential Egyptian statesman, received permission from Pharaoh to settle the twelve tribes of Israel who had immigrated under his father in Egyptian Goshen, it is doubtful that the king would have shown this gracious favor to a man, next to him in rank, if this man had not shared his own faith. Joseph could only have worshipped the sun and other gods accepted by his lord, his country, his wife, and his environment.

The fact that the king arranged Joseph's marriage into an important priestly family testified to Joseph's deep devotion to that religion.

After Joseph, Moses is associated with the Egyptian sun worship. Jewish and Christian commentators keep on referring to this connection but never develop it. Sigmund Freud, in his book *Moses and Monotheism,* was the first to go into this material rather thoroughly. He recognized an identity between the sun worship of Amenhotep IV and the monotheism of Moses.

Like Joseph, Moses was presumably an adherent of the Egyptian religion, which simply means that he followed the native religion of his homeland. After Pharaoh's daughter received him, according to the legend, at the age of three months, he was brought up by her and her court. To this there would have been attached, surely, a court chaplain, as was customary in royal households. This makes us think that Moses could have had no connection whatever with the God of the Bible so long as he sojourned in Egypt.

Every indication points to the fact that he, even more than Joseph, lived and thought as an Egyptian. This implied that he must have known the monotheism of Pharaoh Amenhotep IV. Perhaps he regarded it as the true religion, and after Amenhotep's death and condemnation as a heretic he, together with his supporters, was expelled from Egypt because of this faith. If so, this could explain the first commandment on Sinai, "You shall have no other gods before me."

It is noteworthy that according to the Bible, Abraham and the patriarchs already believed in a single god. This would mean that the promulgation of a single god by Moses would have been nothing special, as monotheism would already have been long established among the people of Israel.

The spiritual innovation ascribed to Moses would represent something unusual only if it differed from that of the patriarchs. The novelty could lie not in the fact that Amenhotep IV raised the sun to the rank of a deity, but in that he saw in it the unique source of life and an all-preserving cosmic principle. Consequently, without ado he deposed the entire Egyptian pantheon not in order to announce a new deity, a unique god, but in order to clear a place for the sun in the universe which rightly belonged to it as the bringer of all life for plants, animals, and men.

That is a grandiose conception for that age of over 3,000 years ago. Modern science is the first to adopt it again in contradiction to all god-based religions. It is a spiritual achievement going far beyond the concepts of the Jewish and Christian religions. This conception of the heretic king is known to us through Egyptian funerary texts. Speaking about the sun in his great Hymn to Aton, Amenhotep IV says among other things:

O living Aton, beginning of life,
Your dawning is beautiful on the horizon of heaven;
When you shine great and glorious, high over the earth,
Your beams embrace every land unto the ends of all you have
    created.

It is you that nourish the begotten in women
And give life to the child within the mother;
You lull the unborn child and soothe away its cry,
You handmaid in the mother's womb;
You bestow the breath that gives life to every child
On the day when it comes from its mother's womb into the light;
You open its mouth at the first cry
And supply it with a livelihood.

When the chick sits in the egg and speaks within the shell,
You give it air that it may live,
You give it strength to break the shell.
And while you were alone you molded the earth
According to your will and created men and flocks and cattle
And everything upon the earth.
You made the distant sky so that you may
Ascend there to survey all that you have created.

There is none like you when you rise
In your form as the living Aton,
Shining and glowing, withdrawing and returning again.

You are in my heart,
No other knows you aright save only your son.

The dwellers of the earth are beneath you,
For you are their creator;
At your rising they live,
At your setting they perish.
You are the very force of life
And through you alone men live.

I am your son, your servant,
I proclaim your majesty as long as your power
And strength shall endure in my heart.
You are Aton living forever and ever
And I am a part of you.

Living after the time of Amenhotep, Moses was familiar with these thoughts and passages and became the apostle of his great ideal and of his sun worship stripped of all supernatural trappings. The following appears to be a likely sequence of events: 130 years after Amenhotep IV, i.e., about 1225 B.C., Pharaoh Merneptah drove some people from Egypt. Meanwhile the cult of the sun as the one and only life principle had been rejected as heretical. As before, Heliopolis again became the capital of sun worship in the re-establishment of the older Egyptian Pantheon. Moses ranked as a priest of the sun God in this temple. He left Egypt with a persecuted minority to be their leader. The sun religion went with them in the form of the only creator of the universe and of life as proclaimed by Amenhotep IV. For its sake he and his people suffered expulsion, scorn, and years of hardship.

History yields various though late proofs for this interpretation. Diodorus Siculus, a Roman writer living in the time of Caesar and Augustus, mentioned an exodus from Egypt. He had gathered this from the writings of the Greek author Hecataeus, who lived about 320 B.C. According to this, there lived among the Egyptians some people who did not serve the gods in the usual, prescribed way. In anger at this the offended gods had unleashed pestilence on the land. Thereupon all foreigners were expelled. Under the leadership of Moses, a section emigrated towards Judaea and erected outside Jerusalem "The Temple which was most sanctified among men."

This account of the Greek writer explains that these foreigners are identical with those who had served the Egyptian gods in a way other than prescribed. That observation cannot apply to a god which was altogether strange to the Egyptians, as, for instance, Yahweh of the Israelites, but can apply to the exercise of the Egyptian ritual in a way which deviated from the indigenous usage. This deviation seems to lie in a continued adherence to the sun monotheism of Amenhotep even after the Egyptians had officially declared it a heresy, although most of them kept on worshiping the sun as one of the chief deities.

Another historical indication for the supposed link between Moses and the outlook of the great Amenhotep is found in the polemic of the Jewish-Roman historian, Flavius Josephus, against the anti-Jewish Greek Apion, in which a communication of the Egyptian Manetho is referred to.

Manetho lived about the same time as the Hecataeus mentioned above (300 B.C.) and was an Egyptian sun priest at Heliopolis. His report, quoted by Flavius Josephus, therefore presumably had its source in the archives of this temple, as the ancient priestly circles were also more literate than other people. He mentions an exodus from Egypt and assigns it to the lifetime of Amenhotep IV, now regarded to be about a hundred years too early. According to Manetho, the king expelled lepers and the unclean were led out by a former priest from Heliopolis. This priest was called Osarsiph, but subsequently changed his name to Moses. He gave laws to his followers, one of which forbade the worship of the gods; another law allowed them to eat animal food, the enjoyment of which had been forbidden in their Egyptian homeland.

In this account, Amenhotep IV is presumably inaccurately given as the Pharaoh of the Exodus. But otherwise Manetho's account fully proves our hypothesis that Moses was a sun priest at Heliopolis and worshiped the sun in accordance with the ideals of the heretical king. The account further on proves that the unclean and the lepers did not mean the physically tainted but the spiritually unclean; the expulsion of the lepers brought back good fortune from the gods to the king.

What has been said likely proves that Moses derived from the thought of Amenhotep IV the idea of worshiping the sun as the one and only principle of the universe and of life; that as a priest of the sun worship at Heliopolis he was banished with his followers because of this heresy; and that he imported his faith into the new land of Canaan in order to save it from destruction after his country had persecuted him and his fellow believers with the most stringent coercive measures. This will perhaps explain a cuneiform inscription which comes out of the archives of Tell el-Amarna and which has hitherto been unintelligible to scholarship. It deals with a report about Amenhotep IV. The clay tablet refers to him as one "who has laid his name forever on the land." The land under discussion was Canaan. Nothing is more probable than the assumption that Amenhotep IV, who called himself Ikhnaton—the beloved of Aton, the sun—had transplanted his sun worship to Canaan, either directly, or, as is more probable, through one of his apostles, whom we are led by everything that has been said to regard as Moses.

It is understandable that this magnificent, cosmically oriented conception of events should find opponents also in Canaan. Much support for this opposition came from other Semitic nomad tribes that joined the migrants from Egypt on the trail northward to the good pastures expected there.

The forms of faith in the Near East, including Canaan, were invariably cults dedicated to polytheism. Among them sun worship took the first place. The chief gods all represented the same feeling for the great miracle of nature, whether it was under the name of Baal, Marduk, Tammuz, Re, Yahweh, or another. Moses and his Egyptians fought against these ancestral customs in vain. His people, meanwhile, had increased considerably in numbers and had greatly changed in racial composition. They worshipped strange gods before his eyes and followed the lead of his brother, Aaron, in making a Baal in the form of a golden bull, slightingly described as a calf in the Old Testament. The change from the great sun nature of all being of the Amenhotep period to the idolatry of Canaan is not surprising, considering the primitive character of people at that time. One cannot suppose that simple nomads had a grasp of the cosmic thoughts expressed by Amenhotep in his funerary texts when he says

I am a part of you, O sun.

Even now, in the twentieth century, after 3,000 years a great part of mankind is not ready for it.

Perception in that ancient period, however, was at least broad enough to give the sun the leading position among all the forces of nature and the deities. Thus the sun god won a kind of hegemony over the other gods and goddesses. Palestine, Egypt, North Africa, Persia, India, all exercised this sun worship in ancient times as their chief cult, as they do in part even today. The phoenix, which gives its name to the Phoenicians of the Palestinian coast, is the "blood red," the sun god. The Indian philosophical religious texts, the *Upanishads,* say in the old Sanskrit tongue:

> Verily the sun is heat, power, might, glory, sight, hearing, self, intellect, zeal, guardian of the world, the unknown god, the unknown primal being, delight, reality, food, length of life, immortality, soul, all-being, highest pleasure, being through itself. . . .

In another early Indian Sanskrit text, the sun is extolled as the creator of all life. It brings the rainy seasons, on the punctual arrival of which all human life depends in hot countries. The sun, identical with Atman, is the universal principle. This fine passage reads:

The holy sun god is the theater of manifold marvels.
From him goes forth everything that exists.
Like birds on the branches, in his thousand rays
the perfected sages and the gods find shelter and a dwelling.
The great god of the wind comes forth from him,
supports himself on the sunbeams and breaks forth in
the vastness of the air.
What greater marvel could there be than this!
Out of good will for his creatures he divides the water

and lets it pour in the rainy season.
What greater marvel could there be than this!
Set in the midst of the orb, the mighty Atman kindles himself
in most piercing brightness and surveys the world.
What greater marvel could there be than this!
He is called the shining one and yet carries in the form
of a dark ray the water in the vastness of the air and
pours it forth in the rainy season.
What greater marvel could there be than this?
And then he gathers the outpouring water in a pure ray into
  himself
again for a season of eight months.
What greater marvel could there be than this?
And in his incomparable gleam dwells Atman himself through
  whom
the seed and the soil are preserved with that which moves and
that which moves not. . . .
What greater marvel could there be than that!

In Assyria it is the sun god Shamash to whom the deepest
devotion is accorded. We read in the Assyrian cuneiform texts of
King Assurbanipal's library already mentioned:

> Shamash, lord of heaven and earth,
> You are the builder of house and city!
> To establish destiny and to determine fate
> Lies in your hand!
> Life's fate is your decree, none other's!
> The utterance of your mouth is sheer life!
> The word of your lips pure salvation!

The Babylonian sun god shares all the attributes for which
the God in the Bible is later praised and glorified. One of the pre-
Biblical cuneiform hymns which have been discovered states:

Among all the gods of heaven none is powerful as you. . . .
Of all countries, however different in language,
You know their strivings, you observe their ways;
All mortals unite to rejoice in you.
O Shamash, all the world yearns for your light. . . .

You stand by the traveler whose road is hard;
You give courage to the wanderer over the sea
Fearful of the surging billows. . . .
O Shamash, the wicked shall not escape your net,
Nor any evil-doer slip out of your snare.
He who breaks his oath, him you strike suddenly;
He who fears not holiness, lies in your clutches.
Your net is spread out wide for him who works mischief
And for him who lays eyes on the wife of his comrade. . . .
When your weapon is turned on him, he has no redeemer;
When he is brought to trial, even his father will not stand by him.
Like the water of eternal springs, there shall be everlasting seed
For the doer of good deeds, honest in all his dealings.
He who has evil thoughts, his name will be recorded with a pencil.
Those who do evil, their seed shall not endure. . . .
You guide all precepts and whatever is bound you loosen.
You hearken, O Shamash, to prayer, petition, and adoration,
To humble submission and kneeling, to worship, and to the
    whispered pleadings of the heart.
In his hollow voice the feeble man cries out to you;
The miserable, the weak, the mistreated, the enslaved man,
Ever he implores you with prayer and penitential psalm. . . .
Those who kneel to you, them you reward with holiness;
Those who come to you in meek adoration, you accept their
    prayer,
They serve you with reverence, they honor your name,
They praise your greatness forever. . . .
Lord, you that make the darkness to shine
And make bright the countenance of man,
Merciful god, you raise him up who is bowed low
And are a shield to the feeble. . . .
Shamash, king of heaven and earth, you that guide
All that is above and all that is below,
Shamash, to bring the dead back to life
And to free the fettered lies ever in your hand.
Incorruptible judge, leader of mankind,
Noble offspring of the bright and rising Lord,

Strong, glorious son, light of all the countries,
Creator in heaven and on earth forever and ever—
All these you are, O Shamash!

When we read this deeply religious, pre-Biblical heathen poetry,
we remember what we have been taught, namely, that belief in
gods is idolatry and spells unheard of wickedness and moral
degradation.

It was a light task for the Biblical authors to write down great
thoughts since they could draw from this ancient literature deeply
rooted in tradition. Before their time this literature had been given
a wonderful form, and since the Jewish writers had no understanding of the true religious depth of the heathen peoples, they
regarded the great thoughts borrowed from this literature as a
special gift from God given exclusively through Moses to his
chosen people.

How familiar to us all are these early heathen psalms in the
later tones of the Bible and how humbling is the knowledge of
their true meaning for everyone whose eyes are not blinded by
ecclesiastical zeal! The unknown author of the prophetical book
of Isaiah obviously quotes ancient psalms and is paying homage
to the sun god rather than to Yahweh when he says in chapter
60, verses 2–3:

> For behold, darkness shall cover the earth, and thick
> darkness the peoples: but the Lord will arise upon you.
> And nations shall come to your light, and kings to the
> brightness of your rising.

The old worship of the sun lies at the root of all the higher
forms of creed and as long as the human race survives it will
always be implicit or explicit among men as the traceable foun-
tain of life. This axiom is valid for every historical period. On St.
Helena, Napoleon says to his physician-in-ordinary:

> If I had to have a religion I would pray to the sun be-
> cause it is the source of all life; it is the true god of the
> earth.

The Japanese emperors traced their pedigree back to the Japanese goddess of the sun, and this led the people to accord them divine veneration down to 1945.

The Jews, too, know about sun worship. In the Talmud there is a description of the popular religious festival of the Feast of Tabernacles. At this festival there is a procession of priests accompanied by music and dancing. After the priests, blowing trumpet blasts, have reached the east gateway, the Talmud runs:

> They turned to face away from the east towards the west and said, "Our fathers turned their backs to the temple and their faces to the east in this place, and towards the east they cast themselves down before the sun, but we turn our eyes towards God."

The image of the sun, the undying lamp, stands in every church. It is the eternal fire prescribed in Leviticus 6:13 with the words:

> Fire shall be kept burning upon the altar continually;
> it shall not go out.

This symbol of light and fire set in a consecrated place always contains the notion of assigning a place of honor to the sun god in centers of worship. It was the same, too, in ancient Persia when an image of the sun set in crystal shone over the royal tent. As soon as the army marched in a campaign under its leader, this holy image as well as the undying fire was carried along on an altar.

The primeval sun worship of the temple at Heliopolis, Prometheus in Greek antiquity bringing man fire from heaven, the old Persian sun cult, and the honor accorded to the sun by many other peoples, all these find their continuation up to the present age in the undying lights of the Jewish and Christian churches and the Mohammedan mosques.

The Sabbath is set apart as a day of rest in honor of the sun god. It is clear from the ancient cuneiform inscriptions that this day, in prosperity as in misfortune, assumed a special place in the Assyrian-Babylonian religion. Like so much else, the seven-day cycle as announced in the Bible with the words "So God blessed the seventh day and hallowed it" is something taken over from ancient Babylonian religious ritual.

The chief occupation of the idolatrous world which keeps the day of rest is the worship of the gods and especially of the highest of the gods, the sun god. He is symbolized in fire. That is why the Jews may not do anything on the day of rest that would recall the old usages in the veneration of fire, the image of the sun god. The embargo on kindling flame on the Sabbath, the day dedicated to God for rest, is designed to prevent any relapse into sun worship. That is why this embargo is the one specific stipulation within the legal framework of a general ban against work on Sundays in the Bible (Exodus 35:3).

Closely linked with sun worship is the idea of its holiness. Nothing unworthy or unclean may be undertaken in view of the sun. Ancient India meets the holy sun with great reverence when it decrees:

> None may set his eyes on the rising sun or on a foreign
> woman when she is naked.

In the Bible, those who have infringed the laws of hygiene are regarded as unclean until the evening. For instance, anyone who carries a dead rabbit becomes unclean until the evening. The reason for limiting uncleanness to daylight is that all evil must shun the light of the sun. When the sunbeams can no longer be insulted by the sight of the evil-doer, as when darkness falls, only then may he be regarded cleansed. The book of Job tells us that the dawning of the sun takes hold of the skirts of the earth and shakes the wicked out of it. Here the sun not only brings wicked deeds into the open, but also exposes the perpetrators to the scorn of their fellow men.

One of the most noteworthy reasons adduced in the Old Testament for venerating the sun relates to blood guilt. If one catches a thief breaking in, one may slay him without incurring punishment thereby. But, says Exodus 22:3,

> If the sun has risen upon him, there shall be blood
> guilt for him.

Slaying a thief by night entails no punishment, but by day in the face of the sun it is murder, a crime.

Is there need of any further proof that the ancient Egyptian, Canaanite sun god still lives on in Holy Writ? Have not Amenhotep IV and Moses, his sun priest, left their mark upon the Bible? Scripture gives the fullest possible account of the way the Israelites worshiped the sun in Biblical times.

Scripture relates among other matter that the people of Israel began to commit fornification with the women of Moab who had invited them to sacrifice to their gods. The Israelites are said to have eaten with the foreign women and to have worshiped their gods. Moses accordingly ordered the arrest of all the chiefs of the people and executed the following commandment which he had received from God: "Hang them in the sun before the Lord." (Numbers 25:4) Two rivals were waging a bitter struggle. Yahweh humbled and showed up the powerlessness of the Moabite sun god by executing his worshippers before his face.

The deep roots of sun worship and idolatry in early Israel are proved not only by the Bible but independently by finds excavated at ancient Israelite towns. There are fragments of clay pots derived from the workshops of a king of Judah bearing the royal stamp of a winged sun disk, the ancient Egyptian solar emblem. This shows that the sun was a cult object in the kingdom of Judah. According to the ancient oriental point of view, the sun acted as the preserver of justice and hid salvation under his wings. This idea the prophet Malachi proclaimed with the words

> But for you who fear my name the sun of righteousness
> shall rise, with healing in its wings. (Malachi 4:2)

The sun, recognized by men of all times as the creator and protector of life, is the foundation of every creed and religion. The one and only God of Israel and God the Father of the New Testament, and indeed Jesus and Allah, are no exceptions to this. This fundamental principle in the religions of the ancient world unmistakably survives in the present forms of these religions.

4. THE GODS OF MAN

Biblical research has clearly established two facts. The first is that Yahweh is not only the God of Israel. The second is that he is not identical with the God originally worshiped by Abraham and the patriarchs. A third point may be added: Yahweh was also not the God of Moses. As the God of the Bible and of the Jews, he was turned into the Lord of Israel by the Biblical authors in a slow process, many centuries after the supposed time of Moses, gradually attaining a character out of accumulating oral transmission.

The name Yahweh or Yahveh, commonly known as Jehovah, was present in Babylon and Egypt in pre-Israelite times. It is historically established in cuneiform inscriptions from about 2000 B.C., i.e., before the time of the alleged patriarch Abraham and hundreds of years before Moses. The British Museum has three tablets of the Sumerian king Sin-Muballidh from this period. The name of Yahweh appears in these. Cuneiform scholars have explained its meaning in the translation "Yahweh is God."

In Egypt, the God is called Yao or Ihaho. Friedrich von Schiller mentions in his treatise "The Mission of Moses" that nobody was allowed to enter the temple of the Egyptian divinity Serapis unless he carried on his brow and breast the name "Yao." It is said that no name in Egypt was ever uttered in greater awe than his. It is said of him, "He is one and self-existent and to him alone all things owe their being."

Here, as everywhere in the ancient pre-Israelite East, we meet the universal god, the creator and defender of all, mostly in the person of a sun god who only differs in essence from the much later Biblical God in the one respect that there are other gods besides him, though they do, however, all recognize this chief of

41

the gods as their father. Originally the God of Israel was essentially the same as this God of Gods (a designation also applied to Yahweh in the Old Testament) and only gradually did he become differentiated from the other.

As the sun bestows life, so other natural phenomena stir the hearts of men. Solar and lunar eclipses, earthquakes, storms, and natural catastrophes arouse alarm and terror by their weird activities and inexplicable power. Wished-for rain and the flooding of rivers to irrigate the parched countryside make men rejoice and render to the gods thanks, sacrifice, and praise. From Babylon there is preserved a hymn to the storm god which describes the phenomena of nature as manifestations of the wrath of god, in the following words:

> When the Lord is angry, the heavens quake before him;
> When Adad is full of wrath, the earth rocks before him.
> Great mountains break down before him.
> At his wrath and at his anger,
> At his fury and at his raging,
> The Gods of the sky mount up to heaven;
> The Gods of the earth go into the earth,
> The sun is darkened in the depth of heaven,
> In the high reaches of heaven the moon vanishes!

The storm god, son of the most high god, is responsible according to the Babylonian notion for punishing men who do not believe in the gods. In a hymn from the end of the third millennium it is said:

My son, arise and go forth in radiance!
Who can lift himself against you as an adversary?
If the land of the enemy does evil against your father who begot
    you,
Who can lift himself up like unto you? . . .
Hurl your small stones and your large stones against it,
That your right hand may destroy the land of the foe,
That the long arm of your power may cast it down.

For men who are ignorant of nature it is always the gods who control its course. Egypt depends for its fertility of soil upon the

Nile alone, and it is brought by the gods. With Amenhotep IV, it is the sun who brings the overflowing of the river. In his great hymn to Aton he says this about it:

> You make the Nile in the underworld,
> You bring it forth as you desire
> To give life to the people [of Egypt]. . . .
> You have set a Nile in heaven
> That it may descend for them
> And engender waves upon the mountains
> Like the great green ocean
> To water their fields by their towns. . . .

In the ancient Indian religious books it is the god Rudra who afflicts man with the thunderclap. In Babylonia, home of the cult of the moon, an eclipse of the moon caused great fear of coming disaster and this used to make all of the country tremble. Its unexpected onset increased the anxiety further since astronomical prediction was still unknown.

In the Babylonian texts, a ritual was laid down for the king to follow when a lunar eclipse began. The religious exercises varied with the months in which the lunar eclipse occurred. In the month Nisan, he could avert disaster only if the priest hung red drapery on the door and offered to the god Anu a censer of holy incense and a similar one to the chief god Enlil. After the eclipse of the moon had passed, the king had to fall on his face toward the south and to produce a mixture of red sap and cypress oil and anoint his bed with it. That would keep the disaster far at bay. Should the eclipse fall in the month of Ab, the king had to lie behind a door, wash himself with spring water, speak in a secret place, and kiss the face of a crone. In carrying out all this properly, "he will make a name for himself and have none to equal him." For every month there was a similar ritual to perform, sometimes easier, sometimes harder.

The ancient Babylonians would have venerated highly a living being which might be supposed to have a life especially influenced by the moon. Modern science supposes that this is true of the palolo worm which lives today in the coral reefs of the Pacific. Each month on the day before the moon enters its last quarter, the female worms detach their hinder parts in such great numbers that the ocean fairly teems with them. These detached parts are about a foot long (much bigger than their mothers) and are capable of forming new worms. If the Babylonians had seen this event and been able to establish the connection with the moon, they would have built a temple to the worm and would have venerated it as the living symbol of the moon goddess.

Among the people of Israel, the moon cult was known just as the sun cult was, being widespread among them as it was everywhere in the Near East in antiquity. The day of the new moon ranked as a holy day, called *rosh chodesh,* and on it no work was done. Later it yielded to the Sabbath, but it continues up to the present to be marked by a half holiday, and in the Jewish liturgy it is honored by a special prayer.

In the Bible the progress of the heavenly bodies and events of nature are ascribed to divine intervention. In Psalm 29 the might of the storm is extolled as the glory of Yahweh. There it is said that the God of glory thunders, and the voice of the Lord breaks the oak trees and flashes forth flames of fire. The final thought is "the Lord sits enthroned over the flood." In the poetry of most oriental people of old, the description of natural catastrophes occupies the foremost place, an indication of how terrible their results are for mankind.

The Biblical myth of the deluge probably refers to a flood between the Euphrates and the Tigris. Similar floods occurred in other parts of Asia and among them one is reported from China in 2300 B.C.

Despite some change of climate since Biblical times in the Tigris-Euphrates area, a disastrous deluge occurred there in 1876. Lashed by a cyclone, accompanied by storms with cloudbursts, a monstrous wave poured with tremendous power over the peaceful land. In a very short time over 400,000 souls had fallen a sacrifice, drowned.

Just as the Bible represents the deluge with its annihilation of almost the whole human race as a punishment from a god, so the prophets declare that it is a judgment from a god when drought hangs over the parched land. Again and again the writers of the Bible can only help themselves against idolatry by believing that they must employ the heavy artillery of famine, brought on by divine interference with the rain. It is the same theory of reward and punishment that the Babylonian priests used long before the period of Israel. From it is derived the primitive conception of nature which generally obtained over all the antique period, and to it the clever post-Biblical scholars of the Talmud were no exceptions.

In defiance of all modern science, this belief in divine reward and punishment has not changed even in the twentieth century for the bulk of the faithful in various regions and religions. Services of intercession to a god for rain prove this. Prayers by Japanese Shintoists for rain to combat the conflagrations were publicly offered after enemy air attacks on big Japanese cities in 1942. In time of prolonged drought in Catholic countries, aid is sought from Bishop Adalbert of Prague, who died about 997 and is the saint appointed for rain and the competent intercessor for rain with the Christian God. When the showers come, Catholics still offer services of thanks in our century to St. Adalbert for his effective negotiations with their God.

When simple pious souls are asked whether they believe in the Genesis myth of a God creating the world and Adam and Eve, the alleged first human beings, they are astonished at the question and answer that they do believe it. With them belong the orthodox Jews, who constitute a unique group not to be compared with any other. These pious people are an active, living reality within an internal and external seclusion chosen by themselves and hedged about by an indifferent world around them. They regard hard destiny as divine punishment for their own and their fathers' sins against their God, as the Bible proclaims a hundred times. They do not know when the bondage of their suffering is to end and so live in continual fear of new disaster to be sent on them by an outraged and terrible God.

Indeed, a God choosing a people to propagate faith in him and then letting them suffer martyrdom for 2,000 years for fulfilling their divinely appointed task is as repulsive as it is inexplicable.

Herein lies the tragedy of the Jews. Out of fidelity and piety to past generations, they have accepted the fear of a god as the subject of their faith, and thereby this attitude of soul has become a heritage of the generations and has broadened out from fear of the deity to fear of the world. They remain in this way stuck fast in the thoughts of a two-thousand-year-old past. So they are slighted and persecuted and always pray ever and again to their god for redemption, and as he was once present to their fathers in lightning and thunder, so he is still present to them in war and in the enmity of men. For they are only suffering punishment because they and their fathers were unfaithful to him.

Thus does the sturdy faith of Jewry in its truly magnificent tenacity of belief present itself to us in its unmodified ancient form. It suffers everything for the will of a god and it stirs our amazement and pity alike. Its watchword is "So God wills!" They are constantly suspended between fear and hope, and of these one has never played them false: namely fear, which they will never lose as long as they regard the ignorance of their forefathers as the highest good in the questions of being. With these forebears they share fear of the name of their god, who spells for them a holy secret. Here, too, they lean upon ancient prototypes.

The museum in Cairo possesses a papyrus dating from the sixteenth century B.C., about a thousand years before the Bible was committed to writing. This papyrus speaks of the God of Gods: ". . . who hides his name from his children, in this his name Amon." Another papyrus from the same period contains a myth about the gods portraying the secrecy of the dreaded holy name.

According to this myth, the name of Re, creator of the universe, is not even known to the other gods. The cunning and crafty goddess Isis is restless because the other gods do not know. She causes Re to be bitten by a poisonous serpent and she alone can save him from the consequences of this bite. As soon as the gods learn of his mishap they hurry to him, grieving to help him. Isis asks him his name, and he answers as follows, "I am it." That is not enough for her, for she wants to know his secret name. She promises to stop the action of the poison, and in return Re lets his secret name pass out of his body into hers. From then on she guards it as the greatest mystery.

This tale has given rise to many interpretations, and it shows the pains taken by the Egyptian priesthood to veil the earthly origin of their divine characters from the people. As the Egyptian creator of the universe was created by the priests, the other gods and the whole universe have him to thank for their existence, and furthermore, it is equally important that the name of this source of all being should be unknown and always feared. Only those of the priestly cloth may know it; for the laity, it must always remain swathed in the terror of mystery.

In an Egyptian funerary text the god Re says of himself:

> I am yesterday which saw millions of years. . . . I am the lord of eternity.

Another papyrus records Re's words:

> I am who I am

(Nu pu nuk), the same as the words spoken by Yahweh in the Old Testament (Exodus 3:14), many hundreds of years after the Egyptian writing.

In Hebrew the divine name Yahweh consists of the four consonants, IHWH, without vowels, the so-called tetragrammaton. The name Jehovah consists of these four letters with the introduction of three vowels, but it is not the secret name of the Jewish God. This secret name remains hidden and forms for the Jews a deep and dreadful mystery. Only once a year, on the day of Atonement, according to tradition, was it uttered in the temple at Jerusalem (before the Romans destroyed the city) by the high priest as "Yehauwo," and then only in a whisper and during a loud general prayer, at which the faithful cast themselves down so that no one could understand it. Even today in the synagogues of the world the holy and dreadful name is uttered only on the day of Atonement by the highest officiating rabbis.

Nothing can express the idea of a god with greater depth and holiness than this name. Even the most sacred objects of the Roman Catholic Church, the monstrance and the wafer of the Holy Communion, the host, do not arise to the significance of the holy name of the god in the Jewish religion; for these most venerable objects of the Roman Catholic ritual lack the dread which Jewry attaches to the name in an especial way. Unauthorized utterance of the name of this god counts as the worst kind of blasphemy. In Leviticus 24:16 is an amplification of the commandment against taking the name of the Lord in vain:

> He who blasphemes the name of the Lord shall be put to death.

The above is the wording of the Revised Standard Version. In the Jewish version this passage runs:

> He that names the name of the eternal one, he shall surely be put to death.

In this connection, the Talmud relates the following passage: A scribe was arrested for some crime and had to answer before his judges. When he was asked why he had occupied himself with the Torah (the five books of Moses) he answered:

> Because the Lord, my God, commanded me.

The Talmud continues:

> Then they passed sentence forthwith that he be burnt, that his wife be executed, and that his daughter be turned over to a brothel. That he be burnt because he had uttered letter by letter the name of God. And that his wife be executed because she had not prevented him. And that his daughter be turned over to a brothel because when once she went past some Roman patricians and they made the remark that this maiden had an elegant walk, she flounced even more.

This Draconian judgment clearly aims to fulfill the priestly idea of keeping the faithful from finding out the earthly and human origin of the figure of God, and to surround it with a thick veil of mystery and terror so that they should never doubt the supernatural character of this deity.

Akin to the utterance of the secret and highly hallowed name of the god, forbidden under pain of death, stands this other commandment (Exodus 20:4):

> You shall not make for yourself a graven image, or any
> likeness of anything that is in heaven above . . . .

The basis for this ban is the same as that for the name of the
god: concealment of the human and priestly origin of the figure
of the god. Ever and again we meet such ideas in various religions.
In the overlordship of the gods there is lurking the overlordship
of the priestly caste. This priestly caste gives directions which
serve man but which also profit the church, and therefore it
installs the gods as the supreme power.

Exclusively endowed with human characteristics the gods must
live in an unknown and splendid world, the blessed goal of desire
which can never be attained in human life. To enhance the sanctity men desire for the gods, their origin remains undisclosed to
human thought, the divine name remains unuttered, and the
preparation of an image is forbidden.

Egypt concealed and put a ban on divine images before Jewry
did. In the museum at Berlin there is a wooden group from
ancient Egyptian times, portraying a treasurer of the sun temple
at Thebes. The inscription says among other things:

> God travels through the sea of heaven and gives light
> to both lands. His images are hidden from mankind. . . .

This is a pointer which says more than merely that there is
no likeness of him. It contains the further thought, that since
there is no image of him, nobody can make any. This idea goes
beyond the Mosaic law, for there is no need to publish a commandment against making any image of a god if his image is
hidden from man, for then it is impossible to make an image of
him. It is, however, surprising that Amenhotep IV pronounced
a ban on making any image of the sun, his sole symbol of belief.
Apart from the extraordinarily striking and illuminating parallel
with the later commandment by Moses, we marvel at the reasoning
of the royal thinker: the true God does not need any form.

The commandment ascribed to Moses in the Bible against
divine images strikes people in general as extraordinary not because
Moses had attained the high conception of a god never reached

before, but because in this matter Moses was obviously showing great fidelity to his grand model. This gives further support to the "Amenhotep Moses" theory.

The sublime concept of the universe as unimaginable in physical images is not limited to Egypt. India even more anciently expressed the same opinion when it said of the only Purusha, the spiritual cosmic unity:

> Then was the holy one, Purusha the highest who does
> not appear in a definite body, graciously inclined and
> spoke unseen.

Causally connected with the commandment in the Bible against making an image of Yahweh is the further clause against making images of any gods. This was not only directed against the danger of idolatry but obviously also against the temptation toward apostasy from monotheism. The prohibition of images was not always respected, as is shown by an image of Yahweh discovered at Jerusalem and dating from the ancient Israelite period. This image represents the god in human form, traveling on a boat.

Popular sentiment never came to terms with the notion of divine incorporeality as proclaimed by the learned. Indian religion made no concession on this point, as other religions, including Christianity, did. Tertullian, the second-century church father, writes:

> Every image is an idol according to the law, and all
> honor offered to such is idolatry.

Constantine the Great had to convene a Council of the Catholic Church at Constantinople about the question of image worship. It unanimously repudiated prayers to images. The fathers of the church, Eusebius and Epiphanes, gave the following explanation regarding this occasion:

> The angels of the devil taught men to make images
> and set them up for adoration. The invention of images
> was the invention of the devil or of people driven
> thereto by the devil.

The Catholic clergy realized in good time that this attitude, if steadfastly maintained, would deprive simple people who delighted in pictures of the most attractive appeal. Even today every Roman Catholic church contains pictures and images which are adored. The Lutheran confession rather strictly limits the use of color and form, despite some considerable use made of them at the beginning. The Anglican Church of England accepted the original idea of Protestantism but soon linked itself with the ritual of the Roman Catholic Church and is constantly approaching closer to the rites of Rome.

Thus synagogue and church are today further away than ever from the days when an Egyptian Pharaoh apprehended by intuition the cosmic order of nature and rejected the world of the gods, prohibiting the erection of an image of the sun as the true god.

Much water has flowed under the bridge both in a chronological and in a spiritual sense for us since the lofty speculations of Greece, which the philosopher Empedocles in the fifth century B.C. embodied in these words:

> One cannot approach the deity close enough to see him with our eyes or touch him with our hands. . . . For the deity does not have head or limbs like a man . . . but is a spirit, holy and superhuman, which stirs the entire universe and rushes through it with swift thoughts. . . . And this deity is a law for all, extending everywhere through the wide-ruling air and through the infinite light of heaven.

Today we stand amazed before the grandeur of such thoughts. This ancient outlook on the universe remains largely a closed book for the present day, which at least in externals follows the old ways of belief. The kernel of the religions of western civilization remains the God of Israel. Created by human beings in their own image, this God is for them the first cause of all being. Even in respect to divinity man is the measure of all things.

5. THE MORTALITY OF GODS AND ANTHROPOMORPHISM

In the course of time mankind increases its knowledge of the observed phenomena of nature. Consequently, the gulf between the current ideas of mankind and those entertained in the ancient world widens with each passing century. Antiquity knew nothing of electricity or of sound waves or light waves, of the origin of the sun and planets, including the earth itself, or of the reproductive processes of life, including those of man. Man created gods and created them capable of being influenced by sacrifice and prayer, thereby enabling them to direct the fates of men and thus by means of human beings to give the appearance of exercising a sort of control over nature. Every period creates its own divinities in order to achieve through them something it regards as better. On the hypothetical basis of an eternal first cause or of a creator of the universe, man creates for his purposes a system which culminates in the community of the gods upon which he makes his own being dependent.

The Bible does not set forth this ancient development of the world of the gods, or does so only in so far as it silently incorporates into itself part of the contemporary climate of opinion, but it never mentions how the people and the nations evolved their ancient cultural traditions, including the gods. The Old Testament presents the pre-Biblical period as almost wholly a *terra incognita*. Its content begins with the history of creation and the first man and woman, Adam and Eve, and then goes on to Noah and the patriarchs to make, in the covenant under Moses, the nucleus of faith out of which comes Jesus, likewise completely unknown. This being established, some vital conseqences follow for pre-Biblical man.

The Jewish god Yahweh is the basis of three religions—Judaism, Christianity, and Islam—into which two-fifths of all people alive today are born. This god allegedly gave a commission over 3,000 years ago to a man to proclaim legislation ostensibly deriving from him. The mission was entrusted to an Egyptian sun priest, Moses, and he communicated it to a group of people numerically insignificant compared with the population of the time. According to the supposition of modern science, humanity has been living on earth for at least 500,000 years. The basis of knowledge about Yahweh is the Old Testament, and its historical and religious account begins with Abraham, less than 4,000 years ago. This implies that Yahweh had paid no heed to mankind for almost half a million years.

As far back as our knowledge reaches into pre-Biblical times, we know that polytheism and some kind of belief in spirits prevailed, and that it was thought highly creditable of the Jews to have introduced monotheism to mankind through their god and Moses. Clearly, therefore, vast numbers of mankind cannot have known anything about the god of the Bible, since he had not revealed himself to men before the time of Moses. Compared with some 500,000 years of human existence, it is really only a very brief period since man has believed in this god. Hence of all mankind, past and present, only a rather small segment ever believed in the god Yahweh.

This unassailable fact reveals to us a tragedy of colossal dimensions in respect to the theory of redemption. According to the normative Christian conception, eternal hell-fire is the lot of those who have not lived and died in the son of the Christian God, and there is hardly any escape from this, even at the Last Judgment. Moreover, the splendor of the beyond is forever closed to the Jew and to the Muslim who do not accept the Christian concept of divinity and scheme of salvation. This fate is likewise in store not only for the many millions of Buddhists, Hindus, and Shintoists and the rest of the nonbelievers but also for those who died during the myriads of years before God and Jesus had vouchsafed knowledge of themselves. Their souls suffer wholly undeserved torment in the unquenchable Christian hell.

There is no answer to the question why this God did not reveal

himself until so recently in human history and why he sent the
Christian redeemer only yesterday in the ages of human existence.
Or why he for thousands of years tolerated idolatry among the
ancient peoples including Israel, even in Biblical times, and then
declared war on this idolatry, instead of preventing its rise in
the first place. As he is almighty, all knowing, and all wise, he
did not need to let this abomination come about in the first
place if he had not wanted to.

This riddle may be solved by examining theology in the framework of man's evolving history. What happens to a people in
the course of time is conditioned by its soil and its landscape. To
this process also belongs the content of its creed. No divorce can
be made between a god and gods, between people and habitat.
According to the religious point of view, heavenly hosts intervene
decisively in the course of history through war, victory, and defeat.
The priests of all religions accompany their armies, seeking by
prayer to obtain victory from heaven for their arms and extolling
the defeat of the foe in prayer as an act of a god.

With the destinies of kingdom the fate of the gods is intricately
involved. They live and die together. When a feeble enemy state
goes to the wall, its god incapable of protecting it succumbs with
it. The victor, however, enhances the position of his gods because
they brought about victory, national security, and territorial ag-
grandizement. The gods were contrived by men and they stand
and fall with them. Despite the might and power of the former
kingdoms of India, China, Egypt, Assyria, Babylonia, Persia,
Greece, Rome, Mexico, Peru, and other past peoples they and
with them their gods have passed away on the river of eternity.
Every kingdom, every god, and every religion will some day founder on this river. Nothing man has made or conceived, even his religions, is immune to this inexorable law of history.

It is intelligible why the god of the Bible does not come onto
the stage of history before Abraham, who perhaps lived about
4,000 years ago. It is because what was dim prehistory for the
Biblical editors lay before this patriarch. With Abraham a knowledge of Yahweh appears for the first time in history. Yahweh
appears at the same time as does the founder of the people of
Israel. The hopes and thoughts of the ancient Israelites are reflected

in their god as they are among all peoples in the figures of the gods which they have conceived. He cannot be divorced from the life and historical course of the people of Israel. He rises and grows with it, and by a gradual development, he finally grows into the one and only God of the Bible. The great riddle of the universe lies hidden behind him as behind all deities.

Exactly as all the other ancient people before them, the Israelites in this way hit upon a solution, befitting the age, for making the unknown intelligible and familiar. Israel, too, made a god for itself in the image of the people of Israel, just as Re was modeled on an Egyptian, Marduk and Enlil on a Babylonian, and Zeus on a Greek. Israel raised for its god the claim that he was greater and more powerful than all previous gods. They saw in him the one and only ruler of the world, the principle of intelligibility, and the meaning of their existence. They formed their god in their own likeness and richly endowed him with human qualities and peculiarities, just as the people before them and around them did. Thus came into existence the mythical being that supposably guides all human destinies and to whom prayers are directed. Thus came the alleged ultimate base of all moral and material power. Thus came God.

All gods without exception have this human origin. It is therefore understandable that their most prominent traits are human ones. The Greek philosophers had already unlocked this knowledge. In the sixth century B.C., when some of the earliest parts of the Bible were written, Xenophanes said:

> Homer and Hesiod have saddled the Gods with everything which is regarded as disgraceful and shameful among men—theft, adultery, and dishonesty towards each other . . . still mortals fancy that the Gods were born and wear clothes, and have voices and figures like themselves. So if oxen, horses, and lions had hands or could paint with their hands and make works of art like men, the horse would make images of the Gods in the shape of horses, oxen in the shape of oxen, the several kinds endowing their divinities with bodies exactly like their own. The Ethiopians imagine that

their Gods are snub-nosed and black, the Thracians
that theirs are blue-eyed and red-haired.

Thus today the Greenlanders place the site of the beyond
with its blessed glories (for which they hope) not in the sky
but under the sea, for since it brings them food and a livelihood,
the sea alone appears to be an appropriate dwelling place for
their god.

The Jewish god is thought of as a man in all his relationships.
Since it was not allowed to represent him by any image though
his nearness had to be made credible to the people, the priests
had an ark constructed. Of this the Bible says (Exodus 25:8):

> And let them make me a sanctuary, that I may dwell
> in their midst.

This holy ark the Hebrews regarded as the resting place of their
god, who continually sojourned with his people, without being
visible. Whatever paths they traversed on the journey toward
Canaan, they carried along this ark amid sustained ritual ceremony
performed by a priestly class specially chosen for the purpose,
whose service was devoted to the sacred sanctuary of their god.
Its construction is precisely described in the Bible. It corresponds,
remarkably enough, to the holy arks occurring in well-preserved
pictures from pre-Biblical periods in Egypt and Babylon.

On journeys and in military campaigns the sanctuary was carried
along before Israel. It accords with the motto "God with us"
used by all people holding to a god. The presence of their god
in the ark helped the Israelites to victory. When the ark went to
war with them, Moses said (Numbers 10:35):

> "Arise, O Lord, and let thy enemies be scattered; and
> let them that hate thee flee before thee."

As a home for this sanctuary a tabernacle was made, constructed
so that it could be taken apart and transported, and in this sanctuary the invisible god was sheltered and could be consulted as
an oracle. Moses undertook the service of the oracle, as this god
had unveiled himself to him alone.

One can infer from the Biblical account that Moses apparently
exercised a most extraordinary influence on the people. Moses

betakes himself to the tabernacle in festival procession; the people stand full of awe before the wooden hut or tent and gaze at the mighty one until he reaches the sanctuary which is covered by a cloud. As soon as he has vanished into the interior, the cloud slowly sinks down, lingers in front of the door of the holy tent, and begins to speak to Moses. Unheard by the people, while they remain standing in a devout and bowed attitude, there now takes place the conversation between Moses and the god as the people suppose. It is the moment when he is receiving divine instructions for the future. After the interview has ended, Moses steps forth with shining countenance and announces what the god has said.

In this description the composers of the Bible repeated the approximate course of a royal audience. The only difference is that here they replaced the person of the king by the ark and the cloud. Islam is familiar with a similar event. Allah, too, never reveals himself in any shape. In the Koran (Suras 42-50) it is said that Allah never addresses a creature made of flesh except through revelation or "behind a curtain."

In spite of the prohibition against images, it is quite impossible to conceive of a god in any but a thoroughly human shape. The prophet Isaiah sees his god in a form which is closely related to his home background. His god is the shepherd and he says of him (Isaiah 40:11):

> He will feed his flock like a shepherd, he will gather
> the lambs in his arms, he will carry them in his bosom,
> and gently lead those that are with young.

In Christianity this beautiful peaceful picture gets adopted as the dominant motif in representing the god, to which the art of many centuries has given sublime expression.

The Talmud gives a proof of the way the divine world is derived from the familiar experiences of human life. The following is part of an imaginary conversation between his god and one of the descendants of Noah as the representative of the human race. It runs:

> Lord of the world, have then the Israelites, who have
> taken upon themselves the Torah, kept its command-

ments? The holy one, let his name be praised, will
answer them, "I testify for them that they have kept the
Torah." They will reply unto him, "Lord of the world,
can then a father give testimony for his son? It is expressly said, 'My firstborn son is Israel.' " The holy one
will answer them, "Heaven and earth shall give testimony for them that they have kept the whole Torah."
They will answer him, "Heaven and earth are pre-
occupied with bearing their testimony. . . ."

This passage of the Talmud presents a judicial hearing in
heaven, in which Israel is the accused, a descendant of Noah the
examining magistrate, and their god the witness. In a prayer which
is still repeated, there is a similar transference. The person at
prayer thinks that none of his sins can prevent his god from
bestowing blessings on him because all of his sins are forgiven
on the Day of Atonement. By way of making even more sure
that he has not been overweening in his prayer, he asks his god,
"Hath the slanderer [Satan] anything yet further to bring forth
against me?"

Between God and Israel and every individual Israelite there
stands the covenant, and this implies a relationship such as exists
between two men who have made a contract. If the Israelites
contravene the contract, then the other party to the contract
should not bear too great a grudge against them. The prophet
Jeremiah laments the punishments which the god threatens to
bring upon Israel for its faithlessness (Jeremiah 14:21):

> Do not spurn us, for thy name's sake; do not dishonor
> thy glorious throne; remember and do not break thy
> covenant with us.

And as its god thinks lovingly of Israel, the prophet Hosea has
him say (Hosea 2:19):

> I will betroth you to me for ever.

The forms in which the covenant with the god is drawn up
derive purely from the relationships of human beings with each
other; a prayer contains the petition that this god may forgive

the sins of the "nation bound to him as a brother." The thought continually recurs that this god should pardon his people and should not be too angry with them for their fickleness. A prayer runs thus:

> We have sinned, O cast us not away . . . when we cry aloud, hide not thy face; when we fail, requite us not! . . . When we fall away, do not thou fall away! . . . When we slide backwards, do not thou slide back from us!

This anthropomorphism reaches its zenith when the god himself appears and pleads, as in the question which the prophet Micah has him utter (Micah 6:3):

> O my people, what have I done to you? In what have I wearied you?

Finally this omniscient god does not know the reason for their falling from him, for Jeremiah puts these words in his mouth (Jeremiah 2:5):

> What wrong did your fathers find in me, that they went far from me, and went after worthlessness, and became worthless?

This god does not spare his reproaches, and in the prophet Micah he recites what he has already done for them (Micah 6:5):

> O my people, remember what Balak King of Moab devised, and what Balaam . . . answered him . . . that you may know the saving acts of the Lord.

If this god knows everything and predetermines the destiny of the peoples, then such thoughts in the minds of the prophets are blasphemy on a lofty scale. But the prophets are only men; they see the idolatry of their people around them and that their god does not intervene. Perhaps they themselves begin to doubt. But things dare not reach such a pitch. This god must himself speak to his people and reproach them for their shameful behavior.

As for these reproaches and questions so understandable among men—if the children of Israel in the face of idolatry will not surrender themselves to the god of the prophets (a god who arose in the prophets and dwells in them), then what is left for these prophets but to lend to their god human thoughts and expressions in complete accord with their own?

Considering the national misfortune continually befalling Israel, one could not attribute it to anything other than punishment for persistent disloyalty to their god. It was up to the people themselves alone to effect a change for the better. As a stern father speaks to his children, so the prophets make the god of Israel speak. Such are the words of the prophet Joel (2:12-13):

> "Yet even now," says the Lord, "return to me with all
> your heart, with fasting, with weeping, and with mourn-
> ing; . . . Return to the Lord, your God, for he is
> gracious and merciful, slow to anger, and abounding
> in steadfast love, and repents of evil.

If they would only listen, these incorrigible sinners; they do not really deserve such great forbearance. It is not until post-Biblical times that it becomes possible to lead the wandering back to this god, and again it is in the Talmud that we find the legal formula suitable for men. It sounds like a lawyer's deed when it says:

> We have sworn to the holy one that we shall not
> exchange him for any other God, and he has also
> sworn to us that he will not exchange us for any other
> nation.

The prophets, the scribes, and the composers of the Bible use images drawn from the life around them to make the concept of their god intelligible to themselves and understandable to the people.

People in the ancient East had a sense of actuality to which intelligent men, including the prophets, paid respect in giving the Bible its form and content. This sense forbade any speculations on the idea of a god which flew too high away from the earth. Not until the rise of a scientific knowledge of nature was the idea of a personal god reduced to an abstract religious and philosophical concept, as has been done to some extent by Protestant Biblical scholars.

Judaism did not follow this path. The Old Testament con ceived of its god as a person just as practising Jews, orthodox Christians, and the Moslems still do. This god is almost purely human. Israel chose for itself a god so earthbound that hardly any other god has been created in a similar guise. He makes a covenant with Moses and gives to the Jews and to them alone the Torah. This great legal work, according to the Talmud, was not appreciated by other nations; for it supposes that this god offered his teaching around to each nation, but they all rejected it until he finally came to the Jewish people and they accepted it. Here again is a thought derived altogether from human ex perience. It leads to the conclusion that Israel regards itself as the chosen people of a god.

6. THE CHOSEN PEOPLE

The Old Testament gives no particulars about the reason why this god chose the Israelites as his people; ostensibly this choice rests on a revelation, an act of divine grace. The origin of any form of belief always remains veiled in mystic darkness and is inexplicable by natural means. For the given content of the Holy Scriptures, it is a question of "faith," there being no room for proof. This faith is the basis of all supernatural religions.

How can we explain a national belief that a god has chosen a people and made a mutual covenant with it? We know that Moses, as seen in the light of the Bible, had a thoroughly earthly orientation. In contrast with other religions, his faith sought the happiness of mankind on this earth. The "future world" is an idea which crept in only during later Biblical times. It is from Egypt that Moses derived his attitude toward life, limiting it to this world. He knew the climatic influences that govern life in his homeland, and was aware of the significance of the sun and of irrigation by the Nile on which the welfare of the country depended.

These simple matters had been observed for generations and were esteemed in accordance with their value for the community. The people of the Exodus knew them too and agree in every particular with the thoughts of Moses respecting them. When the Exodus was accomplished, they became witnesses of phenomena they had never experienced in Egypt and which they had never heard of. These included the natural marvels of ebb and flow. They were amazed to see how the sea slowly retreated from the shore and allowed them to pass over in a narrow and shallow part of the Red Sea, dry-shod. Moses may have heard of this phenomenon before at the court of Pharaoh, and he may, as described in Exodus, have raised his staff and thereby represented himself to the people as a medium of this supernatural

power in order to give a correspondingly strong foundation to his
leadership.

We may suppose that the passage of this presumably large
number of people with wagons and horses may have lasted an
appreciable time; but at any rate it was concluded before the
return of the tide. Perhaps Moses had found out the most pro-
pitious times for crossing from natives of the Sinai peninsula
who had joined his party and who knew the tides.

The Egyptians were unfamiliar with the tides or at least with
their actual high and low periods. They saw Moses and those
with him emerging safely from the sea floor on the other side,
and so they gave pursuit. Meanwhile the tide turned. Pharaoh's
cavalry and infantry were alike drowned, and he himself with
them. It is exactly what happens today to a careless person who
does not know the tides and risks the passage of the mud flats
of the North Frisian islands.

Such is the very simple way in which these great miracles of
the Bible find a natural explanation, and the same applies to the
events on Mount Sinai. Exodus 19:16 tells of thunder and lightning, and a thick cloud upon the mountain, and a very loud
trumpet blast so that all the people trembled. Exodus 19:18
relates that "Mount Sinai was wrapped in smoke, because the
Lord descended upon it in fire; and the smoke of it went up like
the smoke of a kiln, and the whole mountain quaked greatly."

All this points to a volcano not yet fully come to rest; such
intermittently active volcanoes are still found in various parts of
the world. Indeed one could not reasonably expect to find a
better description of a volcanic eruption than that given in the
Exodus verses cited above. The observer omitted no essential
detail. This stupendous natural phenomenon must have made an
immense impression on a people who had no experience of the
like before and were then in a nervous mood produced by suffering and persecution. To them it must have been the veritable
sign of a god saying,

> You shall pray to me, for do you not see my might
> and my majesty with your own eyes and hear them
> with your own ears?

Would not a man like Moses make use of this unexpected and unprecedented occurrence? It would be hard to understand if he had not profited by this opportunity. After the miracle of the Red Sea this yet clearer sign now came from heaven and must have made a strong impression even on Moses. He began to believe in his mission as divinely appointed and regarded the destruction of the Egyptian army in the Red Sea as an act of heaven. Surely he knew it and all the people with him. A god was leading them, shielding them, revealing himself in the heavy cloud of smoke on the mountain, in the thunder, the lightning, the rumblings from the bowels of the mountain and in the quaking of the earth.

There are probably still primitive peoples who react in the same way as Moses and his people to this marvel the first time they see a mountain vomiting fire. Such experiences arouse in primitive men a sense of the vast unexplained and unknown. We remember having seen peasants dashing for safety during peacetime at the first sight of an airplane, crossing themselves in confused flight. Who, however, was the god who spoke to Moses and his people out of the thunderclouds of Sinai? Moses had not known about him before, but he and his people were not the only ones who trembled before this frightful display.

Around them assembled the native inhabitants who had always cast themselves down at the outbreak of these uncanny phenomena on the mountain and then kept on praying fervently. These natives worshiped him who once more threatened punishment out of clouds and lightning, out of fire, smoke, and din. They had known this god, Yahweh, from the time of their early ancestors. Now for the first time Moses learned the name of the god who clearly wanted to give a sign to him and to his people. Somewhat like this may have been the birth of the Yahweh religion as postulated in the Old Testament.

Moses learned in Egypt that the sun alone was the highest principle of life, but now he discovered at Sinai that it did not exclusively rule the universe and direct man's destiny. There was also Yahweh, the terrible god of earthquake, volcano, and fire. Perhaps the accustomed, beloved, and friendly sun would grow pale in comparison. Fear of the angry god of thunder now began to tip the scales, and so fear of Yahweh became dominant. The authors of the Bible in Palestine stress this fear of Yahweh even though that country had no volcanoes spewing fire to support their message of terror.

At Sinai, Moses recognized that Providence was indicating a course of action for him and his people. Clearly the new and mighty god had given him a sign. He ascended the mountain and experienced as actual events the things that took place in his mind. The vivid delusion or hallucination was upon him after he descended from the mountain and reported to his people that a god had spoken to him out of the rumbling of the mountain in the thick and heavy cloud of smoke. Such is the origin of all visions, whether experienced by Moses, the prophets, Jesus, Joan of Arc, or Theresa von Konnersreuth in our own day.

From that time forth Moses may have been certain that this god had some special plan for the people of the Exodus. He had a special place prepared for Yahweh in the midst of the people in the empty ark of the covenant; for what could the manifestation on Sinai possibly mean except that this god intended to set these people before all others? At least that is the conception of the Old Testament, in which the full pride of the composers is expressed in the notion of divine favoritism. Hence other nations are as nothing in the eyes of this god, for he has given his teaching to Israel, and to no other nation. Still, they act as though they did not know that hundreds of years earlier or, if one dates from the final redaction of the Bible, about fourteen hundred years earlier, the Babylonian king, Hammurabi, had published the main essentials of the Jewish law in his stone book of the law, the Code of Hammurabi.

The Bible and later the Talmud adhere to the notion that in the gift of the commandments on Sinai this god created something grand and unique for Israel alone. On this the prophet Isaiah remarks "Those who war against you shall be as nothing at all" (41:12). In the Biblical view these heathen peoples serve no purpose except to punish Israel for any apostasy from this god. Such were the Assyrians and the Babylonians and also the Romans, until finally at the behest of this god these heathen states destroyed the kingdoms of Israel and Judah because of their disloyalty to him.

According to the Jewish scribes and learned men, it was Yahweh's sole purpose to single out Israel. But Israel does not have a monopoly on this line of thought, for there are other religions which regard their tenets as particular marks of a god's grace, as Islam does its Koran.

What is peculiar is the assumption that a community is sanctified by its literature. Every member of the covenant with this god is automatically hallowed by this divine legislation. The Jews of the Bible do not acquire their special merit by outstanding human attributes or efforts, or because they descended from Abraham or belonged to any allegedly superior racial affiliation. There is not a word about this. The writers of the Bible are not in the least interested in that; indeed they appear deliberately to portray their people as altogether lacking in any special merits. For the more unworthy the Israelites are, the more striking is the fact that this god has chosen precisely them out of all peoples. His choice is not made on their account, as is stressed time and again, but rather for his name's sake and because he has sworn a covenant with the Israelite patriarchs that he would keep faith with them. Indeed, this god expressly declares in Deuteronomy 9:5 that it was not because of the righteousness of the Israelites that he gave them Canaan.

When Jews assert that they are a god's chosen people and when in order to keep their faith pure they set themselves apart in the course of history, proclaiming harsh rules to follow and forbidding mixed marriages with gentiles, they may appear to be arrogant. But one must remember that in their separatism they are motivated not by racial pride, not by self-glorification, but purely by the notion that a god has chosen them above all other peoples and handed the laws to Moses with the explicit statement that Israel was neither more righteous nor more deserving than other nations.

This means that Jews may not be said to have excessive self-esteem in a human sense but that none the less they lack modesty in regard to religion. The Bible and the Talmud often indulge in exaggeration about the relationship between this god and his chosen people. This trait has often aroused irritation among the gentiles and consequent persecution.

Why according to the Bible is Israel a chosen vessel? The composers of the Bible thought of Abraham, hundreds of years before Moses, as the first man chosen by the god to fulfill a divinely appointed task. Without the slightest hint of an explanation, this god abruptly summoned Abraham to leave his home and promised him "I will make of you a great nation, and I will bless you, and make your name great" (Genesis 12:2). Abraham got this promise although up till then he did not even know this god since he had worshiped the local gods of his native town, Ur of the Chaldees. But Abraham must have accomplished something particularly pleasing to this god as he further tells him. "By you all the families of the earth will bless themselves." The reason for this great promise is never revealed.

This god's attachment to the stranger from Ur took on a new form when he proposed to make a covenant with him in exchange for which Abraham was to walk before him and be devout. Again for no apparent reason, he promised him the land of Canaan and established the following token of the covenant between Abraham and himself:

> Every male among you shall be circumcised. You shall
> be circumcised in the flesh of your foreskins, and it
> shall be a sign of the covenant between me and you.
> (Genesis 17:10 f.)

After Abraham, who allegedly got to be a 175 years old, came Isaac, his son. This god repeated to him the promise made to Abraham including the proviso that through him, too, all the peoples of the earth should be blessed. He lived to the age of 180 years, and then the god repeated in a dream to his son Jacob all the assurances which he had proclaimed to the two previous patriarchs, and this in spite of the fact that Jacob did not believe in this god. Nay more, he imposed the following condition:

> If God will be with me, and will keep me in this way
> that I go, and will give me bread to eat and clothing

to wear, so that I come again to my father's house in
peace, then the Lord shall be my God.
(Genesis 28:20 f.)

This passage in Genesis appears remarkable, for if this god
chose Abraham and Isaac because of their steadfast faith to bless
all the people of the earth through them, then here is a powerful
argument against this god's foresight and omniscience if the third
patriarch, Jacob, that is, the third generation, no longer had any
faith in him and actually insisted on proof of his omnipotence
before recognizing him as a god.

In the Bible the covenant continued to remain the nucleus of
divine promises which finally reached their climax in the covenant
with Moses. Thus according to the word of this god, Israel was
right from the start the people to whom mankind is indebted for
its future happiness.

In spite of all the covenants and promises between the god and
the three patriarchs, as well as with Moses, Israel was never
constant for very long. Even in their times the rule was backsliding
from the Lord and worship of foreign gods. A passage in the
Pentateuch lays the blame for this on the god Himself; in it
Moses says:

But to this day the Lord has not given you a mind to
understand, or eyes to see, or ears to hear.
(Deuteronomy 29:4)

This utterance allows of only two interpretations. Either the
agreements with the patriarchs were fully valid and in order,
which would mean that the new covenant with Moses was superfluous and the above Biblical passage is an editorial slip of the
writers; or the covenants and promises with Abraham, Isaac, and
Jacob were introduced into the Bible only to establish the idea
of monotheism as running without a gap from Adam to Moses,
and must be appraised as interpolations. In the latter case, Yahweh
was unknown to the people of Moses right up to Sinai, and hence
it was impossible for them to be faithless to him, and the above
Biblical text consequently obtains its correct verbal interpretation.

Moses was accordingly the founder of the covenant between the god and his chosen people and not just one who renewed it as the Bible represents. Of course, this by no means implies that what the Bible says of the covenant transaction contains any historical truth, for there simply is no natural basis for this or any other alleged revelation. Our purpose is only to point out that the Biblical founding of the beliefs of the Jewish religion on the activity of the patriarchs and Moses entails fundamental contradictions. This does not stop the Bible or the Talmud or the scribes and priests, who draw up the commandments, from praising the people of Israel expressly for their great fidelity toward their god and from rendering thanks ever and again to the Lord for having chosen them before all others.

This exceptionally favored position is recognized by other religions. The Koran speaks, though in a tone of raillery:

O you who are Jews, if you think yourselves of all men to be nearest to Allah, then crave death if you are sincere.

But it exhorts the children of Israel itself and represents Allah as saying:

O children of Israel, think on the grace that I have shown you. Keep my covenant, and I shall keep the covenant with you. . . .

Even Christianity, which began and continued the tragedy of the Jews, has never disputed that Israel is chosen. Paul the apostle poses the question:

Then what advantage has the Jew? Or what is the value of circumcision? Much in every way. To begin with, the Jews are entrusted with the oracles of God . . .
(Romans 3:1-2)

That is the scene at Sinai in which the God made the covenant with Moses.

When Allah explains in the Koran 2000 years after Moses,

> O children of Israel, think of the grace which I have
> shown you, that I have exalted you among those that
> dwell in the world,

it is impossible to blame pious Jews for being of the same opinion.
Accordingly they still pray in our time:

> Thou hast chosen us out of all peoples (ato bechartonu
> mikol hoamim), thou didst love us and didst find
> pleasure in us; thou has raised us up above all nations
> and hast hallowed us through thy commandments.

We thus get a bird's eye-view of the chosen people which can
be summarized in this formula: haughtiness in everything connected with their god, modesty in everything connected with
themselves as human beings. This is to emphasize (against those
who read a national arrogance out of passages like this from the
Talmud: "As the world cannot exist without wind, so it cannot
exist without Israel,") that the consequence of the Biblical message really is: "By you all the families of the earth will bless
themselves." If one tries to understand the early periods and
especially the long epoch of Talmudic writings, if one knows
about the great influence that issued from those spiritual centers,
the Jewish universities, serving likewise as the highest courts for
religious legal decisions, only then does one grasp the Jewish
sense of mission and their pride of faith in being preferred by a
god to all other peoples.

Luther acquired from the Jews the idea of being raised above
others by being entrusted with a task of bringing salvation to
men. He says:

> We Christians are greater and more than all creatures,
> not in or of ourselves, but through the gift of God in
> Christ, against which the world is nothing nor can do
> anything.

This reflects to a hair the Jewish opinion about their being
chosen. They do not reckon themselves more worthy than others
on account of their services or their qualities, but only because
a god has taken them as his. Thus too Luther: "Not in and of

us," but because a god has chosen them through Christ. According
to the writers of the Bible this god will preserve the world from
ruin for the sake of the Jews whom he has foreordained to be
the salvation of mankind; Luther also held this same belief when
he says, "It is the Christians for whose sake God spares the
whole world."

The founders of the Jewish and Christian creeds were of the
opinion that they had established them for all time. Even death
does not infringe this principle. The New Testament says:

> If we live, we live to the Lord, and if we die, we die
> to the Lord; so then, whether we live or whether we
> die, we are the Lord's.
>
>   (Romans 14:8)

The Talmud gives expression to identical thoughts for the Jews:

> The Israelites are therefore likened unto an olive tree
> to tell you that just as the leaves of the olive do not
> fall either in summer or in the season of rain, likewise
> for the Israelites there is no ceasing, either in this world
> or in the world to come.

The assumption of an eternal covenant between Israel and its
God is based on the view that the mercy of this god will endure
in the face of any and all sins the chosen people ever committed
or could ever commit in the infinity of time. Consequently the
Bible must heavily stress the continual readiness of this god to
forgive his people, as otherwise the sins of Israel would prevent
the covenant and therefore the Jewish religion from reaching
its goal.

Endowing this god with the peculiarity of continually being
ready to forgive is the only conceivable way of uniting the
Biblical task for the world and that backsliding from their god
which the prophets thrust so firmly into the foreground.

On this note of reconciliation all the disappointments end
which the chosen people cause their god by their idolatry. There
is always a happy end, for if the children of Israel repudiated
their god, the covenant would break up. That repudiation would
mean nothing less than the destruction of the Jewish faith and

therefore the annihilation of this god, for he lives only in the belief of his people. Therefore the final conclusion of religious wisdom is, as the prayer on the Day of Atonement has it, "The eternal one casts not off his people and forsakes not his inheritance."

The Biblical writers nevertheless appreciated that the forebearance they ascribed to their god in the face of flagrant idolatry was a weak point in the structure of their thought. So they let the sinners know that they did not deserve this everlasting grace of forgiveness and that they should not be led by it to suppose that their god forgave them for their own sake. The prophet Ezekiel expresses this clearly:

> It is not for your sake, O house of Israel, that I am about to act, but for the sake of my holy name, which you have profaned among the nations to which you came.   (Ezekiel 36:22)

With the fall of the Jewish national state idolatry gradually let up but did not finally cease until the post-Biblical period.

The forebodings of the prophets about the destruction of the kingdom reached their fulfillment later, if it is not to be assumed that these prophetic pronouncements of divine punishments for idolatry were not committed to writing until after misfortune had already broken in over the kingdom of Israel. This latter view receives support from various circumstances revealed by Biblical research.

Biblical history dwells too amply and too copiously on the struggle of the prophets and their god against idolatry, and by protesting too much validates everything else rather than the faith the Israelites put in their god. Only the Talmud succeeds later in fulfilling the special task of the Old Testament, namely, to make the Jews god-fearing. For the Talmud a short interval of faith towards this god is an event which ensures his good will toward the people. In those early days of deepening faith in their god the Jews, already beginning to be dispersed through the world, placed an especially high value on every one of their so-called divinely inspired utterances. On this subject the Talmud has its god say,

Even when Israel performed but few acts pleasing to
God just as a hen pecks in the dung, so do I gather
them together to make a great heap.

The Old Testament prophets fruitlessly proclaimed the creed
of Yahweh to the ever-unbelieving masses of the people of Israel.
In the same way, Talmudic scholars, exploiting the national misfortune with greater success, later took up and continued the
thoughts of their predecessors. They erected their edifice of thought
with pillars resting on two bases. These were Israel's mission to
the world and the fall of the kingdom through the punishment
of the god as foretold by the prophets because of idolatry.
Apostasy from the god liberated the forces driving toward a renewal of faith. The blasphemous deed of an entire people whom
their god had chosen became the occasion for the rescue of their
religion. The description of idolatrous abomination set forth in
the Bible, especially by the unknown writers of the prophetic
books, bore rich fruit in the Talmud. After the loss of political
independence, post-Biblical men of God made Israel what it had
seldom or never been during Biblical times—the chosen people
true to their god.

Thus idolatry came ironically to renew and maintain the
Yahweh religion of Israel, which today still has ten million adherents. By means of the national disaster joined with the fear
of their god, the priests and scribes made a remarkable diagnosis
of the disease, and on the anvil of idolatry they hammered out
for Israel its alleged mission of being the chosen people.

7. IDOLATRY

Though many details of the development of Biblical monotheism cannot ever be traced back through the darkness of the
distant millennia, still no doubt remains about its ultimate origin
in polytheism. The Israelites and all the other people of the
ancient past, too, for that matter, worshiped divinities whose
power they thought they could detect in the everyday course
of nature. They felt indebted to their household and community
gods for everything, and it went against their grain to suppose
that the familiar rites and practices accorded to these gods were
nugatory. Their customs had been linked with polytheistic cults
for generations. But suddenly there came a demand in Israel to
expunge everything which appeared to the one and only new
god to be superstition, sin, and depravity.

Mosaic monotheism grew out of the realization that there is
only one source of world order, and for the plain man it was too
vast, too lofty, and too peremptory in its consequences for the
course of daily life. The teachings of his ancestors sufficed to
reconcile him to his destiny in his primitive way, albeit that
destiny often treated him roughly. He did not wish to change
what had been right for them; it constituted a tradition which
had been given him in trust. Let the innovators believe in whatever
they pleased, even in a one and only god; he did not mind that
but he wanted them to leave him alone in peace. To him it was
no sin to do as his fathers had done. If it were, as they said, a
lie and a fraud on which he was depending, then this old lie of
his ancestral faith was still much dearer and holier to him than
the new truth of the iconoclasts. Besides, who told him that their
message was really true?

Custom and simplicity are at all times the obvious characteristics of the masses, and they are slow to take on new ways. If the habitual is so strong in our enlightened modern world, how much more likely a revolutionary opinion, such as the expulsion of polytheism by a single god, would come up against unsuspected opposition among ancient peoples. If Moses was the founder of this monotheism and if his life is correctly assigned to a date 1,300 years B.C., 600 years would have elapsed before this faith, sporadically held, arose anew in the reign of Josiah, King of Judah. This indeed was the result of the discovery of the Deuteronomic code in the masonry of the temple which was under repair. Until then, the generation of the Israelites in whose time this event occurred was largely ignorant of both the god and Moses.

The transmission of religious ideas and forms requires more than sagas and legends such as the ancient East created in luxurious profusion. A living medium is needed in the form of a people as a whole, a community. Let us assume that the book of the law was really found as reported and that it was an ancient document as asserted and not the work of priests, say, of the preceding generation, then it follows that 600 years after Moses, Yahweh was hardly known in Judah. This god was not even one among the many gods whom the people worshiped in the reign of King Josiah. Since that generation knew little about faith in this god, the extirpation of polytheism was accompanied by the creation of an essentially new faith.

It is only after this event that the Old Testament comes into being. Not until then did the five books of Moses, the Pentateuch, begin to be written. Then gradually the books of Samuel, Kings, the Prophets, and the other texts of Holy Scripture were revised or newly written down. This took several centuries of work. The nucleus of this structure of faith is the eternal one, the god of the Jews, who ostensibly revealed himself to Moses on Sinai in the gray past. Thus the Bible came into being, the book of books, comprising a synthesis of the thoughts of its authors with the marvelous tales many of them orally transmitted from the ancient past. Its beauty of language, skill of composition, and contents assure it a place of honor in world literature.

The authors of the newly proclaimed faith were unable to

overcome one difficulty. Every day they saw with their own eyes the idolatry of their people, and this presented a danger to their new work right from the very start. Therefore, in their Biblical accounts they could not risk presenting as the sole source of their faith in all periods the god of the ancient time of Moses when he had allegedly just been rediscovered. Furthermore, one would be speaking much too harshly of contemporaries if one asserted that the generations before them had been pious worshipers of the Lord and that only they were abandoned apostates.

According to the Bible, idolatry cropped up as soon as the Exodus from Egypt began. For the god said to Samuel, the Judge:

> According to all the deeds which they have done to me
> from the day I brought them up out of Egypt even to
> this day, forsaking me and serving other gods, so they
> are also doing to you.
>
> (I Samuel 8:8)

As already related, the god made a covenant with all three patriarchs, but Jacob was so little impressed by it that he made his recognition of this god depend on the above-mentioned condition that he must first give him a fortunate return from a journey. He is going to test this god's qualities before he believes in him. His favorite wife, Rachel, the mother of Joseph and Benjamin, worshiped the household gods of her father and stole them from her father before starting on her journey from Mesopotamia to Canaan. It is only at the behest of Jacob that his tribal dependents put away these foreign gods.

The significance of the household gods derives from the instructions Moses passed on to the people directly after he received the commandments on Sinai. These prescribe that a slave who is going to remain with his master after six years' service is to be presented before the gods. His ear is to be pierced with a bodkin into the doorposts which are dedicated to the gods. Recourse must also be had to the household gods for clearing up a theft. Pious readers of the Bible must get qualms from these and similar passages relative to the gods because they contradict the commandment, "You shall have no other gods before me." (Exodus 20:3)

Accordingly the Jewish version of the Bible reads not "gods" any longer but "god." The Lutheran reading is judges instead of gods. Only the German Catholic and the Anglican versions let the word "gods" stand unchanged. Probably the passages cited retain ancient cult forms which the writer of Exodus thought it wrong to eliminate even after the proclamation of the new legislation of Moses.

Moses led his people through territories inhabited by idolatrous heathens. These lands constantly threatened Israel with the danger of religious corruption. The writers of the Bible could not pass over the fact that the non-Israelite natives were polytheists; so they produced reasons for their existence:

> They were for the testing of Israel, to know whether
> Israel would obey the commandments of the Lord,
> which he commanded their fathers by Moses.
>
> (Judges 3:4)

This is a very remarkable passage, for it altogether ignores the fact that the continual struggle of the Biblical writers and their god against idolatry and the continual need of the Lord to forgive this sin would lead one to expect this god to do anything except to tempt the Israelites and to lead them into idolatry.

Images cast from silver, gold, and other metals were employed in the practice of a kind of idolatry which was especially widespread throughout the whole of Canaan. Immediately on his return from Sinai, Moses accordingly forbade the making of these molten images. But he had scarcely turned his back to receive the stone tables of the law from his god when the rule was broken. The man who committed this sacrilege was the high priest Aaron, his own brother. The people had to give their ornaments to him. Out of them he had a golden calf executed to his own design. When Moses returned from meeting with his god, he could only ascertain that in the interim divine honors had been paid to this calf, which represented the god Baal. To it offerings had been brought with dancing and feasting.

At the god's command, Moses had a brazen serpent set up for use as a fetish and as a remedy against snake bite. But the god had not foreseen the sequel, for King Hezekiah of Judah saw to it that this brazen serpent was smashed, because the children of Israel offered it incense and adoration as if it were a god.

The original Canaanite population continually tended to seduce the Israelites to idolatry. "Moses" could only reply with incessant admonitions and the demand that they should tear down the altars of the idols and obliterate everything used in their worship. Above all they should destroy the pillars and the places of prayer on the hills and mountains and under the green trees. For here people conducted services to Baal and Astarte and worshiped the sun, moon, and stars.

Every measure failed. Worshiping images of the gods is a part of man's ancient birthright. The most beautifully built temple can hardly wean him from it. The warm and sunny climate of Canaan gives a sense of inner communion with nature and this is not limited to humanity. Plants and animals, too, are living testimonies to nature's all-embracing power. The Bible teaches us indeed that a god created man and all nature, but this leaves untouched the eternal secret of generation.

The seed-corn is transmuted by an incomprehensible change into the full ripe harvest. Year in and year out this miracle of the tilth and of the mother's womb is sent to man. Is this unworthy of worship? Must it be a sin to sacrifice, to give thanks, and to bring forth festivals to Baal, the god who creates all, and to Astarte, this goddess of fruitfulness? No. If a religion neglects this vast mystery and regards the generation of fruit and of men merely as an act of divine providence and grace, it fails to recognize the deep feeling for life in the mother-to-be and knows nothing of the glory that thrills through a man the first time he sees the love between him and his wife turned to flesh and blood in a babe in her arms. A primitive humanity near to nature does not want to give up its fertility cult goddess for a divinity it cannot see; it wants to remain true to the goddess who gives more than all else—the child that carries on the race and food which nourishes mankind.

Neglect of this complete humanism and failure to allow for it in rite and ritual is the great defect of revealed religion, created as it was for a people who tilled the land and raised their cattle in the warm climate of the Near East, where rain was scarce and where they awaited in fear and prayer the benison bestowed by the fruit. The faith of Yahweh cared nothing for this fundamental attitude of a people who were indissolubly linked with their countryside; and so it was doomed to founder as long as the people of Israel remained settled as an independent entity on the soil of Palestine. The real birth of the Jewish religion was probably not achieved until the kingdom fell and the Jews were scattered to the ends of the earth; this birth the composers of the Bible by way of poetic imagination set back in the time of the patriarchs.

The fertility cults of the Canaanite people dedicated to the Baalim and especially to the goddess Astarte were adopted by the Israelite invaders. The Bible attacks these fertility cults unmercifully. These cults attributed importance to human sexuality to the degree it served as a basis for divine worship, and to the degree the sex act was not merely regarded as a natural function but was given a place in open temple services. This was the institution of hierodules, temple prostitutes (Kedeshes), dedicated to the deity; and their cult in the Jerusalem temple itself was what the prophets lashed at more than anything else because they saw in it an occasion for apostasy from their god. These young women were servers in the temple of Astarte, goddess of fruitfulness. They were dedicated to her service in forms which included the act of copulation.

Such cult practice was almost universal in the Near East. The sanctity of this usage, too, is clearly revealed by records which have been discovered. In the days of Sumer, over 2,000 years before the time of Moses, the young female priestesses in the temple had to put themselves at the disposal of everyone who visited the sanctuary. Every degree of priestess, right up to the top one, was under this obligation. Submission in the sanctuary to a stranger did not count as a disgraceful transaction bringing the priestess shame. On the contrary, the priestess was bound by her deity with the duty of putting herself at least once at the disposal of a stranger so that she might achieve in the holy place the sacrifice to her god of her greatest treasure, her virginity. The priestesses and the men who submit themselves to this duty suffered no loss of respect but were exalted by their god through the ritual. Thus the emphasis was not on the sex act for itself but as a cult service to the god. Blame must fall on the Old Testament writers for letting their religious fanaticism heap shame on the good repute of the idol-worshiping Israelites by stressing the sexual aspect of their fertility cults.

The Bible presents these usages as hateful only because the sexual act in the temple represents a worship of the fertility gods. Moses had already given instructions on this point: "There shall be no cult prostitute of the daughters of Israel, neither shall there be a cult prostitute of the sons of Israel." (Deuteronomy 23:17) This contemptuous designation is used in the Old Testament of women who seduce Jewish men into apostasy from their god. The service of these hierodules, the dedicated priestesses described as temple prostitutes, ranked as an act of apostasy. In ancient Babylon there were towns for harlots dedicated to the god Anu and to the goddess Ishtar (Astarte).

The men of the Bible who regarded themselves as responsible for the worship of Yahweh were continually enraged against the Astarte worship, which was spread over the whole of Palestine and Mesopotamia. As it was impossible for them to abolish the institution of hierodules, they addressed flaming words to Israel in their war against this kind of idolatry. The prophet Amos lamented that wickedness was so widespread that father and son resorted together to these whores, shamed the holy name of God, caroused before the altars of the idols, and drank wine in the heathen temples. Hosea breaks out:

> I will not punish your daughters when they play the harlot, nor your brides when they commit adultery; for the men themselves go aside with harlots, and sacrifice with cult prostitutes, and a people without understanding shall come to ruin . . . A band of drunkards, they give themselves to harlotry; they love shame more than their glory.   (Hosea 4:14,18)

We have seen above that this sexual traffic in the temple was practiced in a god's honor, and the Bible is wrong in regarding it as immorality. If it had only been a question of sexual satisfaction, there would have been no need for divinely sanctified establishments. For that, the everyday opportunities offered to man and woman are quite enough, and in the East even today arranging such opportunities is nothing unusual.

Neither the punishments of the Jewish judicature nor the fear of Yahweh prevented an Israelite, male or female, from uniting with a foreign partner whether inside or outside of marriage. But in the ancient East it was a universal principle that a woman had to be bound to her husband and remain completely faithful to him in spite of the polygamy which he was allowed. Only the hierodules could enter into relations with several men without loss of reputation or breech of the law, and apart from this she was untouchable as a wife to any third party. Thirteen hundred years B.C., the Assyrian table of the law of King Assuru-ballit gives a picture of this sanctity of marriage even though the double standard of morality limited this to the wife. The old cuneiform inscription now in the Near Eastern Museum at Berlin reads:

> Suppose the wife of a man goes to the house of another man and commits adultery with him, and he knows she is married; then both are to be punished with death.

The next paragraph in the inscription considers a similar case, but with the qualification that the man did not know the woman was married. In such circumstances the woman was liable but the man remained exempt from punishment. Nevertheless the law does not prescribe death for the woman but orders: "The husband shall deal with her as he pleases," a wonderful testimony to magnanimity. War conditions were also foreseen. If a woman's husband went away on military service without leaving her sufficient means or without sending home something for her to live on, then the woman was bound by royal law to wait five years for her husband before she might live with another man. She became free to do this at the commencement of the sixth year. If she then took another husband and her first husband subsequently returned, "he may not come near her as she is the untouchable property of the new husband."

Apart from the old oriental view, often still held to, that man is superior to woman as expressed in Genesis 3:16, ". . . and he shall rule over you," the old cuneiform law expresses a lofty moral conception in sharp contradiction to the immorality ascribed in the Bible to the surrounding heathen world. The modern world is ill qualified to sit in moral judgment, for it far excels the ancient world in the realm of sexual hypocrisy. The fact remains, even in the teeth of the Biblical writers, that long before them and even during their times the sacred dedication of temple priestesses and the purity demanded of wives were thoroughly compatible.

Similar ideas were known in ancient India and these represented a higher degree of sexual morality. In the religious texts of the Upanishads is given a prayer that accompanies the sex act. This prayer consecrates the aspect of procreation by which alone the birth of the desired male child can take place. Accordingly there is a relevant ritual prescribed if the married couple want to beget a child that will excel in wisdom, knowledge of the Vedas, or any other qualities. Right from the start these precepts try to suppress the pleasure of cohabitation in favor of the sanctity of the moment. The following translation from the Sanskrit shows how the act of procreation is here, too, thought of only from the point of view of the utmost sublimity. It reads in part:

> . . . .or if he wishes for a learned and celebrated son to be born. . . . then both [husband and wife] must eat rice cooked with meat and with butter poured over it; thus they should become able to beget such a son. Let it be the flesh of a steer or bullock. . . . When morning approaches let him add the melted butter to the food cooked in an earthen pot and offer a spoonful from the dish to each with the words: "Hail to the God Agni [fire]," "Hail to the Goddess Anumati [divine feminine favor]," "Hail to the God Savitri [enlivener, the sun] whose procreation is sure." After he has sacrificed with these words, he takes out what is left and eats part of it and after he has eaten offers her some of it too. After having washed his hands, he fills a vessel with water and sprinkles her three times with it. Meanwhile he says:
> Get away from here, Visvavasu!

Seek other maidens for yourself
Full of wantonness; but you must leave one,
A wife with her husband.
Then he approaches her and says:
I am the heaven and you are the earth.
So let us now go to the work,
And mingle our seed together,
And make ready a child, a male child!
Then he caresses her gently, stroking her three times
as the hair lies, and says:
Let Vishnu prepare your womb,
Let Tvashtri shape the limbs well,
Let Prajapati pour in the seed,
Let Dhatri put in you the germ of the fruit!
O Goddess with the wide tresses,
Sinivali, proffer, O proffer her fruit!
The Asvins, the divine pair, the sun
And moon, crowned with lotus,
Shall create fruit in you!
Gold is the wood that the Asvin Twins
Use for twirling forth a flame;
We pray that you may happily succeed
In bringing forth fruit in ten months!
As the earth nourishes the germ of fire,
As heaven is pregnant with storms,
And as the wind impregnates the four quarters,
So do I lay in you the child.

While the bridegroom recited this prayer, the act was completed
and the holy rite finished. The man had to have learned the
prayer by heart previously, as the appeal to the deities and the
precise wording were just as important for success as was the
observation of the prescribed ceremonial preludes. Consummating
the act of copulation under such circumstances was not primarily
conducive to sensual gratification. The accompanying religious
aspiration for propagating the race invested cohabitation with
the deep seriousness of a consecration rite.

We owe a debt of gratitude to those whose learning has given us an insight into the culture of ancient India. In this classic example they demonstrate how earnest faith can transmute man's loftiest sensual experience into a sacrament that fills the heart and soul. What obtained in the Far East also held in the Near East. And the performance of their duties likewise filled the male and female hierodules of Canaan and Israel with an overflowing holiness.

In addition to priestesses, men also observed the service of Astarte's temple by offering themselves to women who visited the temple. This sexual traffic was undertaken expressly to bring about fruitfulness. Holy Scripture objected no less sharply to this service than to that of the temple priestesses. The book of Kings says:

> and there were also male cult prostitutes in the land.
> They did according to all the abominations of the nations which the Lord drove out before the people of
> Israel.   (I Kings 14:24)

The Old Testament always signifies idolatry by this phrase so that there is no doubt about the nature of the cult. For its practice, money had to be paid to the sanctuary both by men who visited the priestesses and by women who came to the temple servers. As it was raised for idolatry, the Bible covers this money with the expression "hire of a harlot." It says in Deuteronomy: "You shall not bring the hire of a harlot, or the wages of a dog, into the house of the Lord your God. . . ." (Deuteronomy 23:18) By "the wages of a dog" is meant the payment to the men, which was credited like that of the women to the temple treasury. This arrangement was widespread in antiquity and can in no way be regarded as a custom first started by the Jews.

The conduct of people is always to be judged against the moral maxims of their own age. We cannot apply present-day standards to the conduct of a remote period. To stress this appears necessary if we want to avoid attributing to antiquity feelings which are right and unassailable for us but were unknown to the past.

It has been the custom of contemporary writers to approach the cult of Astarte and similar forms of fertility worship from the angle that the real reason the ancient world served the various fertility deities was to abandon itself to dissolute sensuality. Without a doubt under the intoxication of the senses and religious enthusiasm, men attain the uttermost height of ecstasy they are capable of. To be sure, though, among the numerous partakers at these festivals there no doubt were impure elements that neither sought nor obtained edification in the religious sacraments and ceremonies. To dispute that would be idealistic unworldliness. All the peoples of the Near East celebrated these fertility rites, but there is no evidence to show that any people as a whole—priests, princes, the nobility, and all ranks of society—ever felt these rites to be an expression of moral depravity or unbridled lust as they partook of them with pious faith and voluptuous ecstasy.

In Greece, likewise, large masses of people celebrated religious festivals honoring the phallus as in the worship of Dionysus, god of fruitfulness. These ancient festivals, called *Lenaias*, were for promoting fertility and growth; hence, conforming with the innocence of that age, these cult rituals were crowned with the act of procreation in honor of the divine giver of fruitfulness. A fragment by the Greek philosopher Heraclitus of the fourth century B.C. confirms the view just presented. It reads:

> Their processions and phallic hymns would be disgraceful exhibitions if they were not done in worship of Dionysus. But Dionysus, in whose honor they rave and celebrate the Lenaian festival, is the same as Hades.

Thus the deity lay behind the whole usage. All the doings were intended to worship him and to gain his grace. The moral attitudes of the ancient past are revealed to us in many documents. We have the Hammurabi code, one of the sources of the Mosaic law. We have established that a high conception of marriage was embodied in Assyrian tables of the law 3,000 years ago. The Old Testament bears witness in the Psalms and other books to the deep moral experience of ancient Jewry, even if it tries to pillory idolatry with every method of vilification for reasons which are intelligible enough. But there was an inner meaning and a holiness of purpose in the ancient pagan fertility festivals when their outlook on ethics and morals is considered

in relation to that period; and these ethical and moral views are
not to be perverted into their opposites simply because the present
age fails to understand the true meaning of the ancient practices,
an age which lives in more of a glass house so far as ethics and
morals are concerned than did nearly any previous age in human
history.

Worship of the gods was conducted principally in the open
air, depending on nature and the climate of the country. In the
book of Isaiah, the god sternly complains about the disobedience
of his people, who sacrifice in gardens and burn incense upon
altars of brick to strange gods, and

> who sit in tombs, and spend the night in secret places;
> who eat swine's flesh, and broth of abominable things
> is in their vessels   (Isaiah 65:4)

The prophet Hosea rebukes the people's apostasy from the Lord
and says that it is full of whoredom and wine and new wine.
The people inquire of a thing of wood and

> They sacrifice on the tops of the mountains, and make
> offerings upon the hills, under oak, poplar, and tere-
> binth, because their shade is good. Therefore your
> daughters play the harlot, and your brides commit
> adultery.   (Hosea 4:13)

These passages not only reveal the practice of the cult of
Astarte but also at the same time confirm that the handing over
of brides to temple cult uses had in the popular mind been turned
into a kind of religious "jus primae noctis" whereby the priest or
the male hierodule assumed the position of the lord.

The Bible strongly condemns Israel not only for the "whoredom" of its women but also because like all other people of the
ancient world it engaged in other cult practices. A passage in
Jeremiah makes an allusion to this; it says:

> Who say to a tree, "You are my father" and to a
> stone, "You gave me birth"
>   (Jeremiah 2:27)

In another place it runs:

> She polluted the land, committing adultery with stone
> and tree,   (Jeremiah 3:9)

In the same vein is Isaiah, who thus words his castigation:

> For you shall be ashamed of the oaks in which you
> have delighted; and you shall blush for the gardens
> which you have chosen.
>   (I:29)
> You who burn with lust among the oaks, under every
> green tree.   (57:5)

The Bible so describes this idolatry as to show that it consisted of worshiping the phallus, venerated as the bringer of fruitfulness in the religious usages of antiquity. In statues of the gods the generative function of the phallus or lingam, the male member, was emphasized by fashioning this organ huge out of all proportion to the other parts of the divine bodies; it was accorded adoration in the form of the god Priapus in the Near East and in the form of the god Shiva in India.

Primitive peoples marveled at the miracle of reproduction throughout the living world, and at the same time they understandably paid religious veneration to its appointed mediator, the phallus. Thus arose a cult which has not yet vanished even today. The extraordinary prominence given to this part of the god's body expressed not impure erotic thought but the highest conception of life, the power that calls everything into being.

To our way of thought there is a certain grotesque extravagance in the plastic representation of the phallus. But who can definitely assert that bronze statues with exaggerated phallic members excavated at Pompeii were a subject of ribaldry instead of worship by the Roman women?

Figures and accounts preserved from Egypt, ancient India, and other parts of the world as in Greece, leave no room to doubt the religious value of the male emblem. Phallic images made of gold are known which deviate so extraordinarily from their natural prototypes that they were carried round in the holy festival processions on gilded wagons, as the other gods were.

A relevant account by the Greek writer Athenaeus has been

preserved from the Ptolemaic period (ca. 200 B.C.). Furthermore, there is considerable evidence that the women of classical antiquity used this symbol of reproduction made out of stone or other materials. It is not surprising if the mute invitation to ribald jesting presented by the object itself may have led to abuses and indeed occasionally to scenes of indecency, for it is not reasonable to suppose that the ancient world was more restrained than the modern one.

A statue was erected at Rome to the god of reproduction endowed with a male organ of immense size. Roman brides were placed upon this in a solemn religious ceremony before marriage so that they might be blessed with children by the giver of fertility, the god which bred descendants. This sacred action assured the propagation of the race. To the Romans this was obviously an act of divine service unmarred by any secondary thoughts of obscenity.

Oaths in the Bible were not taken by raising the hand toward heaven or by touching some consecrated piece of temple equipment. The man who took an oath put his hand "under the thigh," that is to say, on the private parts of the father or overlord, and then swore. Divine veneration paid to the phallus survived in the way the Israelites took an oath. From the same origin comes the present-day Moslem practice of swearing by the phallus of Allah.

The offering of fruit in a sacrifice is a consequence of the holiness attributed to the gods of fertility in countries like Canaan, where stockbreeding and agriculture were pursued. Even in pre-Biblical times the firstlings of beasts and fruits were offered to Baal, a usage which was adopted by Israel and comprised a substantial part of the sacrifices in the Temple at Jerusalem. The Babylonian cult of Baal meanwhile did not limit itself to these gifts, for the firstlings of men were also sacrificed to Baal in the form of the god Moloch. The eldest child was offered to Moloch in the fire. Jewry adopted these ideas, but not their form. Every first-born son belongs to God as Numbers (3:13) declares: "for all the first-born [of Israel] are mine. . . ." This demand, however, derives not from the Canaanite usage of sacrificing the first-born but allegedly from the Lord's smiting all the first-born in Egypt to punish Pharaoh for not letting the children of Israel go. But it was impossible for Pharaoh to let them go even if he had wanted to, because the Lord told Moses, "I will harden his heart, so that he will not let the people go." (Exodus 4:21) In spite of this, Pharaoh and all his subjects were severely punished with the murder of all their first-born male children.

The god expressly takes the blame for this deed when he says, "for all the first-born are mine; on the day that I slew all the first-born in the land of Egypt, I consecrated for my own all the first-born in Israel." (Numbers 3:13) According to a later command of the god, the first-born child could be redeemed if it was offered on a dish in a religious rite to be performed in the house where the baby was and was then bought back for money from the officiating priest as the representative of the god. In our own day, pious Jews still perform this ceremony of redemption (Pidyon Haben). The Old Testament account of the god's dubious behavior toward Pharaoh is nothing more or less than a bad misinterpretation of the old usage of sacrificing the first-born as practiced by the Canaanite people.

Even in Holy Scripture, albeit only as an exceptional occurrence, there are signs of sympathy with child-murder. The sacrifice of Isaac shows that Abraham was ready, at the god's command, to slay his own son without raising any protest. He had already brought the knife near to complete the prescribed holy act of killing his son when a ram miraculously appeared and fell as a sacrifice to Abraham's knife. Antiquity knew a similar legend which was committed to writing at about the same time as were portions of the Bible, an indication that in the sacrifice of Isaac, too, we are dealing with part of the common stock of Mediterranean story material. The Greek poet Euripides composed in the fifth century B.C. a splendid tragedy, "Iphigenia in Aulis," in which he described how Agamemnon's daughter, Iphigenia, was going to be sacrificed to the goddess Artemis, to enable the Greeks to conquer Troy. A messenger reports the scene of the sacrifice to Iphigenia's mother in the following beautiful words:

> Then the priest took his steel and prayed and searched about her neck to strike it cleanly. A terrible grief came over me and my heart failed me; suddenly we beheld a

marvel. All heard the sound of the stroke clearly, but no one saw whither the maiden vanished. Then Calchas the priest cried aloud and all the army cried, as contrary to all hope a vision appeared before their eyes, one sent from Zeus; though seen yet it found no belief. Then a doe lay sprawling on the ground. It was of tall growth and beautiful. Its fresh blood moistened the sacrificial hearth of the Goddess in streams round about.

Here, too, as in the sacrifice of Isaac, a blooming human life destined for death was expiated by the sacrifice of an animal and so was brought to a happy ending. Surviving pictures prove that similar ideas were known to the ancient Egyptians. They show a man prepared for sacrifice. He is fettered and his throat is about to be cut, but there at the same time lies on the sacrificial altar an animal designated for sacrifice in his stead. In the Old Testament, the book of Judges gives the story of a less fortunate end to the sacrifice of a child. Jephthah had promised to sacrifice to his god after a victory over the Ammonites "whoever comes forth from the doors of my house to meet me." He was returning in joy from triumph in battle when his first and only child, his daughter, met him. According to her wish, he granted her two months for lamenting her early death with her companions, and then he sacrificed her to fulfill his vow to the god. This is the only incident of the sacrifice of a child occurring in the Old Testament and it took place in one of the rare periods when Israel was faithful to its god. On the other hand, the Bible describes the worship of Moloch as a demonstration of idolatrous practices. Even before the immigration into Canaan, Moses allegedly issued the warning:

> You shall not learn to follow the abominable practices of those nations. There shall not be found among you any one who burns his son or his daughter as an offering . . . for they even burn their sons and their daughters in the fire to their gods. (Deuteronomy 18:9-10, 12:31)

The second book of Kings reports that the kings of both Israel and Judah and their peoples sacrificed children to the glory of Moloch.

A faith must be terribly strong if it can stifle the deep sorrow of having to offer one's own child to a god. If anything is capable of demonstrating the superiority of the idolatry characterized in the Bible as whoredom over the religion of Yahweh, it is the fact that the Israelites remained loyal to the old usage of child-sacrifice, even though love of children and a deep family feeling are reckoned their most pronounced qualities. Parents able to make this most difficult sacrifice to the gods of their country should find it easy and pleasant to perform any other cult ritual. Now we can understand why the prophets were doomed to failure with their unceasing lamentations over the idolatry of the children of Israel and with their continual admonition to believe in the god.

The Biblical writers were eye-witnesses of idolatry and they themselves realized their own impotence, without being able to assess aright the real reasons for their failure, or if they did understand them, without being able or willing to express them. Indeed Holy Scripture has no room for the statement that Baal and the rest of the old Canaanite divinities are greater, more comprehensible, and accordingly more holy than the god of the Bible.

The Biblical writers must accordingly explain why Baal, Astarte, and the rest attract people more than Yahweh does. They finally adduce the sex urge, the most powerful human passion, as the reason for idolatry. The hereditary evil is the foreign woman with charms and wiles who is bent on seducing the Israelite men to idolatry.

Proverbs ascribed to Solomon warn against wantonness leading to death:

> The lips of a loose woman drip honey, and her speech is smoother than oil . . . Rejoice in the wife of your youth, a lovely hind, a graceful doe. Let her affection fill you at all times with delight. (Proverbs 5:3, 18-19)

Here the meaning of "loose woman" is not prostitute but a non-Jewish woman seducing believers to idolatry.

The seventh chapter of Proverbs gives an exact account of such seduction as witnessed by the writer personally. A young man void of understanding met a wily woman, loud and wayward, with the attire of a harlot on the street in the twilight. She seized him and kissed him, and with an impudent face she said to him that she had offered sacrifices so that she might find him. She described her couch bedecked with colored spreads of Egyptian linen and her bed perfumed with myrrh and cinnamon, and she bade him come and take his fill of love as her husband had gone on a journey. He followed her "as an ox goes to the slaughter, or as a stag is caught fast till an arrow pierces its entrails; . . . he does not know that it will cost him his life." (Proverbs 7:22-23) Thus she has laid many a victim low, and her house is the way to the grave. Seduction to idolatry by a foreign woman is likened to death. On this question the Talmud gives the following account:

> He set up tents . . . and he placed harlots there, an old one without and a young one within. When an Israelite ate, drank, and was merry and walked the street for pleasure, the older one spoke to him, "Do you want any linen?" She offered it to him at the right price, but the younger one offered it for less. After this was repeated two or three times the younger one said to him, "You are like a member of the family; please be seated and choose something." Jars with wine of Ammon stood before her, and as non-Jewish wine was not yet forbidden at that time, she said to him, "Perhaps you would like to drink a glass of wine?" When he had drunken and his spirit was roused, he said to her, "Give yourself to me." Then she drew her deity out of her bosom and said, "Worship this." He answered her, "But I am a Jew." "What's wrong with that? I'm only asking you to empty yourself before this. Moreover I won't let you go until you have denied the teaching of your master Moses."

This episode throws light not only on the manner of the seduction but also on the method employed by the scribes to strengthen the

Biblical understanding of the sexual danger of foreign women. The scribes contrived situations in which the idolatress provided the background with her loose morals. Thus a story like the above grew, revealing its author's psychological insight and knowledge of actuality both in the sequence of its events and in its whole construction.

A Talmudic law runs:

> If a wife of foreign extraction is imprisoned for a matter of money, she is allowed access to her husband; but if she is involved in a criminal matter, she is forbidden to her husband.

The reason for this is that in a money matter she may be spared because of the fear the gentile has of losing the money. In a serious case of crime involving risk of death for the woman, she might have surrendered herself to the idol worshipers to save her life. She is therefore unclean through the mere suspicion and is forbidden to her husband.

If Jewish justice as derived from Biblical ideas were strictly enforced, correspondingly Draconian punishments would be the result. A magistrate following Talmudic directions would have an Israelite beaten to death for living with a gentile woman. The faithful children of Israel lived in dread of the abominations of heathen worship; so both in the Old Testament and in the Talmud this fear is predominant in all measures and legislative rulings taken to protect the faith in Yahweh. One passage says that wicked people who have to spend time in purgatorial fire would be rescued by Abraham and taken out, "except it be an Israelite who has lived with a gentile woman." Another legal precept explains that he who has slept with a gentile woman should be crushed down by the zealots. But the Jew was not granted the right to kill his gentile woman to avenge outraged honor; that was far from the lawgiver's mind. Any member of the Jewish people who was enraged at the crime of such adultery with a gentile woman, with its idolatrous consequences, might slay the evil-doer with impunity. The Talmud explains the justification for this: "If anybody lies with a gentile woman, it is exactly the same as if he had married an idol." The inner meaning of this concept is perhaps derived from what has been said elsewhere about the phallic cult.

This license to kill amounts to practically a declaration of outlawry against any Jew who ever spends a lover's hour with a gentile woman. It reveals the most violent religious fanaticism, such as is wholly unknown anywhere else in this context. At all periods, the young people have been rather free to choose their mates according to their own standards.

The extraordinary severity with which the priests and scribes proceeded is based on a demand in Deuteronomy:

> If your brother, the son of your mother, or your son, or your daughter, or the wife of your bosom, or your friend who is as your own soul, entices you secretly, saying, "Let us go and serve other gods," . . . you shall not yield to him or listen to him; . . . but you shall kill him; your hand shall be first against him to put him to death. (Deuteronomy 13:6-9)

For the Bible and the Talmud, the worst of crimes is apostasy from the god. A passage in the Talmud runs: "The law about idolatry outweighs all the other laws."

Besides the penal laws, preventive measures were taken which far exceeded anything ever conceived of by other religions and peoples. The Talmud proclaims a decree amplifying the prohibition against images:

> The inscriptions under figures and pictures may not be read on the Sabbath [prohibition on work]. The pictures themselves may not be looked at even on a weekday, as it is written: "You shall not turn to idols."

Here is the root of the artistic poverty of the Jews which lasted nearly two thousand years.

Excessive anxiety about idolatry caused such preventive measures as the prohibition on trade issued in the Talmud. For carrying on commerce with heathen neighbors constantly offered new solicitations to idolatry. In this way, too, familiarity with foreign women began, and this was not limited to the early period. A prohibition says:

> An Israelite merchant on his outward journey may do business at a heathen shrine, for he may well go back home again; but he is forbidden to do so on his homeward journey because then he will be so taken by the place that he will surely return to it. . . . Hence an Israelite merchant is forbidden to carry on this trade on his way home because one may then assume that he has trafficked in idols and is carrying the profit with him.

Courts of temples often served as market places. But if a Jew bought anything at such a market place during a heathen religious celebration:

> He must hamstring any cow bought; he must let rot any fruits, garments, or gear; he must cast gold or metal utensils into the sea.

This implies the suspicion that the purchased objects may have already been used for idolatrous purposes or at least been intended for them.

Perhaps some pious people may see merely isolated examples of idolatry in the various passages we have cited. They may suppose that these instances found mention in Holy Writ just because they were so isolated. But the Bible itself disposes of this objection as dipping only superficially into the Old Testament will show.

In the time of the three patriarchs, belief in Yahweh was not firmly rooted. This can be understood in the light of the knowledge derived from the Bible story that Abraham was an idolater from birth and that even his grandson Jacob did not put his faith in this god unconditionally. It was, however, different with Moses, the true founder of Old Testament belief. At his time idolatry was so firmly implanted that he took stringent measures against the children of Israel. From that time onward, right up to its final redaction, the Old Testament was not mainly concerned with widening and deepening the faith among the chosen people, but with vindicating the concept and religion of Yahweh against the Israelites themselves. Practically all the books of the Old Testament are classic witnesses to this fact.

One of the periods when the denial of the god Yahweh was strongest was during the kingdoms of Israel and Judah. These centuries put everything else in Holy Scripture in the shade in respect to the idolatry described. They present an almost continuous development of idolatry interrupted only seldom and then only partially and for short periods by a belief in Yahweh. At other times the Bible may repeatedly inveigh against the outbreak of idolatry; yet everything else grows pale compared with the time of the kings when the worship of the gods of Canaan was the rule and that of Yahweh the exception. This fact has a very deep significance for the history of Israel, because the children of Israel rejected this god Yahweh precisely at the time when they were politically independent.

The admonitions, prophecies, and threats of punishment by the preachers of the god neither weaned the people from their traditional gods nor had any effect on the rulers, for these, too, were only human and subject to the same temptations as everybody else. Again it was the woman who, according to the Bible, led the king astray into idolatry. It is said of King Solomon:

> He had seven hundred wives, princesses, and three hundred concubines; and his wives turned away his heart. For when Solomon was old his wives turned away his heart after other gods. . . . And so he did for all his foreign wives, who burned incense and sacrifice to their gods. (I Kings 11:3-4, 8)

The god threatened King David with dire punishments, because he took to wife a beautiful woman he saw bathing on a roof, after he had had her husband put aside. But, as the second book of Samuel reports, the Lord was filled with wrath less because of the murder than because of the contempt heaped on him by the marriage with the foreigner. The god let their child die as a punishment for the blasphemy. To judge from the Talmud, however, David may have received only a light requital from his god, since he is supposed to have fathered four hundred children on women whom he had captured on his campaigns alone. This number would have weighed all the more heavily in the balance if these women were captured from the seven idolatrous tribes of Canaan already forbidden by Moses.

Abraham, too, made a mixed marriage with the Egyptian handmaid Hagar, through whom he became the father of Ishmael, the tribal ancestor of the Mohammedan Arabs. It is obvious that in spite of all divine commands, union with foreign women was the rule for the chief characters in the Bible. Even Abraham's wife Sarah did not believe in the god. Abraham married her in his old home of Ur in Mesopotamia as an idolatress. Their son Isaac married Rebekah, a Mesopotamian woman, whose father, a brother of Abraham, was also a native of Ur. Their son was Jacob, who got his name Israel from contending with the god at the ford of the Jabbok. He had, according to what we have seen, a pair of grandparents on the paternal side of non-Israelite stock. On the maternal side both grandparents were pagans. Jacob's father, Isaac, was a first generation Israelite by conversion; his mother Rebekah was a complete pagan, the daughter of the Mesopotamian Bethuel.

This shows that according to the text of the Bible the children of Israel are descended from three patriarchs who were born of idolatrous parents and grandparents. The third tribal ancestor, Jacob, took to wife the maid Bilha of foreign stock and by her became the father of Dan and Naphtali, ancestors of Israelite tribes. Jacob also married Zilpah, a pagan, who gave him the ancestors of the later tribes Gad and Asher.

This shows that according to the Biblical account the god had to allow the seed of idolatry in the field of Israel right from the beginning and that without this intermingling with idolatrous peoples, Israel never would have arisen. Joseph, the founder of the tribes of Ephraim and Manasseh, likewise married an Egyptian sun-worshiper. Moses was probably, as we have traced elsewhere, an Egyptian sun priest; but, even if we ignore him, the Biblical facts adduced above show that the Israelites derived from a pagan origin going back to Abraham, Isaac, and Jacob, the three great patriarchal founders.

Idolatry during the exile fostered by mixed marriages with the indigenous Babylonian women led Nehemiah to summon together the children of Israel:

> And the Israelites separated themselves from all foreigners, and stood and confessed their sins and the iniquities of their fathers. (Nehemiah 9:2)

The Temple was no longer the center for worshiping Yahweh but for the exercise of idolatry. As Nehemiah confirmed, a portion of the children born from the marriage with gentile women could no longer speak their father's tongue. For this he punished them with blows, cursed them, and put them under an oath never again to let their sons and daughters marry gentiles. His invective has the old theme:

> Shall we then listen to you and do all this great evil and act treacherously against our God by marrying foreign women? (Nehemiah 13:27)

Thenceforth for all time up to our day, mixed marriages have been prohibited and forbidden. In this respect, orthodox Jewry remains unchanged to the present. The gentile partner in a marriage perverts the Jewish part into apostasy from the god and from Jewish beliefs. Only when the gentile partner is converted to Jewry can an exception be made; otherwise mixed marriages are forbidden to orthodox Jews. They also regard Christianity as idolatry.

Jewish thinkers cannot escape the dilemma presented by the contrast between the omnipotence of their god and the hopeless struggles in the Bible, and especially of the prophets, against idolatry at every period of Old Testament history. They reflect upon this and find that the enduring persistence of their faith testifies to their deep religious perceptivity and to their intellectual power disciplined over many generations. The question why the almighty did not destroy the pagan gods out of hand is simple and reasonable; remarkably, the Talmud itself poses this question. A learned scribe answers it this way:

> If the idols people worship were things not needed in the world, God would have destroyed them long ago.

But people also pray to the sun, moon, stars, and planets. Should God annihilate them because fools worship them?

A logical objection could be raised that the god should at least destroy the things used in the cult of the gods which are not necessary to the world such as images of the gods in animal or human shape. The Talmud's answer to this objection is that the worshipers of sun, moon, and stars could then be of the opinion that these really were true gods, as the god had not destroyed them. In the final analysis, the explanation of the Talmud only says that the god cannot set aside the symbols of eternity because his own eternity dwells in them. If the realm of the stars were annihilated, then the eternal one lacking an object through which to declare himself would be snuffed out.

That is the conclusion of Israelite thought about idolatry. The god, indeed, had the means to stop it, but he could not apply them or he would have exposed to annihilation the universe which he had created and with it his very own self. Meanwhile his chosen people were not so precious to him that on their account he would destroy the world. So the god constantly had to be indulgent toward his chosen people; for he could not, according to the account in the Old Testament, bring them round to have faith. And the book of Job frankly declares that the God's indulgence to the godless is a puzzle.

Thus according to the Biblical account, the god found himself in a quandary; out of all peoples he had chosen only this one single thankless Israel. With it he had concluded a covenant; if he had let Israel perish because of its disloyalty, then he would have lost the only people who were supposed to believe in him. All other people were heathen, and did not know him because he had not revealed himself to them. Thus with the destruction of Israel, the god Yahweh would have ceased to be the god of man; along with Israel he too would have fallen a prey to nothingness. Hence a way had to be found leading out of the unbridled idolatry of Israel, causing the worst sins and crimes against the god; this way could only be found in the divine grace of forgiveness. The prophet Micah reduced these thoughts to a formula:

They (Jewish idolators) shall lick the dust like a serpent, like crawling things of the earth; they shall come trembling out of their strongholds, they shall turn in dread to the Lord our God, and they shall fear because of thee.

Who is a God like thee, pardoning iniquity and passing over transgression for the remnant of his inheritance? He does not retain his anger for ever because he delights in steadfast love. (Micah 7:17-18)

That was the belief of the prophets who imputed to the god the knowledge that he would live on in his people if he forgave them. The prophet saw in him the savior who would some day let his people fulfill their duty to the world, the subject of the covenant.

In post-Biblical times the god Yahweh became truly the god of the Jewish people, which he scarcely ever was in Biblical times. The Biblical writers never surrendered him, and he clung to his people through his continual forgiveness. The post-Biblical priests and scribes elevated him to such power and might as he now assumes among orthodox Jews. Now the road was clear. The creator of the universe and Lord of all became the highest and most awe-inspiring god, recognized at last by his people after they had caused him so much sorrow.

A mighty concept was formed of this great and only god. The later authors of the Old Testament sang his praise in the poetry of the Psalms. In him the loftiest qualities found their dwelling. Freed from idolatry, Israel created its god of the Old Testament who was soon to become God the Father in the new Christian faith of the New Testament.

8. THE THREE CAPITAL S's (SOUL, SIN, AND SATAN)

A god allegedly breathed the breath of life into Adam. According to Christian dogma, this inhalation is repeated with each newborn child, but it is really no supernatural occurrence eluding scientific inquiry. The point of view of modern science is this: The manifestations of the soul are a matter of brain function, for psychological events originate in the brain.

> The spiritual is an aspect of the living and therefore in men, too, must be seated in the smallest living entity of the cell. There can be no shadow of doubt that the spiritual aspect of man is especially closely related to the nervous system and its main center in the midbrain.
>
> (Jores)

The interconnection of spiritual activity with the brain was correctly recognized as long ago as 400 B.C. by the Greek doctor Hippocrates. About 300 B.C., Erasistratos made an estimate which is astonishing for its time, explaining that the seat of the capacity for thought is in the furrows and convolutions of the brain. Modern science confirms this theory that the centers of the senses and of the activities of the psyche lie in the fifty billion or so nerve fibers of the cortex of the brain. Upon the functioning of these interdependent fibers depends our thought, our sensual perception, the unity of our consciousness; in short, everything which we call intellect, emotion, and life of the soul.

These discoveries bear directly on the nature of the soul; advance in knowledge has wrested the soul from dualism and will be decisive in shaping the religious views of the future. It is precisely the belief in the immortality of a superterrestrial, incorporeal

101

soul, which is the sheet anchor of the religious moral law with its theme of reward and punishment; for the supposed continuance of its life after death is the strongest pillar in the structure of the faith of the revealed religions.

Jews, Christians, and Moslems believe that a god breathes a soul into man, but they in no wise agree on the origin of the soul. According to the Talmud, God fetches it from a place called *guph* in which the souls of the still unborn children are waiting ready. The Roman poet Lucretius in the first century B.C. criticized this theory; for him it was an axiom that body and soul are naturally inseparable. He said on this point:

> Surely it is utterly ridiculous to suppose that a number of souls are continually lying in wait in order to enter swiftly the body of a new being the moment it is conceived or born and to occupy that body until it becomes dilapidated or disintegrates and then to begin anew its quest for a dwelling.

Christians view souls not as waiting ready for the god's purpose in a special preserve but as created anew each time for every newborn child. But since every man is born already burdened with the sin Adam committed in Paradise, this original sin taints even the new souls just originating with the Almighty himself.

The pure and blameless souls of children become defiled from the first moment of their entry into the body, thanks to the long-past misdeed of Adam and Eve. The god cannot or will not shield them from it. Thus every Christian child is born with a spotted soul. Jesus is supposed to have appeared and died for men in order to redeem them from this sin and the evils that stem therefrom. But then the soul is immortal and in death is freed from the body in the nick of time, a theory deriving from the Greek philosopher Plato. This opinion of his later found its way into the teaching of the Fathers of the Church and they erected upon it the edifice of the Christian Church.

For the Jews the soul dwells in the blood and, escaping at death, it goes back to the god. (cf. Ecclesiastes 12:7) This is the reason for the strict rule against any partaking of blood. The charge of ritual murder has played a tragic part in the life of

Jewry and it is raised anew ever and again; but it exhibits not only the vileness of those who invent it but also their total ignorance of Holy Writ, because they either do not know one of its most important laws or they prefer to ignore it for their evil purposes.

Orthodox Jews still observe the precepts against the partaking of blood with all strictness. To prepare certain fresh meats they rub in salt and leave it for a time so that the salt can draw out any residue of blood that may still be in it, thus removing the bearer of the divine soul. Human blood is forbidden not only by this precept, but also by the commandment "Thou shalt not kill." The special method of slaughtering beasts prescribed in the Jewish ritual, "kosher" butchering, is designed to drain all the blood from the animal killed so as not to infringe the rule against partaking of blood as the bearer of the soul. Deuteronomy says:

> Only be sure that you do not eat the blood; for the blood is the life, and you shall not eat the life with the flesh. (Deuteronomy 12:23)

According to Christian teaching, the soul is an incorporeal substance which severs itself from the body shortly before death. A dying person breathes out his soul. In the moment when he draws his last breath, the soul vanishes.

Whatever the differing opinions of these three religions, Judaism, Christianity and Mohammedanism, may be concerning the origin, seat, and nature of the soul, they are all united on one point, that the soul comes from a god and is consequently the most valuable part of a man. For Philo Judaeus, a forerunner who helped to prepare the way for Christianity and lived about the beginning of our era, the soul is the breath of the god and a part of the Holy Spirit. In the Bible and Talmud it likewise ranks as the divine portion of a man. In Catholic teaching the immortal soul is the most precious part because it is created in the image and likeness of the god.

Unanimity prevails yet further in the belief that the link between body and soul is to the advantage of the body and that a lasting union of the two is impossible because of the comparative worthlessness of the body. Again it was Plato who first promulgated this teaching. The body, in which the divine soul must dwell during a man's lifetime, is something evil. Plato is for that reason of the opinion that the two must be put asunder. He accomplishes this in his theory by declaring the soul immortal and at the same time divesting it of all corporeality.

But this theory leads to a difficulty. If the soul journeys directly to the god after the death of the body and is accepted by him again in all honor, then during a man's lifetime it may safely indulge in all the wickedness it possibly can with the body, for no punishment follows. In other words, the most abominable life a body and soul can lead together entails no bad consequences for the soul. That would mean victory for immorality. Plato dared not let his theory be pushed so far in his idea of an immortal and divine soul separable from an evil body. Accordingly he made it responsible for deeds done jointly with the body. It cannot infallibly count on the god receiving it in grace at the last breath of the dying person.

Plato subjected it to the principle of reward and punishment after the death of the man. The soul finds in the god a moral judge. The newly founded Christian Church adopted this edifice of thought about five hundred years after Plato and made the Greek philosopher's theory of the soul the basis for its moral teaching. Now, in accordance with the god's judgment the soul is received in the heavenly kingdom near his throne forever for its good conduct on earth; or, so far as it has done evil, it suffers a painful cleansing in purgatory; or, if it has committed mortal sins, its lot is eternal relegation to the pains of hell. Thus the beyond, with its heaven, hell, angels, and devil is the ineluctable consequence of the Platonic construction of the soul and its responsibility after death.

The great Democritus went sharply after Plato. He said that those evildoers who have been wantonly wicked with impunity during their lifetime fear that someday they might be punished, and hence they invented the beyond with its court of justice so that they can say they, too, will ultimately be punished.

Plato's theory of the soul with no escape for anybody from his judge exerts a powerful influence on man because of the daily spectacle of innocent suffering. This means that the arguments of Democritus and other sages do not get a hearing. Western people coming after Plato have in their ignorance supposed that he perceived the true nature of reality: that body and soul, the universe and God, this world and the next, are concepts of entities which are real but completely independent of each other. The one is always corporeal and sinful, the other pure, noble, and spiritual. Plato, with his ideas borrowed in part from the old Orphic teaching, was accordingly the founder of the dualism at the heart of three great religions today—Judaism, Christianity, and Islam. It is still the means whereby some thoughtful modern people seek to find their moral place in the universe.

Six hundred years after Plato the Neoplatonists repeated his teaching and expanded it. Thus the idea of the sinfulness of the human body in contrast to the soul reached its zenith in the philosopher Plotinus, who is ashamed of having a body at all. Early Christianity is strongly under the influence of this attitude. Jerome, the Latin Church Father, is convinced of the wickedness of the flesh and of the world. His opinion is:

> It requires great strength and unflagging attention to overcome what you are from birth; to live in the flesh but not after the flesh and to struggle with yourself every day.

The precipitation of this attitude is found in modern Catholicism, especially in monasticism, where it is the foundation of cloistered life. In the New Testament we read:

> Do not love the world or the things in the world. If anyone loves the world, love for the Father is not in him. For all that is in the world, the lust of the flesh and the lust of the eyes and the pride of life, is not of the Father but is of the world.
>
> (I John 2:15 f.)

The Jews also follow the general ill opinion of the body. This is apparent in a prayer still used which runs:

> Thou [God] knowest well that this earthly creature is a
> vain thing, a withered leaf, a dried blade of straw, an
> earthen potsherd, a something of no worth . . .

This unworthiness of the body is a commonplace of all monotheistic religions and in them the scales of faith are especially
heavily weighted in favor of the divine and pure beyond against
the sinful earth. It is a solution which assures men the prospect
of justice for the wrong suffered in life and which thus makes the
burden of existence tolerable for them.

Real life begins after death for those blameless ones who have
been sorely tried, or such is the expressed belief. Depending on the
religious beliefs obtaining among the various peoples at various
times, the soul goes direct from the realm of the dead into heaven,
or to a region where dwells the god who watches over the souls,
or it may, after the resurrection, return to its former body again
to enjoy the kingdom of heaven. Among the Egyptian hieroglyphic
texts on the graves at Amarna, there is found on the entrance of
a tomb a prayer which the dead one himself utters:

> Place me for ever in the abodes of the blessed and in
> my tomb of holiness; but draw forth my soul that it
> may behold your sunbeams and eat of their sacrificial
> gifts. Let my name be called when the words of the
> sacrifice are spoken that I may share in the gifts which
> are delivered. I partake of bread, cakes, and pastry,
> roast and broiled meat, water, wine, milk, and every-
> thing that is delivered to me out of the temple of Aton
> in Ekh-Aton [Akhe-Taton, Akh-en-Aton].

This funeral text, dating from the fourteenth century B.C. and
composed in the reign of Amenhotep IV, proves that the belief
was current that the soul leaves the body after death, regains the
daylight, and begins to eat of the sacrificial gifts which represent
the favorite foods of the departed. The dead man remains in the
protection of the great Egyptian god Osiris; before him his heart
is weighed and tested by Thoth, judge of the dead. In his company
is found the Devourer of the Dead. This Devourer has, according

to a hieroglyphic text, the head of a crocodile, the trunk of a lion, and the hinder parts of a hippopotamus.

Regarding the relation of body and soul, it is noteworthy that in ancient Egypt there was felt to be an antithesis between heart and soul. Hearts were embalmed and preserved in special vessels in the graves of mummies, the places where funeral epitaphs are found, just as is now done for canonized saints in the Roman Church four thousand years later. Special prayers were said for the heart, because the soul could come forward as a witness against the heart at the Day of Judgment. A passage in the Book of the Dead, now in the British Museum, describes the weighing of the heart by Thoth. It runs:

> Thoth, who decides justice, [says to the nine judges of the dead who are seated before Osiris]: Hear this charge with righteousness. I judge the heart of [here follows the name of the departed], whose soul has come forth as a witness against him. His being is recognized as righteous upon the great balance, and no wickedness is found in him. . . . He carried no crime about with him while he was upon the earth. . . . He has no sin and shall not suffer any punishment from us. The dog may not make himself master of him. . . . Bread and beer that are delivered by Osiris shall be delivered to him, and he shall for ever fare as do the servers of Horus.

Horus is the son of Osiris, the god of the dead. These and similar ancient Egyptian texts show us that the essential components of later creeds were known long before Moses, more than a thousand years before Plato and more than fifteen hundred years before Christianity. Such was the dichotomy between body and soul and the judgment after death with rewards and punishments. We can recognize Cerberus and hell itself in the Egyptian dog (to whom the dead who are found to have sinned are abandoned), the Devourer of the Dead, as he is called in one text. That the soul can bear witness against the heart shows that the soul is exalted over the body. This demonstrates how deep in antiquity

the roots of the Orphic-Platonic-Christian concept of the beyond
are traceable.

The Books of the Dead of the period of the Pharaohs mention
the ascension of the dead to attain a divine nature. The ceremony
of the cult of the dead is a subject of great sanctity and great
secrecy. For it the Egyptians created especially sublime forms,
which possibly served as a model for freemasonry *via* the offices
of medieval builders. Keeping secret the Books of the Dead is
enough to assure the dead person that the promises made to him
will be fulfilled.

Such a hieroglyphic text runs:

> Every illuminated one for whom this book has been
> accomplished, his soul shall have power among the
> Gods, unless they reject him. These Gods encompass
> him and they know him and he shall be like unto one
> of them. This book is indeed the deepest mystery, and
> the laity among the people shall not see it for all
> eternity. It shall not be read to any man and it shall not
> be repeated to the laity. No ear shall hear it and no
> man shall see it, except the one who knows it and the
> one who taught it to him. Write not the sentences with-
> out it be for yourself and your trusted ones. . . . It is
> food for the illuminated in the Underworld, it feeds
> their souls and gives eternal life. . . .

The body must be preserved by embalmment to make life possible for a person after death. A ritual recording how the dead
were embalmed to turn them into mummies has been partially preserved. At the end the legs are wrapped with linen fabric which is
soaked in a solution of natron, resin, and gum. After the mummy
is made ready, it is anointed with holy oil. Then the ritual goes on:

> You see your name in every province, your soul in
> heaven, your body in the Duat [the place where the
> dead wait], your statues in the temples. You live in
> eternity and remain young forever.

In this ancient conception, too, the soul is already regarded
as traveling back to heaven by itself. That is the fundamental

notion retained in the three later monotheistic religions. According to the Talmud, this occurrence takes place in a rather more circumstantial way, as this passage describes:

> The body remains preserved for twelve months and the soul ascends and descends. Thereafter the body decays and the soul ascends never to return.

This is contrary to the opinion generally obtaining elsewhere, that the soul escapes from the body immediately upon death. This theory of the Talmud is all the more extraordinary because the Jews had already come to regard the living body as an impure and unworthy place for the divine soul, not to mention a dead one, which has to submit to the action of worms and other vermin. No other religion went so far as the Yahweh religion of the Jews in teaching the salvation of the soul for the god's sake and integrating that idea into its thought, even though the concept of a beyond providing highest blessedness was originally foreign to Jewry.

Martyrdom for believing in the god remained for a long period of Jewish history the highest form of service, and there were many thousands of instances to demonstrate this, especially in medieval Europe. For at that time the Jews firmly believed that the god took up the soul of a man burned at the stake directly into Paradise and there bestowed upon it every heavenly bliss. A Jewish contemporary and eyewitness wrote on the occasion of the massacre of the Jews in Mainz during the Crusades:

> What does it matter, so long as our souls go into the eternal light of Eden unharmed. Blessed is he who suffers death for the sake of the name of the Only One. There above he will be enthroned together with the righteous who lost their lives for the sake of the Holy One.

It is the same fundamental idea found earlier in Egypt and then in Christianity. The soul is received by the deity outside the earth, to enjoy there an eternal reward in return for the unmerited sufferings which it has undergone in the man's lifetime. In accordance with the more luxuriant imagination of the East, the souls of dead

Moslems experience an exceptionally fine eternity. On this subject the Koran says:

> You that believe in our sayings and have humbly acknowledged Allah. Enter into paradise; you and your wives shall be happy. Around you are set dishes of gold and cups there within, the soul's desire and delight of the eye. There you will stay for ever. And this is the paradise that you inherit for what you have done. There within are many fruits from which you shall eat.

Good food, and as far as possible his favorite dishes, reward the soul of the dead in Islam as well as in Egyptian and other religions. Most important of all, this exhibits a Justice correcting inequalities—as is to be expected after death in Paradise, in the beyond, in heaven, or whatever the superterrestrial dwelling place of the souls may be called. For hunger is the most pregnant expression of physical human suffering, with the exception of bodily aches and pains. Enough to eat is the prime demand of mankind. It is more immediately important than anything else, for on it depends the daily preservation of life. So, as those who believe in the soul suppose, food must be equally necessary after death. Since it is the function of the body to take in food, the soul has to have the body to enjoy this physical gratification. Luther agrees with this when he says:

> I want to live not merely according to the soul but according to the body. I will have the body with me too. . . .

Some people, though faithful to religion, have not been wholly convinced that a future life is in store for the soul after death. People often entertain doubts even if they do not wholly discard this belief, as the Greek philosophers of the early period before Plato did. In the Bible the Preacher inquires, "Who knows whether the spirit of man goes upward?" (Ecclesiastes 3:21), for souls must first leave the earth once and for all in order to be able to share in the comforts of heaven. This above all is needful: to meet the doubter head-on and to prevent him from spreading doubt.

The Koran is well aware of the danger of thought and says:

> O you that believe, ask not about matters which only
> bring you sorrow when they are made clear to you.

It is a candid remark meriting especial attention because sentiments like it are rarely found in holy books. For this is the way
things work out: The simple believer, feeling secure and con-
tented in his faith, should not ask questions lest he discover things
and fall into doubt not only about his god but also about man
as well.

If anyone opens the eyes of a deeply God-fearing person full
of the presence and activity of a god and without any urge for
enlightenment, he is burdening himself with an intolerable responsibility. He should consider the spiritual wilderness into
which he might lead people whose faith he could possibly eradi-
cate swiftly, without then being able immediately to offer them
any inward support with the insight that he himself possesses.
Respect for the faith of another, when it is a faith that brings deep
happiness, must be inviolable for all, for there is as much beauty
and as just a claim to respect in the pious dream of a believer as
there is in the profound consciousness of life in a man who cuts
out the indirect approach through a superterrestrial and imaginary
god and draws his spiritual and moral strength directly from that
universe of which he is a part and with which he knows he is
united.

Only the crowds, the great hordes, who make an outward display on the countenances of their faith as they flock to church
on Sundays and holidays, must ask themselves this. Can there be
apart from the body such a thing as a soul that can be employed
to put aright the injustice on earth? After death, will the soul
have things better in a hereafter in proportion as the man has
endured more in this world? For these people, doubt is not only
permissible but reflection is compulsory, because a worthwhile
future for all can only be built by men themselves. Voltaire, who
never quite emancipated himself from belief in supernatural
powers, once said in his ironic way, "God, if there is one, be
merciful to my soul, if I have one."

Great minds do not need the background and knowledge of modern science to grasp the natural bond between body and soul Napoleon asked his aide-de-camp, Gourgaud, on St. Helena:

> Have they ever found a soul under the scalpel? Where is its seat? In what organ? I say there is no doctor that believes in God. My dear Gourgaud, when we are dead we are as dead as mutton. What is a soul? Where is the soul of a man when he is asleep? Where is the soul of a madman? Or of a newborn child? The soul develops with the body, it waxes with the child and wanes with the old man.

The general found it difficult to give satisfactory answers to Napoleon's questions.

Modern science has succeeded in throwing light on the problems of the soul. The idea that the intellectual and spiritual has no separate corporeal or conceivable reality is an established principle of psychology, the science of the mind. Everything included in the concept of spiritual life is a process which proceeds out of the living organism, and which, as mentioned above, has its origin and starting point and its seat in the human brain.

The soul is not something that can exist outside the body or can have any existence independently of it. There is no such thing as a soul in the sense that it is a power divorced from the body, with independent thought, feeling, and will. The inner life or consciousness which we experience is impossible and therefore inconceivable apart from the life of the body in which it takes place. Soul is only the name for the total range of experiences, ideas, feelings produced in a man's nerves and brain in the course of his daily living, and manifested in thought and feeling.

It is this feeling, above all, which easily leads men into psychological errors. Feeling comprises those psychic events which are hard to put into lucid thoughts and which generally produce only blurred ideas. Given some reflection and the necessary will, one can understand these dark feelings, unless one dotes on basking continually in these deliquescent sensations. For in the blurring of clarity and in surrendering to vague subjective fantasies, sensitive natures given to great emotional instability are tempted to suppose that these fantasies contain more bottom than reason allows them.

When these feelings dominate, logical thought is blocked, for union between the two is impossible. They are interpreted as the great unknown whose murkiness is "felt" to harbor something vast although inaccessible to human wisdom. Then fear takes a hand. So perhaps there lurks behind it all a power to whom we are responsible at least in life and perhaps even after death. So it seems better not to disavow the god, even though, to be sure, one has precise knowledge about the physics, chemistry, and astronomy of the universe and assumes that in a heaven at about absolute zero no god conceived in the image of man could exist.

Lack of inward clarity about the eternal laws of the universe, also operating in man as part of the universe, turns into a vague feeling, a wicket of escape for personal safety. Even if they reject the personal god of the Bible, some people still think that a god might exist as a supernatural power permeating everything and manifesting itself in this obscure feeling. So these people invent new structures in which a god is proved not by thought or reflection, as in Descartes and Hegel, but by mere feeling. The profound experience of true reverence is totally different from this superficial way of trying to come to an understanding of the universe, and it is to be respected under all circumstances.

He who relies on his feelings also postulates an immortal soul separable from the body. And thanks to the promise of a beyond, this soul enables him to bear the woes of life patiently. He resigns himself to the thought that everything comes from a god and is predestined by him. But these facts confront the reflective person with two questions. Whence does injustice come into the world, and why must man endure it? Religion can give no answer to the first question. The fact of unmerited human suffering remains; indeed the good person often fares ill, while the evil person for all his wickedness often prospers right up to the end of his life.

If divine guidance and providence is in control, then the evil constantly present in human history must be explained. Let us

suppose there is a god, an absolute monarch of all the universe as
the faithful Moslem puts it, and that he is able to do exactly as
he pleases. Still he is helpless in the face of injustice in the universe, for only man can do anything about that. Faith postulates
that man has "free will" to do good and evil. A saying of the
fathers runs, "All is foreseen, but free will is given." But wicked
deeds cannot remain unpunished. So in the face of evil he cannot
or will not eliminate, this god is put forth as the executor of
justice, or because of wickedness on earth it is said that a god
is necessary to dispense justice. Now the way is clear. A god
leaves it to men to behave well or ill; then he can reward or
punish them as justice demands although not on earth but after
death in the beyond. The existence of a god is thus vindicated by
the presence of evil in the world. This is what Christian theology
calls "theodicy" or "vindiction of divine justice."

It can be seen that faith stands upon veritable feet of clay, when
the so-called omnipotent Ruler of the worlds and Creator of the
universe owes his very existence to the misconduct of the men
whom he created. If they were all virtuous there would be no need
for any reward in the beyond or for any hell, for they would be
sure of Paradise anyway.

Since the existence of the god depends on the dispensation of
justice, there has to be a place where men can do evil to each
other. We know from our own experience that there is no lack
of this in our earth. Religion accordingly calls the earth a "vale
of tears" and contrasts it with the beyond with its promise of
reward and threat of fearful retribution. It requires no further
preparation for the god to punish the souls of the dead, for
Satan and his cohorts are always ready to lend a hand. But there
is no corresponding arrangement to guarantee divine reward. We
have already seen that Christians conceive of mankind from Adam
onward as being born in and burdened with original sin. It is impossible for mankind to free itself therefrom by faultless earthly
conduct alone. However great and meritorious their deeds, men
can never free themselves of their inherited sins; only the God can
do that. If anyone believes in Christ and in the redemption of sin
through Jesus, he becomes justified by virtue of this belief and by
the grace of the god which comes through it. Only thus can the

soul of the departed count on reward in the beyond for his good deeds. The path to this is cleared symbolically by the purification given by baptism. Then at the Last Judgment, all the people dead for untold years will rise from their graves, the drowned from the seas, the burned from their ashes, as physical and spiritual beings; the believing Christians to go into an eternal life, the unbelievers to eternal damnation in a hell.

To support its legend of Jesus, Christianity often appeals to Old Testament passages as foretelling the coming of the son of the god. But how much easier it is to demonstrate from the Old Testament that the god is responsible for evil in the world than to support the Christian vindication of the god.

The Biblical writers could not foresee the emergence of this Christian doctrine when they reported occurrences which present the god as the originator of evil. Before Moses came out of Egypt with his followers, it was the god who "hardened" Pharaoh's heart so that he refused permission for the Exodus. The consequence was the series of terrible plagues the god let fall on the land of Pharaoh, and that merely because this god had induced him to treat Moses ill.

In the book of the prophet Ezekiel, the god explains,

> And I will give them one heart, and put a new spirit within them; I will take the stony heart out of their flesh, and give them a heart of flesh. (Ezekiel 11:19)

If the god can prevent man's hardheartedness, it means that his will is not free but is determined by the god. In the book of Joshua the god decided

> to harden their (the Hivites') hearts that they should come against Israel in battle, in order that they should be utterly destroyed, and should receive no mercy but be exterminated, as the Lord commanded Moses.
> (Joshua 11:20)

This disaster would not have struck the Hivites if the god had not hardened their hearts to oppose Israel.

When the god says in the prophet Isaiah "I . . . create woe" (45:7), that makes the whole "vindication of God" untenable and disposes of the need of a beyond and of punishments after death, for if the god is the occasion of evil deeds he cannot simultaneously be their judge. The New Testament too knows nothing of man's free will, for the apostle Paul says of the Lord,

> So then he has mercy upon whoever he wills, and he hardens the heart of whomever he wills.
>
> (Romans 9:18)

Islam is of the same sentiment in the Koran:

> Allah lets one go astray and leads another on the right path just as he chooses. He is almighty and all-wise.

Mohammed emphasizes especially that it is precisely the soul which Allah influences for evil. A verse of the Koran runs,

> . . . and with the soul and him who shaped it, making it evil and god-fearing.

According to the religious expositors, Satan is the evil active in man, and according to Holy Writ, he is the very principle of corruption.

Satan is supposed to be the one who incites men to acts forbidden by the god, the begetter of mean desires and immoral deeds. Satan, however, is not free to act on his own impulse; he is not exempted from the omnipotence of the god.

The book of Job tells how one day "the sons of God came to present themselves before the Lord, and Satan came also among them" (Job 1:6). The Lord assured Satan of the righteousness and integrity of Job and cast in his teeth ". . . you moved me against him, to destroy him without cause" (Job 2:3), a thing which is irreconcilable with the god's goodness. In a further conversation, the Lord gave Satan premission to try to get Job to deny the Lord, if he could make Job do it.* Satan boldly said, "Skin for skin . . . put forth your hand now, and touch his bone and flesh, and he will curse thee to thy face." And the Lord said to Satan, "Behold, he is in your power; only spare his life." (Cf.

---

* This passage Goethe cleverly lays under tribute in a scene between the Lord and Mephistopheles in *Faust*.

Job 2:4-6). Thus Satan, the principle of evil in man, was commissioned by God and took his orders from the Lord.

All this proves out of Holy Scripture itself that the god is also answerable for the evil man commits. So man has no free will, and reward and punishment lose their meaning along with the whole belief in souls and the other world.

In all religions, to doubt or deviate from the creed calls forth laments and reproaches. The following psalm is known from the library of the Assyrian King Assurbanipal.

O strange things are seen everywhere.
I gazed backward, and affliction followed me,
Like one who did not make ready the gifts for the God's altar,
And let his thoughts rove at the meal for the Goddess . . .
Like one, from whose lips came not prayer and supplication, . . .
Who taught not his people to fear God and honor him, . . .

Without beating around the bush, the Talmud explains:

> Seek not for that which is veiled from you. Meditate
> on things lawful for you and do not busy yourself with
> mysteries.

Another passage says:

> He who broods over things, what is above and what
> below, what is before and what behind: for him it were
> better if he had never come into the world.

Doubters and unbelievers are threatened in all ages with divine punishment. Here, too, we will give the very words of the writers of the holy books, so as to let the believers express their own opinions directly for themselves. An old Sumerian cuneiform text, of about 4000 B.C., says:

> He who does not fear his God is like a broken reed,
> his members are cut through like straw. He who has
> no Goddess for refuge, his flesh decays, like a star in
> the heavens it vanishes, like water in the night it passes
> away. He who just meanders along runs into an im-
> passe; a storm batters him, he is dashed to pieces. He
> runs about like one frantic; he vaults up like one whose

heart has been torn out; he burns like one that has
been tossed into the fire . . .

Catholicism keeps the majority of its faithful in check with the
fear of purgatory and hell. It is a mistake to suppose that primitive
ideas of hell have dissolved into refined ethical considerations in
the twentieth century. That is simply not true in Catholic countries. There even the people in the cities are constantly in fear
of this spiritual and clerical discipline, and the simple country
people as a rule still believe in devils, witches, and angels.

These crude notions have largely disappeared from Protestantism. Of course, Luther was still of the opinion that the god
condemns a part of every generation to eternal damnation, a
theory Calvin especially espoused. In suras 19 and 22 the Koran
presents this prospect to Mohammedans so far as they are
unbelievers:

So by *your* Lord! We will most certainly gather them
together and the devils, then shall We certainly cause
them to be present round hell on their knees.
Then We will most certainly draw forth from every
sect of them who is most exorbitantly rebellious against
the Beneficent God.
Again We do certainly know best those who deserve
most to be burned therein.
And there is not one of you but shall come to it; this
is an unavoidable decree of *your* Lord.
And We will deliver those who guarded [against evil],
and We will leave the unjust therein on their knees.
                                    (Sura 19, verses 68–72)
. . . then [as to] those who disbelieve, for them are cut
out garments of fire; boiling water shall be poured over
their heads.
With it shall be melted what is in their bellies and
[their] skins as well.
And for them are whips of iron.
Whenever they will desire to go forth from it, from
grief, they shall be turned back into it, and taste the
chastisement of burning.
                                    (Sura 22, verses 19–22)

The Koran expresses more clearly than any of the other monotheistic religions the motives for these threats of punishment. It thus declares:

> I proclaim the tortures of punishment for those who store up gold and silver and spend it not in the path of Allah. They shall be made red hot every day in the fire of hell and they shall be marked with its burning on their brows and their sides and their backs.

With good reason priests are solicitous about more than proclaiming punishments after death. They also set up and keep control of measures to check the people from straying into sin, like the prohibition on reading profane literature not approved by the priests.

The Talmud enumerates a series of people who have no share in the future world. According to Rabbi Akiba, this includes those who read "outside books." Only censored literature is allowed, for another passage tells us:

> An uncorrected book can be kept for thirty days but no longer, for it is written: there shall be no abomination in your house.

Jews were never allowed to read the Bible in any other language than Hebrew. When the distinguished Jewish philosopher Moses Mendelssohn published the first German translation of the Bible for Jews, it aroused strong indignation in orthodox Jewish circles of Germany. The zealots of the eighteenth century proclaimed this translation criminal. The anathema of the synagogue fell on possessor and reader alike.

Reading the Bible in the vernacular has certainly led to apostasy more than anything else. In view of this danger, the watchdogs of religion have done all they could to keep rational minds from getting firsthand knowledge of the Bible. Hence a pious Jew will read the Torah and Talmud only in the original Hebrew.

The Roman Catholic Church is even more restrictive. It not only prints part of its twentieth-century prayer books in Latin, a language unintellible to its communicants, but it also reads the Holy Scriptures in Latin at its church services. To avoid the incessant threat of infernal torment, a Catholic may buy books only in a Catholic bookstore. Only thus can priests and laymen be certain of getting books that are not on the Index, a contrivance devised in 1542 by the Grand Inquisitor in Rome under the title of "Index Librorum Prohibitorum."

Thus, freedom of thought is abolished for Catholic Christendom. From then onward every book was placed on this Index which contained anything contrary to the interests of the Roman Church. In the course of four centuries thousands of books have fallen under this religious proscription. Here, too, we encounter the same fear that we found in the Talmud of people reading the Holy Scriptures in the mother tongue.

In the time of the Reformation, the Bishop of Bologna under Pope Julius III issued an authoritative statement, which says:

> Finally, of all the counsel we can now give, the most important is to strive with every effort to see to it that nobody be allowed now or hereafter to read even the smallest part of the Gospels and especially not in the vernacular . . .

The New Testament as we know it was something quite foreign to early Christianity. Parts of the Gospels were known, but the early Christians were strongly forbidden to read them; they were allowed to get only the teachings verbally imparted by the priests. On this point Lessing writes:

> I subsume under the term Christian religion all those teachings included in the creedal expressions of the first four centuries. . . .The heart of that confession of faith was called among the earliest the *regula fidei*. It is not derived from the writings of the New Testament; it was in being before a single book of the New Testament existed. It is thus even older than the Church. . . .The first Christians in the lifetime of the apostles were satisfied with this *regula fidei,* and in the same way the succeeding Christians of the entire first four centuries considered it wholly adequate for Christianity. Therefore not the Scriptures and not Peter and his successors but the *regula fidei* is the rock on which the Church is built.

9. PRIESTS AND SCRIBES

Facts require no proof. Things that actually, really exist manifest themselves through perception. They are physically accessible and require no subtle corroboration. Likewise intellectual processes enacted in the brain need no demonstration of their truth. Nobody will dispute that seeing and hearing are facts established by experience. A sound person thinks; it would not occur to anybody to doubt that, even though we cannot physically analyze the process of thought. There are things and ideas we know beyond reasonable dispute.

If the existence of a god could be explained in the same simple and natural way, there would be only a single religion, a single creed, and a single god. They would be self-evident to everybody. Since there is no need for any special study of the obvious, the institution of churches and priests would be superfluous and dispensable. God, religion, and creed would then be facts essential to human life and as natural as breathing and circulation of the blood. They would be present as a part of life and their existence would require no finespun demonstrations.

It is hard to conceive of anything whose very existence has to be proved. The existence of a god is therefore improbable just because religions are so bent on proving it. Since there is no foundation in nature for the existence of a god, no god can reveal himself. Men are needed to assert his existence and to canvass for the idea, i.e., the clergy. They must convince people of the existence of a god or gods in order to make themselves spokesmen of this idea. They regard themselves as intercessors between their gods and men. They assert that a special divine grace has called them to this mission and qualified them for it. As a consequence, they rank themselves above other men and unite into independent groups to fulfill their so-called divinely appointed duties and to look after their own priestly interests.

The common people believe that the priests are endowed with divine power. By exploiting this popular belief, the priests dominate the people and found castes open only to the clerical elite and priestly families. Outsiders never get to examine the organization. Ancient Egyptian documents teach us that the written directions laid down for serving the gods and carrying on the related cult usages were to be made accessible only to initiates. Divulging the divine promises to the laity automatically nullified them. Egyptian funerary texts always counseled the initiates to maintain the strictest secrecy.

A burial formula dating from pre-Biblical Egypt runs:

> When you lay this Goddess on the throat of the trans-
> figured one, you shall say: "O Amon of Amon in
> heaven, turn your face toward the body of your son
> and let him be hale and hearty in the nether world."
> This book is a great secret. Let nobody see it. It is an
> abomination for it to be known. Hide it. The name of
> this book is Mistress of the Hidden House.

In early historical times the elevated rank of the priests over against the common people endowed them all the more with the halo of sanctity and sublimity. Moreover, the priestly organization profited only the great ones of the realm. The plain man was spiritually, socially, and materially too far removed from the haughty priestly caste to be an object of its interest or solicitude. In this respect there is no real difference among the various religions. The plain man could not go to an oracle with weighty questions. The Talmud explains this:

> Let the high priest question the oracle. Let him question
> it however only for a king, or a judge, or some other
> important personage in the congregation.

In ancient times there was never a lack of arguments to prove that a priestly caste was necessary. Apart from their spiritual means of power, the priests also required considerable temporal property to ensure their domination over high and low. The sanctity of divine service excluded the priests from pursuing profitable activities. The people had to raise money to meet the church expenses. All imposts were described as decreed by the god, for only thus would the masses recognize and fulfill these obligations. Any evasion of laws about taxes due to priests or temples infringed the god's commandment.

Priestly service and religious exegesis are closely linked with the special worldly prosperity of those who exercise these functions. This phenomenon is always observed when divine hermeneutics becomes a career for a section of the community interested in it. An inscription on a cliff has been preserved from ancient times in Egypt in which Pharaoh Zoser, in the third millennium B.C., mentions an edict which he issued for the temple of the god Khnum on the island of Elephantine in the Nile. In this stone decree, the ruler provided as the property of the temple and its priesthood a tract of land stretching along the banks of the Nile on both sides of Elephantine. The following gifts and taxes were settled on the god:

> All fishermen, all trappers, the hunters on the water together with all lion hunters in the desert—I tax them with a tithe of all that these earn. Furthermore a tithe is to be exacted from the gold and ivory, woods and minerals, and all timber and all things, which the Nubians of the Sudan bring to Egypt together with any man who comes in common with them. No vizier may issue any order in these places and raise taxes from them so as to lessen in any way what is to be delivered to your temple. I grant you this field with the stones and good fruit land, and nothing is to be taken away from it, and with all things that heaven gives it, to satisfy your scribes together with the inspectors of Upper Egypt who check on all things. . . .

This charter drawn up by the priesthood assured exceptional wealth to the temple and to its priests with a luxurious mode of life for them.

In spite of all their supernatural advantages, the men of God do not wish to renounce their temporal property which the god has awarded them. If they are understandably grateful to their god for this, he is by the same token beholden to the people for the taxes on their produce delivered on behalf of the priests. Compare that with the following:

> Bring the full tithes into the storehouse, that there may be food in my house; and thereby put me to the test, says the Lord of hosts, if I will not open the windows of heaven for you and pour down for you an overflowing blessing.   (Malachi 3:10)

The priests assert with good reason that their office is ordained of the gods, for apparently only this claim makes the priesthood endure. Called "by the grace of God" is ever the warrant for kingship too; in antiquity kings were also the high priests. Three thousands years ago the great Assyrian king Tiglath-pileser I proclaimed in the foundation of a temple:

> You great Gods who govern heaven and earth . . . who make mighty the realm of Tiglath-pileser, the sovereign, the beloved of your hearts, the exalted shepherd, whom you chose in your true hearts and decked with a lofty crown, and have called to lordship over the land of Enlil, to whom you gave governance and heroic grandeur . . . whose priestly majesty you called to serve in the temple for ever.

It is the goal of earthly kings to become like gods and often enough they give out that they are gods themselves and have their people worship them as such. The Roman Emperor Augustus forbade paying him divine honor in the temples of Rome but could not prevent the people of his empire from diverting their worship from the gods to him. Virgil, Horace, and Ovid, great contemporary poets of this golden Augustan age, hailed in Augustus the god who had come down from heaven and at long last brought true peace, freedom, and happiness to mankind.

In early Egypt none but the pharaohs communicated with the deities. The reigning monarch appointed priests to help him and from their number he chose the high priest as his vicegerent for managing the cult. In the Catholic Church, too, the priestly order is founded on divine right. A priest exercises his functions as the vicar of the god and not as a human official. As a corollary to this doctrine, orders of Pope Boniface VIII include:

> We declare, announce, and define that every human creature is subject to the Roman pontiff and that no man can be saved unless he believe this.
>
> (Bulla—*Unam Sanctam*)

The concept of sanctity embraces everything dedicated to the god, whether it be the animal chosen for sacrifice at his altar, or whether it be the priest who officiates in these matters and who has dedicated his life to the deity. From this idea it is but a short step to the assertion that the priests are like the god.

Roman Catholic canon law of the Middle Ages refers to the fact that Constantine the Great, who proclaimed Christianity equal before the law with the heathen cults in 313, forbade all lawsuits against priests. The preamble runs: "Priests are Gods and so can only be judged by God."

This prohibition entails obligations the priests do not always approve. The chief obligation is that a wife and sexual intercourse are incompatible with the sanctity of a priest. The fleshly lusts of the body are set in sharp contrast to the sublimity of the soul. Even in pre-Christian religions, woman was the source of all evil. Ancient India declared:

> A man heaps up evil works for the sake of a woman; therefore he must suffer pain in the beyond and already here on earth.

Association with women was reckoned so debasing that men who worked alongside women got counted among the despised classes. They were pariahs, and with them a clean man would have nothing in common.

The real reason for debasing women has always been the danger of sexual intercourse, and men who follow women's occupations are more liable to this than the representatives of other trades. Roughly four thousand years ago, the Codex Hammurabi held it offensive for lawfully married members of the priesthood to have sex relations. It specified:

A priestess has the right to marry but not to become
a mother. For this purpose she may give a concubine to
her husband.

A priestess had no right to bear children, for being dedicated
to the god she had to remain barren. The act of parturition dis-
graced her and made her unworthy of serving the gods. Catholicism comes close to this thought when it prohibits priests from
marrying. Under Pope Gregory VII, the prohibition of priestly
marriage became law in 1074 and still remains in force in the
Catholic world. This decree about celibacy stipulates that no
married priest may officiate at the rites and offices of the Church.
The people are forbidden to attend masses celebrated by priests
who keep "concubines," as lawful wives are designated in the
decree.

This enactment met powerful opposition. The Roman clergy
declared the decree inconsistent with the teaching of the apostles
and preferred resigning their priestly offices to putting away their
wives. A pastoral letter in the New Testament says regarding
servants of the church:

> Now a bishop must be above reproach, married only
> once. . . . and likewise, Let deacons be married only
> once, and let them manage their children and their
> households well.
>
> (I Timothy 3:2, 12)

The Bishop of Constance commented on the decree about celibacy
that it would be better for the priests to live in wedlock than
that they should practice prostitution under the appearance of
chastity. Only when Gregory VII had sent out among the common
people a circular letter declaring that the masses performed by
married priests were unholy and ineffective, did the people expel
those of the clergy who would not repudiate their wives and
children. Thus, after a long struggle, the papacy finally reached
its goal and removed the clergy from all secular influences beyond
papal control.

The Catholic law of celibacy never succeeded in creating in
the eyes of the populace any special aura of holiness by the pro-

hibition of priestly marriage. As medieval and modern history demonstrates, the ban on marriage effected a devastating deterioration of morals, which the Church regarded as the lesser evil compared with the advantages of monastic life.

Jewish rabbis may get married, but Ezra and Nehemiah required evidence of ancestry for a priest's bride. Only members of unimpeachable families had the prospect of entering upon priestly marriages. As the Talmud has it, those who came back from Babylonia to the land of Israel were "sifted like fine meal." That means they had been previously winnowed according to the various degrees of their caste at birth. A regulation carefully stipulated which of the ten castes could intermarry. Only two of these could furnish wives for the priests.

Of some of the Jews who had returned from Babylonia the book of Ezra says,

> These sought their register among those enrolled in the genealogies, but they were not found there, and so they were excluded from the priesthood as unclean.
>
> (Ezra 2:62)

At no time was the priesthood esteemed more highly than in the period when Ezra and Nehemiah re-established the faith. Here again the Talmud hits the nail on the head. There was an Israelite of a distinguished family who wanted to marry a priest's daughter; he had to examine the bride's family closely, including the mothers, grandmothers, and great-grandmothers on both the paternal and maternal sides, to tell whether she had a fit and spotless ancestry. (As is well known, Hitler in perpetrating his crimes against the Jews ostensibly to maintain Aryan racial purity adopted the practice of scrutinizing the ancestry of his victims.)

After the priests, it was the Jewish scribes, the commentators on the Torah, who generation after generation created the Talmud; thereby they provided Jewry with the spiritual armor of its faith, which has lasted until today, with a view to shielding it as completely as possible from its contemporary surroundings in its worship of Yahweh. This enables us to understand why these ancient Jewish scribes created in their literature the same exceptionally privileged position for the priests, just as the Bible prescribes it. The Far East, in its modesty and humility, is almost innocent of this continual emphasis on the superiority of the priests over the common herd. The stress the Moses-Jesus legacy laid on priestly superiority marks this legacy as a distinct spiritual retrogression in comparison with the earlier periods.

An Indian sage inquiring about the weaknesses of man asks:

> Wherein does the godliness of the Brahmans [Indian priestly caste] consist? Wherein their worth? Wherein their worthlessness? Wherein their humanity?

His answer:

> In studying the Veda lies their godliness. In their vows lies their worth. In evil reports about them lies their worthlessness. In their mortality lies their humanity.

Our generation sadly misses the words of another Indian sage, which he wrote over two thousand years ago in the "Song of the Sublime":

> Those who faithfully believe in other Gods and humbly revere them, they too worship only me though not quite in the proper manner. . . .I am the same to every creature, having neither friend nor foe.

In the days when the Bible was first taking shape and prophets and priests were engaged in a forlorn struggle to establish the faith of Yahweh among the Jewish people, China was creating a religion for itself. Then two great thinkers, Confucius and Lao-tsu, founded a peaceful state religion based on an understanding of the universe with no god and no priestly caste. In the first century of the Christian era, Confucianism was made the religion of the state, thereby becoming the official moral code of China. Its ethical foundations are the two cardinal virtues set forth by Confucius: love of neighbor and reverence, which are broadened out into a universal love of mankind. The Chinese *Book of Manners,* written in the time of the sages of the Talmud (ca. 200 B.C.), says this about the scholar as the true teacher of the people:

He finds it hard to enter upon an office but easy to resign. He does not strike one as having any special skills. He treasures neither gold nor gems, but conscientiousness and reliability are his treasures. He does not strive for landed property; righteousness is the land upon which he dwells. He does not combine with others when doing so would be unrighteous. If anyone tries to intimidate him with weapons, he will not change his principles in the face of death. The scholar is open to love but not coercion, he is approachable but not compellable, he may submit to death but never yields his honor. Even a cruel government cannot change his standpoint. Even in the midst of besetting dangers he remains true to his convictions and does not forget the needs of the people. He does not deliberately associate with the lowly in order to be thought noble. He does not fit together many trifles to impress people by the multitude of his achievements. He neither agrees unthinkingly with his own party nor condemns unheard those who are against him.

The scholar is not cast down by poverty and lowliness, nor does he become overweening in wealth and honor. He is not abashed before princes and kings, he does not let himself be stopped by officials of the state. Therefore he is called a scholar.

These are words from a past that lies more than two thousand years behind us. They were spoken by a wise man, not by a priest of any imagined deity. In them a great man portrayed a record of civilization so limpid and so sublime that two thousand years later we cannot improve it by one jot or tittle.

In Greece, Socrates above all others based his philosophy on man and had a political theory firmly anchored to the earth, remote from the antiquated teachings of faith. In his view, the concept of all wisdom emanates in virtuous action, this being the supreme goal of the inner freedom of man, giving him in turn the right to examine critically anything in existence.

The antiquity of China, India, and Greece was free of the idea of a supernatural god propagated by priests and Bible sages; hence the meditations and reflections of its great thinkers are more congenial and germane to us than the proclamations of the metaphysical powers that be today. For in antiquity, humanity was often enough appealed to as the sole regulator of life; and nobody was called upon to proclaim the idea of a god as the foundation of the universe and to defend it by all means possible. Thus antiquity was spared the scourge of religious wars, nor did intolerance toward doubters and unbelievers ever permit the notion of any particular god to become fixed. Intolerance became a religious duty for long periods in the Middle Ages and modern times. The antithesis cannot be put better than in a sentence from the distant past, which we learn from an inscription carved in a cliff under King Asoka. In this he explains that all his subjects, irrespective of the faith to which they belong, are his children for all that.

10. WAS JUDAS ISCARIOT A TRAITOR?

The tragedy of Jewry has been closely linked for almost two thousand years with the name of a Jew, Judas Iscariot, one of the original twelve Christian apostles. His deed introduced the martyrdom of the Jews, and his name is still a symbol in the civilized world for mercenary treachery. In a twofold sense he is the destiny of the Jews. They are venal for money and they betrayed and then murdered the savior, Jesus Christ, through Judas Iscariot.

History knows nothing of any such individual. The story of the treachery of the apostle Judas Iscariot is not based on any verifiable historical evidence. This should give modern generations food for thought when they consider the gravity of the charge and the fateful consequences derived from it for living fellow men. There is such a lack of original source material that we are exclusively referred to the accounts of the four evangelists when we try to come to grips with the question of the betrayal and its relevant circumstances.

From these we learn: Jesus came out of Galilee from Nazareth and let himself be baptized by John in the Jordan. (Mark 1:9) After that occurrence, he ascended out of the water, and saw a dove descend upon him which he took to be the Holy Ghost. On this occasion a voice addressed him from heaven, "Thou art my beloved son." (Mark 1:10–11) After a pause of forty days in the wilderness, he began to preach the gospel of the kingdom of the god. At the same time he performed miracles and unprecedented healings of sick people.

He selected twelve young men, the twelve apostles, out of the number of those who thronged about him. (Luke 6:13) Among them was Judas Iscariot, who Jesus as an all-foreseeing god knew would later betray him even before he chose him. (Luke 6:16) The New Testament, however, tells us nothing about the reason for choosing him as one of the brothers and preachers of the gospel. Jesus granted it to these twelve trusty ones to recognize him as the anointed, the son of the living god, but he forbade them to talk about it. (Matthew 16:16–20; Luke 9:20–21) He confided in them the task of going forth and preaching to their Jewish countrymen (for Jesus and the twelve were Jews) that the kingdom of heaven was at hand. He commanded them, "Heal the sick, raise the dead, cleanse lepers, cast out demons." (Matthew 10:8)

In short, on the basis of his divine power, he put them in a position to achieve miracles like those which he himself performed. This applied to Judas Iscariot too. This attitude toward his twelve chosen ones testifies that he confidently expected them to fulfill their holy tasks. Meanwhile there is no doubt about the complete devotion of the apostles toward their divine master. The last thing that would be expected is the remark which Jesus suddenly made to the consternation of all—"one of you is a devil"—whereby he alluded to Judas Iscariot, although he did not say so outright. (John 6:70f) He was plainly accusing one of them, but left them all hanging in mid-air as to his identity.

Strangely enough, in the face of this appalling charge, not one of the twelve insisted on knowing whom Jesus regarded as a devil. They did not ask a single question about it, as if there were nothing unusual, nothing disturbing about it, when their god, Lord and master, saw a devil in one of them. It did not, so far as one can see, trouble Jesus either in the least when these twelve, including Judas Iscariot, all proceeded with the preaching of his holy gospel with the concurrence of the savior.

One might suppose that the apostle whom Jesus had branded but not named would have realized that he was discovered. He should consequently have departed forthwith, to let Jesus and the eleven fellow apostles go their way alone, to avoid making himself still more guilty of sacrilege by preaching the holy words of the savior when he was a devil. For it is unthinkable that a devil should act as a missionary of Christ's gospel with the approval and knowledge of the son of God.

But nothing happened. Everything stayed as it was. All twelve disciples continued to share the grace and recognition of their Lord and master, Judas Iscariot too. He remained untroubled, an apostle of God, with no suspicion or knowledge that he was the one accused of being a devil. He did not know it, but Christ knew it. The gospel writer tells us, "For Jesus knew from the first who it was that should betray him." (John 6:64) He said to his apostles,

> Nothing is covered up that will not be revealed, or hidden that will not be known,"
> (Luke 8:17. cf. Matthew 10:26, Mark 4:22)

for like God the father he knew and saw everything both in the present and the future. He must accordingly have had good reasons for hiding from Judas Iscariot and the other disciples that at the given time Judas would become a devil (John 13:27) who would betray him for gold.

It is extraordinarily strange that he should not only have permitted the one who was marked down for the future to go on accompanying him as a messenger of his holy word but should even have required of him, as of the other apostles, not to leave him. For when many of his disciples left him because they found what he taught at Capernaum a hard saying (John 6:60, 66), then Jesus said to the twelve, "Will you also go away?" (John 6:67) These, his most trusty companions, endured with him to the end. Whatsoever he demanded they performed as a sacrifice of love for him.

> If any one comes to me and does not hate his own father and mother and wife and children and brothers and sisters, yes, and even his own life, he cannot be my disciple.
>
> (Luke 14:26)

Then they gave him this assurance, "Lo, we have left our homes and followed you." (Luke 18:28) They fulfilled his requirement,

> he who does not take his cross and follow me is not worthy of me.
> (Matthew 10:38. cf. Matthew 16:24; Luke 14:27)

They all deserted their parents, wives, children, brothers, and

sisters, and took upon themselves every hardship, giving up
everything, simply in order to serve their god. He taught them
the Lord's prayer because they besought him to, and they prayed
with him,

> And lead us not into temptation,
> But deliver us from evil.
>
> (Matthew 6:13)

Judas Iscariot uttered this prayer, too, in common with Jesus
and the other eleven.

In wonder, reverence, and love, they accompanied their god
and savior on his wanderings through their common motherland.
They were eyewitnesses of his miracles and heard with their own
ears the magnificent sermon on the mount. (Matthew, chaps. 5–7)
With amazed astonishment they recognized the superterrestrial
power and might, the divine origin of their Lord. Hitherto had
a mortal ever fed and satisfied five thousand men and their families
with only five loaves (Matthew 14:17–21), or trodden the sea
underfoot, or made the blind see and the dumb talk? Or had a
man dead for four days and already stinking, as his sister said
(John 11:39), ever been brought back to life with the words
"Lazarus, come forth"? (John 11:43) After living through such
things, as Judas Iscariot had done, one would know that Jesus
was a God. The idea of betraying him simply could not enter
one's head. Reward for reverence, loyalty, devotion, would not
just fall by the wayside.

> And he lifted up his eyes on his disciples and said:
> "Blessed are you poor, for yours is the kingdom of
> God."
>
> (Luke 6:20)

But how could Jesus call Judas Iscariot blessed when he was a
criminal, a traitor, and a devil? Certainly, as we shall see, the
savior had command over devils too, but this divine power knew
its limitations, which were not to be transgressed. To prepare
the kingdom of heaven for a devil would imply the victory of evil
over good which would spell the ruin of Christian morality. This
would also abolish purgatory and hell and therewith scuttle the

most effective penal sanctions Christians have to force people to keep on believing in Jesus.

That could not be the savior's purpose, for in his religion this theory of punishment serves precisely as the strongest pillar of the faith and of his Church. But it was also on account of their hard destiny that the apostles obtained the god's blessing:

> Blessed are you when men hate you, and when they
> exclude you and revile you, and cast out your name
> as evil, on account of the Son of man!
>
> (Luke 6:22)

This prophecy, to be sure, was fulfilled in Judas Iscariot. Since the time of Jesus, he has above all others typified the despised Jews, "scorned, shunned, and reviled." Jesus added to the promises to the disciples, "Rejoice in that day, and leap for joy, for, behold, your reward is great in heaven." (Luke 6:23) This also applied to Judas Iscariot.

Jesus ever and again showed his disciples by his conduct that he loved them all and wished for them all joy in heaven as the well-deserved reward of their fidelity. He gave them the strongest proof of his good will by celebrating the Last Supper with them at the Passover. At this feast he transmitted to them the most holy of all the sacraments he instituted. He sacrified himself for them, giving them his flesh in the form of bread and his blood in the form of wine. Again he did not except his disciple Judas Iscariot from this most sublime of transactions. The report of Jesus eating the paschal lamb with his disciples runs thus:

> Now as they were eating, Jesus took bread, and blessed,
> and broke it, and gave it to the disciples and said,
> "Take, eat; this is my body." And he took a cup, and
> when he had given thanks he gave it to them, saying,
> "Drink of it, all of you; for this is my blood of the
> covenant, which is poured out for many for the for-
> giveness of sins."
>
> (Matthew 26:26–28)

Now mark, all should drink of his blood and eat of his flesh; he required this expressly. Judas Iscariot was also among those to whom he addressed this demand. One could scarcely conceive of anything more incredible: in this hour of the most profound religious consecration, Christ willing to yield himself to Judas, a devil.

After instituting the sacrament of the Last Supper, Jesus washed the feet of his disciples. Of this it is said:

> Jesus rose from supper. . . . Then he poured water into a basin, and began to wash the disciples' feet, and to wipe them with the towel with which he was girded.
>
> (John 13:4 f)

Then he challenged them:

> If I then, your Lord and Teacher, have washed your feet; you ought also to wash one another's feet.
>
> (John 13:14)

He told them this about the meaning of this ceremony: "If I do not wash you, you have no part in me." (John 13:8)

If we once ponder on this scene, we shall grasp the greatness of the moment and the profound emotion of the twelve apostles; for in the solemn and holy calm of the room, their god had just sacrificed himself for them and had chosen them for the highest destiny. And at this point Jesus was supposed to have made an utterance which must have come as a stunning blow to his twelve bosom friends; without any warning

> Jesus said to him, "He who has bathed does not need to wash, except for his feet, but he is clean all over; and you are clean, but not all of you." For he knew who was to betray him; that was why he said, "You are not all clean."
>
> (John 13:10–11)

Are we reading aright? Was it all only a farce? Jesus knew that among the twelve there was one unclean, a traitor, a devil. And yet he passed to him his body and his blood, in order to prepare for him eternal bliss in heaven with God the Father! He himself washed Judas' feet, so that the presentation of his flesh and blood might be fully effective through the cleansing of the recipient and that thereby he really might partake of his god.

What a wrench on the feelings of the other eleven this must have been! In the presence of a traitor and he along with them, they were to receive their savior's last act of grace and were to witness how he communicated the sublimest revelation to a devil? And this god asked them to wash the feet of this epitome of all evil and to let their feet be washed by him so that they might mutually belong to each other! No Christian can make sense out of his redeemer here. Even if one were dealing with a mere man and not with one who was also a god, one would still be facing an unanswerable riddle, for nobody reveals his ultimate secret in a circle of intimates when he knows a traitor is present.

Next let us consider how the evangelists judge the character of Judas Iscariot. A person who makes himself guilty, in the Christian view, of such terrible wickedness toward his god might reasonably be supposed to give some other indications of his abysmal depravity. A hypocritical pretense of love and humility toward a master in order to betray him in the end for money marks an unsurpassable baseness. But Jesus is a god.

Even if Judas Iscariot had denied the divinity of his master, and the New Testament never makes any such suggestion, he must have done some other evil things too, because Jesus described him as a devil. Just what he might have been guilty of beyond the treachery is not specified. It is remarkable that the four evangelists contain no information on this point. On a single occasion he was reproached with embezzlement; but we are able to examine that incident more closely.

The story runs:

> Mary took a pound of costly ointment of pure nard and anointed the feet of Jesus and wiped his feet with her hair; and the house was filled with the fragrance of the ointment. But Judas Iscariot, one of his disciples (he who was to betray him), said, "Why was this ointment not sold for three hundred denarii and given to the poor?" This he said, not that he cared for the poor

but because he was a thief, and as he had the money
box he used to take what was put into it.

(John 12:3–6)

In other words: Mary showed the savior a kindness by using
a costly ointment. Judas protested against this waste and calculated how poor people might have been made happy if the
money spent on the ointment had been turned over to him. The
evangelist suggests that he really had not intended to use the
money for benevolent purposes but to embezzle it for himself.
It would have been easy for him to steal the money since he
was the treasurer of the common fund of the disciples.

If the suspicion of theft were justified, he would be an impossible choice as treasurer. Nevertheless he subsequently enjoyed
the confidence of all, including his savior, in the conduct of that
office. There was never a single complaint made about his being
a thief. The other evangelists also give accounts of what passed
at the anointment by Mary. But they say:

When the disciples saw it, they were indignant, saying,
"Why was this waste?"

(Matthew 26:8)

All twelve raised the objection, not just Judas Iscariot. And
Mark says in addition,

But there were some who said to themselves indig-
nantly, "Why was the ointment thus wasted? For this
ointment might have been sold for more than three
hundred denarii, and given to the poor." And they
reproached her.

(Mark 14:4–5)

Mark speaks here of "some"; so it was not the disciples but
others who judged Mary harshly. His apostles would have wel-
comed a favor done to their Lord and their god and would not
have wanted to shame its author.

So appears the only matter given in the New Testament that
might serve as a charge against Judas Iscariot during his whole

apostleship right up to his betrayal. That holy book is to blame for building up Judas as the greatest of religious villains, as Christianity regards him.

The evangelists prepare in advance for the betrayal by stamping Judas Iscariot as a traitor right from the start. As soon as they mention him they add "the traitor" or "he that should betray him." These phrases occur so often and persistently that they inevitably create the impression of having a set purpose. But the evangelists never analyze the motives of Judas. The paltry sum of money, and therefore the motive of covetousness, cannot have tempted him, for he was the treasurer of the apostles. He had only to reach into the purse entrusted to him in order to purloin a substantially bigger sum than the thirty pieces of silver, and that without betraying his god and savior. As we have seen, Jesus had just shared his holiest sacrament with him, that of the Last Supper, and had washed his feet. Judas cleaved to his god with the most submissive faithfulness and devotion; he and the other disciples and apostles were all equally bound by love to their Lord and master.

The evangelists let Judas turn suddenly into a traitor without any reason or motive. The four writers of the gospel all tell of Judas' betrayal but none of them explains how or why it took place.

According to Luke, this event had already taken place before the Last Supper was celebrated. This is what he says about it:

> Then Satan entered into Judas called Iscariot. . . .
> Then came the day of Unleavened Bread, on which
> the passover lamb had to be sacrificed.
>
> (Luke 22:3, 7)

Matthew and Mark also put the planning of the betrayal in the period before Easter and the Lord's Supper at the Feast of the Passover. They write:

> Then one of the twelve, who was called Judas Iscariot,
> went to the chief priests and said, "What will you give
> me if I deliver him to you?" And they paid him thirty

> pieces of silver. . . .Now on the first day of Unleavened
> Bread the disciples came to Jesus. . . .
>   (Matthew 26:14–15, 17; cf. Mark 14:10–12)

These versions suggest that Judas, who kept the money bag, was so strongly tempted by the proffered payment of thirty pieces of silver that he betrayed his divine master to whom he had hitherto been utterly devoted. What is really back of this paltry sum that Judas received we shall soon learn from the Old Testament. In any event, two facts are certain. The money offered to the treasurer of the disciples' common fund could not have tempted him if he is to be regarded as venal at all, and the New Testament gives no proof that he was.

There is also the additional fact that none of the evangelists raised any objection to Judas Iscariot or reported anything unfavorable about him from his election by Jesus as a disciple and apostle right up to the betrayal, save for the anointment by Mary. He not only enjoyed the love of his fellow apostles but also, in a pronounced measure, that of the savior too. The latter as a god, however, knew what the future was to hold. Even if the treachery to take place in the near future should have escaped his attention, and that is not to be assumed of a god, especially when his own future earthly life was at stake, Jesus must have known at least in time that Judas would betray him to the high priests allegedly even before the Last Supper.

By then it had virtually become an affair of the present, not of the future. Nevertheless, the savior let Judas partake of the Last Supper directly afterward. In what light must Jesus then be regarded for having proceeded with the sacrament of the Last Supper in the presence of the traitor and for having offered himself as a sacrifice to him in the bread and wine? If, therefore, the treachery was really perpetrated at all, it could not in any case have preceded the Last Supper.

John gives us the necessary explanation for this. Having described the events as the other evangelists do,

> And during supper, when the devil had already put it
> into the heart of Judas. . . .to betray him
>   (John 13:2),

John tells us something quite new which completely contradicts the report in the three other evangelists. After the supper and the washing of feet, Jesus said to the twelve, "Truly, truly, I say to you, one of you will betray me." (John 13:21)

None of those present felt himself to be a traitor. Then Jesus indicated him with the words, "It is he to whom I shall give this morsel when I have dipped it." (John 13:26) Of this John further reports,

> So when he had dipped the morsel, he gave it to Judas, the son of Simon Iscariot. Then after the morsel, Satan entered into him.
>
> (John 13:26–27)

Not until then did the faithful disciple turn into a traitor and that in a flash. He received and swallowed the morsel and the devil entered into him all in the twinkling of an eye. If Jesus had given the piece to one of the other apostles, then that one would have become the traitor. Thus a morsel of food possessed of the devil became for Judas the act of destiny into which Satan was introduced by Christ himself. For he was also the Lord of evil, too, as the gospel reports,

> And he. . . . cast out many demons; and he would not permit the demons to speak, because they knew him.
>
> (Mark 1:34)

Now we have a lucid account of the origin and sequence of the evangelists' story of the betrayal. God, the Almighty, and Jesus, his son—one and the same person in Christian thought—decided to make Jesus the savior and redeemer of the world, the liberator from evil. They also decided that this could only be done if Jesus died as a man for mankind in such a way that the blame would fall on the Jews. In accordance with the concerted divine strategy, a Jew had to betray Jesus to the responsible Jewish authorities and these had to condemn him to death.

It would surely have been simpler to let the police apprehend and arrest Jesus. But the opponents of the god's son and of the Church of Jesus to be founded by the evangelists were not to get off that easy. It was desirable to set in sharp contrast the sublime divinity of the savior and the low infamy of the Jews. So the most infamous action, the crime of treachery against a friend for base mammon, was set as a foil against the noblest deed, the mortal sacrifice offered for the redemption and salvation of humanity.

The Almighty and Jesus personally carried through the proper course of events. They appointed Judas Iscariot to act as traitor. Then the high priests and Jewish scribes, the official representatives of the Mosaic religion, condemned Jesus to death and delivered him to the Roman soldiery for crucifixion. Thus Judas Iscariot became a traitor, without willing it, indeed without knowing it, and without even suspecting the Satanic infection of the morsel Jesus handed him.

This concatenation of events was the will of divine providence. Judas had to swallow Satan. The power which had been conferred upon him together with the other disciples got thrust aside by an outside power. For according to Scripture, Jesus "gave them power and authority over all demons." (Luke 9:1) Now the disciple could no longer defend himself against evil, even if he had known that the devil was contained in the piece of proffered bread. For Jesus himself handed the piece of bread to the trusting and unsuspicious Judas. His fate was then irrevocably sealed. He, the Jew, committed the religious crime which was to serve as the foundation of Christianity and for the destruction of the Jews. The one whom Jesus had thus appointed to be the traitor was forthwith instructed, "What you are going to do, do quickly" (John 13:27), for the acts of divine providence were to be rapidly fulfilled. The new Christian religion for which the ground had been so carefully prepared could now be set up without further delay. When thereupon Judas went away to betray him, Jesus said to the eleven apostles who remained behind, "Now is the Son of man glorified. . . ." (John 13:31) He knew that he would die and lie dead for three days, so that then he could again reunite with his divine father and participate in his heavenly glory.

The events given above leading to the betrayal are authentic, for they are drawn from the words and purport of the New

Testament and can be checked at every point. Christianity holds that Christ himself is the author of the New Testament. The evangelists were only noting down what he dictated. In this way John, too, wrote his gospel, which we mainly followed in our narrative of the events. This gospel was composed by Jesus, revealed to John, and ranks among the very holiest of scriptures, according to Christians. But this authorship did not suffice Christian writers.

Even though the god ordained Jesus his son to save mankind, this god spoke hardly a word in the New Testament. He revealed himself only in the Old Testament. Accordingly, Jesus tried through the mouths of the evangelists to adduce proofs that his father had already announced his coming and mission in the Old Testament. It is therefore asserted that the life and acts of Jesus were only the fulfillment of what the god had already revealed to Moses, the prophets, the psalmists, and to all the others in the Old Testament. The gospel according to Matthew refers for the betrayal by Judas to just such a supposed Biblical passage which runs:

> Then was fulfilled what had been spoken by the prophet, Jeremiah, saying, "And they took the thirty pieces of silver, the price of him on whom a price had been set by some of the sons of Israel,. . . ."
>
> (Matthew 27:9)

Judas' blood money was reportedly also used to pay for the potter's field, to bury strangers in. (Matthew 27:10) However, it was not Jeremiah, as Matthew suggests, but the prophet Zechariah who spoke of the thirty pieces of silver. In what context?

Zechariah relates that the Eternal one of Israel asked of his faithless, idolatrous children to tell him just how much he (or his shepherd) was really worth to them. Not one of them would give more than thirty pieces of silver for their god (Zechariah 11:12), the value of a slave. (Exodus 21:32) If then God the Father was worth at most only thirty pieces of silver, his son could not be worth more since according to Christian dogma both are one and the same person. Thus the Omniscient one and

Jesus already knew in advance the amount of the reward which
the man they appointed to be the traitor would get from the
Jewish rulers, and they knew this sum long before the apostle
ever thought of betraying his Lord and master. So Jesus was not
at all surprised by the betrayal which he had seen coming, any
more than he was at the arrest which followed the betrayal.
Everything was taking the course willed by himself and the god.
So when one of his adherents grasped a sword to protect his
master at the arrest, he forbade him from doing any violent
deed with these words: "Put your sword back into its place; . . ."
(Matthew 26:52)

Not a single passage in the Old Testament can legitimately be
attached to Jesus or to the betrayal by Judas Iscariot. One must
completely distort the original text, as Matthew does, to contrive
any artificial connection, for none is at hand. Anyway a friend
was to serve as the traitor. A passage was also adduced allegedly
to show that the friend was Judas Iscariot and the sacrificial
victim Jesus. For this John the evangelist referred to a "psalm
of David," which says,

> Even my bosom friend in whom I trusted, who ate of
> my bread, has lifted his heel against me.
>
> (Psalm 41:9)

To himself Jesus applied this psalm ostensibly written by the
legendary King David about a thousand years before. According
to John, Jesus said,

> I am not speaking of you all; I know whom I have
> chosen; it is that the scripture may be fulfilled, "He
> who ate my bread has lifted his heel against me."
>
> (John 13:18)

Here again we see a text arbitrarily chosen from the Old
Testament by the evangelists, serving as witness for the prosecu-
tion for the divinely foretold treachery of Judas Iscariot. It is
most extraordinary that the incarnation of truth and purity, the
savior and son of the god, who himself is this god, should have
displayed such proofs to his evangelists in the New Testament

to explain an event of which he himself was the author. Now anyone with ordinary intelligence knows that such a passage was not written by a god or the son of a god, Jesus, but by men thoroughly bound to the earth as were the Biblical authors in general, be they prophets or evangelists. The thoroughly human character of the four evangelists explains the many contradictions they wove into their story of Jesus.

To make his chosen friend a traitor and to condemn his name to millennia of obloquy would completely contradict the savior's high moral code and pure love of truth, goodness, and humanity. But religious bigotry has not shrunk from branding its most dangerous rival, the Jewish religion, with the price of blood, the kiss of Judas, and the betrayal in order to heap shame on Jewry for all times and in front of all the world.

The authors of the New Testament have attained their purpose in generous measure. For two thousand years Christendom has seen in the Jewish traitor the model of human wickedness. Even today, the Catholic Church has these words in a prayer on Maundy Thursday:

> My friend hath betrayed me with the sign of a kiss, the sign with which he consummated the murder. Luckless man, he never even received the price of blood but hanged himself at the end. . . .Judas, that trafficker in iniquity, came nigh unto his Lord that he might kiss him. Like an innocent lamb, the Lord did not reject his kiss. For a few coins the traitor delivered Christ to the Jews.　　　　　(Great Missal, pp. 839, 840)

We know that this prayer is not only uttered in our days, but what is much worse, is believed as a fact by millions of Christians. Do the men of the twentieth century behave this way deliberately or out of indifference and ignorance? They are more guilty than the zealots of the Middle Ages, most of whom were unable to read. Any Christian in the modern world can read his New Testament. So he can easily find out for himself what it has to tell about the supposed treachery of Judas Iscariot. Also he need not go to the New Testament for a name to designate shameful treason. Among others, that of the traitor Quisling is already adopted into the language used by the civilized world.

Today, though most of us are Christians of one stripe or another or Jews or Muslims or believers or nonbelievers in some god or gods, we do have one thing in common: we are human beings and are to behave as human beings. We must first of all bring home to faithful Christians that for two thousand years they have not read discerningly what is clearly stated in their own Holy Scriptures, requiring for their comprehension, as in the case of Judas Iscariot, neither shifty interpretation nor murky mysticism. In the passage about the betrayal, the sacrificial victim was not Jesus, for he saw that the betrayal accorded with the deliberations of the god and of himself, as he himself said, "The Son of man is to be delivered into the hands of men" (Luke 9:44) and he gave himself up temporarily to death for three days in consequence of divine providence, every detail of which he foresaw beforehand.

All our human sympathy goes out to the wronged and wretched Judas Iscariot, whose destiny, honor, and repute the deity has treated altogether capriciously even if for lofty purposes. The betrayal forms the prelude to the redemption of Christianity. There would be no reason at all to expose him to scorn even if the disciple had brought about the deed as a deliberately criminal act. So it is impossible to understand the evangelist when he says:

> The Son of man goes as it is written of him, but woe
> to that man by whom the Son of man is betrayed! It
> would have been better for that man if he had not been
> born.   (Matthew 26:24)

There is this to add. If Judas Iscariot had not been born or imagined there could have been no Church of Christ today according to the New Testament. For this alleged act of the Jewish apostle was made the starting point of salvation and eternal life beyond the grave for all believing Christians. Only through Judas Iscariot was the way cleared for the mission of the redemption of man, which the god and Jesus desire. Only now can the faithful go to his god and Christ in heaven, divinities who have not yet seen fit to morally obligate either their Church or their priests to desist from charging Judas with an act these divinities themselves brought about and to which Christianity owes its existence.

Two thousand years have slipped by since Christ and four hundred years since Luther, but Christians have given little thought to restoring the honor of the Jewish "traitor" to which he is entitled by the account in the New Testament and by Jesus' own words.

11. THE DEICIDE CHARGE AGAINST THE JEWS

In November, 1964, after nearly two millenniums of teaching and propagating the unjust charge that the Jews murdered Jesus Christ, the Roman Catholic Church revised its official position on this matter and called upon all its adherents to refrain from presenting the Jewish people as one rejected, cursed, or guilty of deicide.

In the closing days of its 1964 session, the Ecumenical Council (Vatican II), begun under Pope John XXIII and continued under Pope Paul VI, approved the text of the document "On the Relation of the Church to the Non-Christian Religions," which was to serve as the approved basis for a final version for adoption by the 1965 Council session.

The document seeks reconciliation with all religions—even primitive religions—and specifically mentions Hinduism, Buddhism, Mohammedanism, and Judaism. But the greatest impact of the declaration on the Western world has been produced by that portion of it that pertains to the Jews.

Following are extracted passages of the document that deal specifically with the Church's attitude toward the Jews:

> . . . In this age of ours, when mankind is being drawn closer together, day by day, and the ties between peoples here and there are made stronger, the church weighs earnestly her attitude toward non-Christian religions.
>
> One is the community of all peoples, one their origin, for God made the entire human race live on all the face of the earth. One, too, is their ultimate end, God. . . .

With a grateful heart, the church of Christ acknowledges that, according to God's saving design, the beginnings of her faith and her election were already among the Patriarchs, Moses and the prophets. She professes that all who believe in Christ—Abraham's sons according to faith—were included in the same Patriarch's call, likewise that her salvation is typically foreshadowed by the chosen people's exodus from the land of bondage. ·

The church, therefore, cannot forget that she received the revelation of the Old Testament from the people with whom God in His ineffable mercy concluded the former covenant. Nor can she forget that she feeds upon the root of that cultivated olive tree into which the wild shoots of the gentiles have been grafted (cf. Romans 2:17–24). Indeed, the church believes that by His cross Christ Our Peace reconciled Jews and Gentiles, making both one (cf Ephesians 2:14–16). . . .

No less does she recall that the Apostles, the church's mainstay and pillars, as well as most of the early Disciples who proclaimed Christ's gospel to the world, sprang from the Jewish people.

Even though a large part of the Jews did not accept the Gospel, they remain most dear to God for the sake of the Patriarchs. This is the witness of the Apostle, as is the utterance that God's gift and call are irrevocable. . . .

Since the spiritual patrimony common to Christians and Jews is of such magnitude, this sacred synod wants to support and recommend their mutual knowledge and respect, a knowledge and respect that are the fruit, above all, of Biblical and theological studies as well as of fraternal dialogues. Moreover, this synod, in her rejection of injustice of whatever kind and wherever inflicted upon men, remains mindful of that common patrimony and so deplores, indeed condemns, hatred and persecution of Jews, whether they arose in former or in our own days.

May, then, all see to it that in their catechetical work
or in their preaching of the word of God they do not
teach anything that could give rise to hatred or contempt of Jews in the hearts of Christians.

May they never present the Jewish people as one rejected, cursed, or guilty of deicide.

All that happened to Christ in His passion cannot be
attributed to the whole people then alive, much less
to those of today. Besides, the church held and holds
that Christ underwent His passion and death freely,
because of the sins of all men and out of infinite
love. . . .

It is expected that this formal exoneration of the Jews for the
death of Christ will serve ultimately as the basis for the removal
from Catholic educational and liturgical texts of all charges that
the Jews murdered Jesus.

What has been the history of this charge of murder against
a whole people?

When one engages in a legal dispute, one must objectively
examine all the data relevant to the case before one draws any
conclusions from them. Now we know that Christians long gave
a decisive affirmative to the question whether the Jews killed
Jesus Christ and whether his death is to be regarded as murder.
Christians have maintained and taught this accusation of murder
in their religious instruction; Christian prayerbooks have described it as an accomplished and incontestable fact. The various
churches and chapels of the Jesus religion may differ in many
items of faith, but they have all agreed that the Jews murdered
Jesus. It has always been stated baldly: the Jews murdered our
savior. Presumably the institutions and individuals recognized as
responsible, like churches and priests, have had extensive proofs
and evidence for this, such as a court would require before judging
a person accused of only a trifling offense.

But not a man on earth can produce any genuine document
whatsoever to support the charge of murder made against the
Jews. For in the first place some proof that Jesus was ever really
killed is requisite. No one can supply this proof simply because

it is not self-evident that Jesus ever lived. Christ is certainly not a historical personality but exists only in faith. We shall not here examine whether Jesus may have lived and, if so, whether his life as the evangelists present it in the New Testament ran so as to copy the prototype given in the previously mentioned Dead Sea scrolls. There is scant historical proof that Jesus ever lived; this is established and the Christian churches do not deny it.

This lack of cogent evidence, the base of every legal decision, counsels the utmost caution in answering the question posed under such remarkable circumstances. For in the modern world there is not a court in a single country which would consent to conduct legal criminal proceedings against an individual, a community, or a nation, if nobody could produce the corpse, if no witnesses or exhibits could confirm the murder, and if no one reported to the authorities that the allegedly murdered man was missing. These are all matters admittedly pertinent to Jesus insofar as one naturally postulates that a murdered man at least had had to live.

No one would need trouble himself about the question of the existence of Jesus—one could merely leave the answer to belief— if living men on account of his death had not been "despised, beaten, and killed"—treatment which the Christians for some two thousand years have reproached the Jews for having inflicted on Jesus.

However great the lack of any secular proof for the life and death of the savior, a thousandfold more demonstrable is the atrocious fate of Jewish men, women, and children in Christian history. For apart from some pogroms in the early period of Islam, the Christians are the only people in the world who have persistently scourged the Jews, for the traditional hatred of the Jews is rooted mainly in the doctrine that the people of Israel murdered the savior. This ancient accusation has expressed itself continually in new kinds of persecution, these having reached an unimaginable climax in modern days.

If, therefore, this question of guilt has historically no legal leg to stand on and is supported only by the reports in the sacred books of the Christians, then we must examine these sources to get some clear notion about the accusation. Our chief concern here is not to level a critique at Christianity or to combat a theory; our sole and only purpose is rather the issues of justice and injustice for the living. We want to decide in the light of the New Testament account whether the Jews at the time of Jesus could justly be charged with murdering him.

For the elucidation of this subject two separate groups of people stand at the bar of world public opinion. These are the Jews and the believing Christians. The former, because since the foundation of the Christian Church they have been unable to get a fair hearing. The latter, because their faith fettered them to the murder doctrine with an unswerving bigotry.

As there is no evidence at hand about the life of Jesus outside the texts of believers, we could without more ado adopt the standpoint that nothing remains for us but to invesigate whether he was murdered and, if so, by whom. We might argue thus if the question were of secondary importance, if nobody had a special interest in the solution, and if the alleged murder had no further consequences. But we know that its results were the foundation of the Church and the downfall and proscription of the Synagogue. What a tragedy lies in simple articles of faith; the Jews made a one and only god for themselves, and from him there came a son who has been their doom for the last two thousand years! The Eternal One of Israel becomes the first and last cause of their fate, for in the Christian view he is one in person with Jesus, and so in Jesus the Jews murdered their own almighty God of Sinai!

The New Testament is the only foundation that we have on which to test the rights and wrongs of the Jews in our inquiry. So we can only occupy the position of this faith if we want to tackle the problem objectively. We accordingly accept for the purposes of our reflections the postulates of the faith that Jesus actually lived, as well as the four evangelists, Matthew, Mark, Luke, and John, the apostles Peter and Paul, and all the other people mentioned in the New Testament for whom there is not much more historical evidence than for Moses and the patriarchs or any other character in the Pentateuch or for the mythical King David or many other characters in the Old Testament.

As for the god, Jesus, and all those great ones of the Bible whose existence can never be proved, we must accept that they might have been or were, just as in Egypt people believed that Isis and Osiris ruled over them, in Greece that Zeus ruled over the Greeks, in India that Brahma ruled over the people, and in Palestine Yahweh, who became God the Father of Christendom. The gods, like Horus in Egypt, Apollo in Greece, Mithras in Persia, and Jesus in Palestine, live only in men's beliefs; likewise, in belief only, exists an after life as expressed in the Elysium and Hades of the Greeks and analogously in the heaven and hell of the Jews and Christians.

We do not propose in any way now to criticize or searchingly to investigate any of these human, all too human, ideas, images, and inventions. We accept them as the well-established matter of actual religions. The faithful had to accept them, or, insofar as the religions have not perished, still have to accept them, if they are to avoid incurring the guilt of mortal sin which allegedly cannot be expiated even in the everlasting flames of hell as in Catholicism. We thus deliberately stand on the spiritual ground of primitive times, or, which comes to the same thing, on that of the contemporary Roman Church as interpreted by many, including the Cardinal Archbishop Mercier of Mechelin in Belgium in the twentieth century. This prince of the Church wrote:

> The Holy Scripture expresses God's word as the Holy Spirit dictated it to the writers of the holy books. . . . Revelation is contained in the Holy Scriptures and also in Church tradition, a word which means transmission of the transmitted word. The tradition is that part of God's word which was first taught by Jesus Christ with his own voice and was thereafter committed by his apostles to the bosom of the Catholic Church which will follow it until the end of time.
>
> (Grand Missal, p. 22)

Thus, in general, the Church is still of the persuasion that Yahweh dictated the basic thoughts of the Old Testatment to Moses and that the son of the Jewish Yahweh delivered the fundamental teachings of the New Testament by word of mouth to the apostles, from whom the evangelists got them and wrote them down. So faith looks upon the Testaments as revealed by two gods and as "Holy Scriptures." This is why Christianity regards the Jewish God the Father and the Christian God the Son as quite inseparable and the two halves of the Holy Bible as united together. Since God's scripture is older than that of Jesus, the Father must declare the legitimacy of his son through the Old Testament. He must provide proofs of the divine sonship. Christendom, therefore, cannot escape adopting the Bible of Moses, for the writers of the New Testament have to derive from it their demonstration of Jesus' divinity and the announcement of his mission.

The Jews, on the other hand, regard their Torah as sacred, it having emanated from their god, besides whom there can be no other gods. Consequently, they reject Jesus as a new god. For them Jesus is no son of a god but the child of a Jewish carpenter and his wife, Joseph and Mary, who begot Jesus when betrothed, which may have been in accordance with local morality at that time as it still is in many places. For his parents, Jesus was a man and nothing more. They probably knew that he was educated for Biblical study, a young man inspired by lofty thoughts and led by the obvious daily misery of his people to reflect upon a remedy.

Such is the least that we can imagine if we are to accept the existence of Jesus at all. The sufferings of his country brought him to the conviction that they are unavoidable and that improvement was not to be expected in this world. He believed that the god had called him through visions to raise men out of their earthly misery. Apparitions and conversations with the god led him eventually to believe that he was the son of this god and destined to redeem mankind; to save mankind was his god-given mission. He would no more direct his yearnings toward earth but toward heaven, for the happiness of man lay in the next world, not on earth.

He began to proclaim his teaching that the kingdom of heaven was at hand, and it found willing hearers among the suffering masses. Instead of having to abandon forever all hope of a happy life, an idea which seemed obviously true in the midst of war, revolt, and oppression by the heathen, there was now to be ultimate happiness for them also. True, it was to come only after death in heaven, but earthly life is short when all is said and done and the few decades are soon over. Eternal happiness on the other hand is long; indeed it never comes to an end.

Post-exilic Jewish religion, to be sure, also promised its adherents this happiness after death in Canaan, the land of their fathers, but nobody ever came back from among the multitudes who had died in this faith. But in heaven, whither all good men would come through Jesus, there already were the angels. Where these dwelled, it had indeed to be fair. So people enthusiastically followed the son of the god, who told them that he had heard a voice at the baptism in Jordan which cried to him from heaven: "This is my beloved Son" (Matthew 3:17), and that it could only have been the god who thus confirmed his parentage as genuine.

People streamed in throngs to the heaven-sent savior. Their jubilation knew no bounds as they finally saw him drawing into the capital Jerusalem. They spread their garments in his path so that his foot be not soiled by the dirt of the ground, and they cry to him: "Hosanna! Blessed is he who comes in the name of the Lord." (Mark 11:9)

These events did not remain concealed from the guardians of divine and political order—the high priests, elders, and scribes. They grew pale at the notion that a Jew was giving himself out as the son of the god with the intention of founding a new religion. That touched both the roots of their faith and their hitherto secure existence. They summoned the instant intervention of the Jewish police, and it managed with the help of a Jewish traitor to secure the person of Jesus though he had been keeping himself in hiding. The double crime of blasphemy and high treason was implicit in his claim to be recognized as the son of the god who had destined him to be king of the Jews. This is what made the great Sanhedrin competent to condemn him to death. The army of occupation was the executor of this decision; so Jesus was handed over to the Roman soldiery, which executed him by its customary method, crucifixion, not without having first satisfied its sadism with all kinds of cruelties.

The Jews are guilty of the savior's death according to this

account, which follows essentially the statements of the New Testament about the course of these events. From their point of view, it was a judgment in accordance with their faith, their conscience, and their law. For Christendom, however, it has been regarded as the murder of the savior, of the son of the god. In the view they long held, the Jews made themselves guilty of the murder of Jesus Christ by virtue of the decision of their judges. If we accept the historical Christian interpretation, the Jews are indeed guilty of murdering the god, and the indictment hits the Jewish judges full in the face.

But we must ask what the Jews of the period after Jesus have had to do with the court sentence and its execution. Is it right for every new generation of Christians to learn, as they still do everywhere throughout Christendom, that the Jews murdered their savior? Is it possible for the innocent youths with their thirst for knowledge to draw any other conclusion than that the living successors of those who murdered Jesus are all criminals as bad as they?

It is the most absurd of paradoxes and nonsense that for almost two thousand years millions of Jewish men, women, and children fell victims to a creed which owes its origin to the murder of Jesus! Though one may regard the physical and intellectual characteristics of Jews as inferior—a view one would have to investigate thoroughly before accepting—still Christian aversion toward Jews has been based on the teaching of the Church of Jesus that the Jews are guilty of murder.

We do not hold other people responsible for crimes their ancestors may have committed, nor do we deliver them over to universal contempt because of them. It would not occur to any sane person to point the finger of scorn at the Catholic Church today because of the murder of Joan of Arc, the maid of Orleans, who was burnt alive by the Catholic priesthood for blasphemy, though in our century she has gained papal canonization for her death. Four hundred years before Christ, Socrates was accused of blasphemy. Though he was a man of great virtue and wisdom, the people's court at Athens condemned him and he had to take poison and perish. It does not occur to anybody to despise and scorn the modern Athenians on this account.

Even if Jesus was murdered by the Jews, the accusation should only be made where it belongs, in the period of Jesus' death, and leveled against his judges. The presupposition for this lies in proving that the members of the great Sanhedrin were actually guilty. Did everything fall out as the gospels described the events leading up to Golgotha, or are there clues indicating other causes for the death of the savior?

We have already seen that in the New Testament the remission of sins is achieved not by the shedding of animal blood as with the Jews but by the shedding of human blood. Not just by the blood of any man you like, but only by the blood of Jesus, shed in the act of crucifixion. This raises the question of who it was that limited the sacrificial blood of salvation to Jesus The crucified one gave the answer himself in these words,

> For I have come down from heaven, not to do my own will, but the will of him who sent me.
>
> (John 6:38)

And so he prayed to the god, his father,

> I glorified thee on earth, having accomplished the work which thou gavest me to do.
>
> (John 17:4)

The text of a Christian prayer explains what this work was. It runs:

> God, who did will that his son should suffer the martyr's torment upon the cross to free us from the power of the enemy.
>
> (Grand Missal p. 8)

Thus it was the Almighty who decided that mankind could be redeemed only by the blood of his son. He prescribed the death of the savior to liberate man from his enemy, the devil, the author of evil.

This is a most important fact. It was God himself, not just the Jews, that demanded the death of the son of man. The death sentence decreed by the great Sanhedrin, the crucifixion by the Romans, suddenly appear in a new light, for neither judge nor executioner could have been acting wickedly insofar as they were carrying out the will of the god. Nor could this have remained hidden from Jesus either. For he, too, knew that the Father had awarded him death for three days, and that he would rise again from the grave alive on the third day. He knew well enough that his situation reflected the will of the god and was inevitable; this is shown by the answer Jesus gave when he had to appear before the Roman governor for a hearing at which he was asked whether he knew that the latter had power to have him killed: "You would have no power over me unless it had been given you from above." (John 19:11) This "above" is the kingdom of the god, his home whence he had come and whither he would return.

> My kingship is not of this world; if my kingship were
> of this world, my servants would fight, that I might not
> be handed over to the Jews; but my kingship is not
> from the world.   (John 18:36)

He was weaker as a son of man than he was as the son of God; his will as a man counted for nothing against his will as a god; it was not an earthly will that was done, but a heavenly one.

His arrest demonstrates this point, too. When one of his companions drew his sword in order to defend him, Jesus forbade him and added in explanation:

> Do you think that I cannot appeal to my Father, and
> he will at once send me more than twelve legions of
> angels? But how then should the scriptures be fulfilled
> that it must be so?
>
> (Matthew 26:53–54)

Jesus wanted to surrender himself to death so that some hazy assertion of the Old Testament allegedly demanding his death might be fulfilled.

It is most amazing that Jesus could give no other reason for the death decreed by his father than the highly dubious appeal to the Mosaic Bible. The god demanded the sacrifice of his son; the latter knowing this did not struggle against it, but declared himself ready to die voluntarily. Not only did the god demand the blood of Jesus; to this very remarkable new fact is added a further real sensation: Jesus wanted to die! He said:

> For this reason the Father loves me, because I lay down my life, that I may take it again. No one takes it from me, but I lay it down of my own accord. I have power to lay it down, and I have power to take it again. This charge I have I received from my Father.
>
> (John 10:17–18)

Nobody took it from him, neither the Jews nor the Romans, for he and the god had the power to prevent his death, but they chose not to use it. On the contrary, both of them wanted to see Jesus crucified, long before even a single Jew had any notion of his existence. Even before the savior's birth as a man, the god had decreed his sacrifice of blood upon the cross; for that purpose Jesus, who had been God in eternity, had to appear on earth in human shape and be born of Mary. He had already known his fate even when he was a suckling in the crib at Bethlehem, for in that newborn babe lay hidden an eternal, omniscient deity. Accordingly, as soon as the son of man became older, he began to speak of his earthly life and of his mission with foreknowledge of the future. Thus everything took place just as he had prophesied to his astonished disciples:

> Behold, we are going up to Jerusalem; and the Son of man will be delivered to the chief priests.
>
> (Matthew 20:18; cf. 26:45)

And so it occurred. Further:

> The Son of man must suffer many things, and be rejected by the elders and chief priests and scribes.
>
> (Luke 9:22)

This is exactly what happened.

> Everything that is written of the Son of man by the prophets will be accomplished. For he will be delivered to the Gentiles.
>
> (Luke 18:31–32)

No prophet ever mentions this with even a single word; but
according to the New Testament, he is delivered to the gentile
Romans.

> They will mock him, and spit upon him, and scourge
> him, and kill him.   (Mark 10:34)

This is exactly the way they treated him.

> You know that. . . .the Son of man will be delivered
> up to be crucified.
>
> (Matthew 26:2)

And he was crucified.

> For I tell you that this scripture must be fulfilled in
> me, "And he was reckoned with transgressors."
>
> (Luke 22:37)

Again nothing relevant to this is found in the Jewish Bible, but
the prophecy he gave to his disciples was fulfilled to the letter,
for he was executed together with two criminals. (Luke 23:33)

We have before us a case which in its way is unique. The
murdered man knows every stage of the wrongs to be committed
against him long before any living soul, including the police, had
any suspicion of his existence. Before Jesus was pursued, arrested,
accused, condemned, and killed, he knew clearly in advance by
whom, where, how, and with whom he would meet his death.
Not the murderer but the murdered man carries out the plan for
the murder. If this bears the stamp of murder, then every murderer who has ever been convicted has suffered a miscarriage
of justice.

Now it might be objected that we ought to guard ourselves
against evil, as the god has given us free will for that purpose,
according to the view of faith. But this argument cannot be
adduced here because it would imply that what the god has
planned for the good of man is evil. But if the intention of the
god was good, then this action of his must be good too. The
Almighty is pure righteousness and goodness; so the condemning
of Jesus Christ to death is a right and good act, for the god so
willed it.

If the Christian theory of free will is to stand in spite of this statement, and if the Jews are accordingly to be branded as the murderers of Jesus, then we must suppose that they acted against their better knowledge. For an attribute of crime is the evil intention, the will to do wrong; so was their action deliberately evil? The Jews had heard from Jesus himself that he was the son of the god; but did they also know the purpose of his appearance on earth, the nature of the mission God the Father had entrusted to him, and did they know the true nature of the savior and why he was sent? Did they pass the sentence of death in good faith or against their better judgment? That is the only decisive issue in this deliberation.

In the epistle to the Ephesians we read of a mystery of Christ and of

> his purpose which he set forth in Christ . . . to unite
> all things in him, things in heaven and things on earth,
> > (Ephesians 1:9–10)

and that

> the Gentiles are fellow heirs, members of the same
> body, and partakers of the promise in Christ Jesus
> through the gospel.
> > (Ephesians 3:6)

To express this in a different way, the subject of the mystery of Christ is the knowledge of the way through Jesus leading man from this earth to everlasting happiness in heaven beyond the grave, and this knowledge was to be communicated to the gentiles. The essential purpose of a mystery is to keep something secret from a third party. Here this third party was the Jewish people. They were not allowed to hear about the matter to be kept secret; there were only Jews and gentiles on earth.

Jesus himself left no doubt about this, for his disciples asked him when he spoke to the Jews about his mission in parables which were unintelligible to them, "Why do you speak to them in parables?" (Matthew 13:10) He answered:

> To you it has been given to know the secrets of the
> kingdom of heaven, but to them it has not been given

. . . .because seeing they do not see, and hearing they
do not hear, nor do they understand.

> (Matthew 13:11, 13)

They were not to understand, and therefore,

> With them indeed is fulfilled the prophecy of Isaiah
> which says: "You shall indeed hear but never under-
> stand, and you shall indeed see but never perceive."
>
> (Matthew 13:14)

So another Old Testament passage was fulfilled, spoken by
a prophet out of a vision long before Jesus and bearing no relation to him; hence the Jews should not come to know either his
mystery or his real nature and function, even though the god
expressly sent Jesus to the Jews, and his disciples were supposed
above all things to preach the gospel to them. For his first charge
to the apostles runs:

> Go nowhere among the Gentiles, and enter no town
> of the Samaritans, but go rather to the lost sheep of the
> house of Israel   (Matthew 10:5–6)

so that, as Paul says, "all Israel will be saved." (Romans 11:26)
But the God also wanted to leave them in the dark about Jesus, as
the God "has mercy upon whomever he wills, and he hardens the
heart of whomever he wills." (Romans 9:18) The Eternal one
condemned Israel to remain excluded from the supreme good of
salvation, however much it may have yearned for it, because the
God had decreed:

> Israel failed to obtain what it sought. The elect obtained
> it, but the rest were hardened
>
> (Romans 11:7),

> for it depends not upon man's will or exertion, but
> upon God's mercy.
>
> (Romans 9:16)

The god and Jesus, however, did not have mercy on the Jews.
These were not to find nor even to recognize their savior in
Christ.

No one can come to me unless the Father who sent me
draws him, he says; This is why I told you that no one
can come to me unless it is granted him by the Father.
(John 6:44, 65)

But God did not draw his chosen people, neither did he give them
salvation.

We thus find a third essential fact demonstrated by the New
Testament, in addition to God's plan for the murder of Jesus
and of Jesus' own wish to die: God and Jesus hid the mystery
of Christ from the Jews in order to use them as a tool for their
purposes. At the same time the two Godheads excluded the Jews
from the salvation through Jesus. The Jews had to bring about
the death of Jesus to ensure the salvation of mankind, without
partaking in it themselves. They did not pass the death sentence
against their better judgment, or from a wicked intent, but in
all good faith, for they did not know the mystery of the savior.

Jesus trusted the devils themselves more than he trusted them;
for when he healed the possessed and drove out the unclean
spirits, the devils, these fell down before him and cried that he
was the son of God. "And he strictly ordered them not to make
him known." (Mark 3:12) The devils could know his secret but
not the Jews, his fellow countrymen and fellow believers. The devil
himself, as we have seen, played a part in the scheme of salvation.
At the given moment he was to enter into the apostle Judas
Iscariot to tempt him to betray Jesus and thereby to introduce
the deed of Golgotha. (John 13:27) The bandage the god and
Jesus placed over the eyes and ears of the Jews could not be
removed, lest they should recognize as a crime a deed they regarded as a duty inspired by their divine creed.

It is a long time since Jesus died, rose again, and began to lead
his life as a god above the clouds in heaven in the presence of
his father and all the angels and saints. But all the while, the
god still keeps the Jews in their impenitent blindness. The Christians, too, notice this and so they direct the following prayer in
church to the Almighty even today:

Let us pray for the unbelieving Jews and implore the
Lord, our God, that He lift the cloak from their hearts

that they may join us in witnessing Jesus Christ as our Lord. Almighty and everlasting God, deny not thy mercy to the Jews according to their lack of faith; hearken unto the prayers which we raise to thee, adjuring thee to lead them out of their darkness so that they may know the light of thy truth, which is Jesus Christ.   (Grand Missal, p. 924)

But these priests and believers prayed to the god in vain. For they did not perceive the contradiction between the treachery and murder ascribed to the Jews on the one hand and on the other the sole and incontrovertible guilt of the god and the savior documented by the New Testament itself. The following promise of the evangelists is empty: "Whatever you ask in prayer, believe that you receive, and you will." (Mark 11:24; cf. Matthew 21:22; I John 5, 15) Presumably this promise is empty because they do not believe that the God will show the Jews the way to Jesus Christ, as they know from the New Testament in which Paul explained:

A hardening has come upon part of Israel, until the full number of the Gentiles come in.

(Romans 11:25)

Only after the non-Christians have become faithful members of the Church of Jesus will the god permit the Jews to become penitent and to accept the savior.

Twenty centuries have not sufficed to reach the majority of all minkind, the goal set by Paul. We cannot expect the billions of living non-Christians and their descendants to embrace Jesus. Paul insisted that this be achieved as a condition before the god shall deliver the Jews from their blindness in recognizing the savior. This would most likely mean that they will never come to Jesus in all eternity, that they will never be redeemed in the Christian sense, and that they will be exposed individually and collectively to eternal torment in hell.

The murder of Jesus does not make the Jews deserve such a fate, for the death sentence and the crucifixion were only possible because the god and Jesus willed it and because divine providence did not unveil the mystery of Christ to the Jews. The deed was good because it was the will of the god. The Jews committed no outrage, but performed an act of salvation, bringing to Christians everlasting happiness and their enduring Church, which alone can redeem. This cluster of events occasions no reign of grief among mankind.

> The whole of creation is in a transport of joy.
> (Grand Missal, p. 927)

> Christ's coming in the world is the climax of human history. (*Ibid.*, p. 419)

But God is invoked in prayer to let those who have at last been redeemed understand that

> the creation of the world was no greater marvel than that which appeared late in time, when Jesus Christ was put to death.
> (Grand Missal, p. 979)

His death becomes "the source of eternal salvation" (Hebrews 5:9), as He has made "us [Christians] a kingdom, priests to his God." (Revelation 1:6) Those passages accord the deed the merciful judgment it well deserves. But men's opinions are inconstant. The Christian churches have not resounded with this jubilant symphony on their organs, but in the name of the god and the savior the massed choir of priests and people have sung these words loud and clear:

> What have I done to thee, O my people; wherewith have I troubled thee? Tell me. Because I led thee out of Egypt hast thou therefore set up a cross for thy savior? Is it because I have been thy leader forty years long in the wilderness and fed thee on manna and led thee into a glorious land, is it for this that thou hast set up a cross for thy savior? Yea, is there anything that I have not done for thee? Thou wast an excellent vine that I planted but thou art become full of bitterness for me, for when I was athirst, thou didst give

me vinegar, and thou hast pierced the side of thy savior
with a lance. . . .For love of thee I slew the first-born
in Egypt, and thou has delivered me up to be scourged.
I drowned Pharaoh in the Red Sea, and thou hast given
me over to the high priests. . . .I have let glory and
honor be thy portion, but thou hast nailed me to the
wood of the cross.

(Grand Missal, pp. 925–927)

The most incomprehensible thing of all, however, is that Jesus
himself launched into grievous complaints against the Jews, he
who knew the true circumstances of his death better than any
Holy Book could ever express.

"Woe to you!" (Matthew 23:13) He cried to them, a cry
which is raised against the Jews in all the tongues the Christians
speak. "You serpents, you brood of vipers, how are you to escape
being sentenced to hell?" (Matthew 23:33) He cursed them:
"Upon you may come all the righteous blood shed on earth, from
the blood of innocent Abel" (Matthew 23:35), "the blood of all
the prophets, shed from the foundation of the world." (Luke
11:50) "O Jerusalem, Jerusalem," he warned threateningly,
"killing the prophets and stoning those who are sent to you!"
(Matthew 23:37)

That is what Jesus said, the omniscient son of the god, very
God himself, as if he did not know that Abel, the son of the
first man, was killed by his brother thousands of years before
there was a single Jew. And he cursed them for every murder
committed since the creation of the world at any place or time
whatsoever, long before the people of Israel existed. Jesus, "the
true light that enlightens every man" (John 1:9), could be such
an unjust judge as to curse a whole people for crimes it never
committed. How could the god of love, truth, and mercy say
this? How can this be reconciled with his word which he said of
the Jews shortly before his death: "Father, forgive them; for they
know not what they do"? (Luke 23:34) We will say nothing about
the contradiction inherent in this utterance when Jesus declared
that they acted out of ignorance in their God-willed blindness and
at the same time prayed for pardon for their act from the very one
who had willed it and had led them to it. But there is the worse

contradiction that he begged for forgiveness for the Jews and at the same time heaped shame and execration upon them for this alleged act. If the savior could be so grossly unfair, we must not be surprised to hear the Church alleging that with the crucifixion of Christ the Jews "committed the worst crime that has ever stained the world" (Grand Missal, p. 909), and further explaining "that the Jews do not say: we did not kill Christ. . . .It is you, O Jews, you indeed who slaughtered Him." (*Ibid.*, pp. 895, 896) The living Jew is here accused of the murder of Christ. It is printed like this in a Catholic prayer book, which until today has been found in the possession of hundreds of thousands of faithful Christians in Catholic Belgium as their principal prayer book, with papal approval. Even in modern times the guilt of murder is the basis for the services during Passion Week, an occasion on which in past centuries bloody pogroms were begun.

As if this were not enough, the faithful have for ages been observing the sufferings of Christ and the murder by the Jews re-enacted on living human beings in the so-called passion plays. These representations kindle religious hatred ever anew. Because of the significance which such passion plays still have for the educated Christian world, we must briefly consider the most famous internationally of these performances, those at Oberammergau in Bavaria.

Schroeder, domestic chaplain to the Pope, considered these performances especially significant for strengthening Christian faith. They have helped to influence the thought and sentiment of whole nations, according to Schroeder. The theme of the treatment at Oberammergau is the hatred of the petty Jewish traders and sharpers who believe that Jesus is hurting their business and are incited by the Jewish officials to encompass the death of the "hated Galilean."

> Their unrelenting hatred is the direct driving force in
> the whole story of the Lord's suffering.

This picture of the Jew as a money-grubbing, unscrupulous higgler for the sake of strengthening religious feeling does no harm to the spirit, the prelate thinks, because all it shows is that the enemies of Christ themselves

do not shrink from stirring up the lowest passions for
the only purpose of consigning the dangerous Nazarene
to destruction and preserving their own threatened
authority,

for in this play lies a religious intention which has been capable
for centuries of imparting to innumerable hearts an effect often
of lifelong duration.

The Passion of the savior is to be presented in living pictures
before well-to-do tourists, as the gospels tell the tale. In this
presentation, the priests incite the people to frenzy, a temple
servant punches Jesus in the face, and the Jewish high priest fawns
upon Pilate

to win him for his plan, as the whole affair was highly
distasteful to him.

After refusing to pass the death sentence, Pilate has Jesus
scourged. Not content with this, the chief priests hasten away
"to win yet more people for their bloody plans. Ever more violent
becomes the demeanor of the priests, ever more menacing the
attitude of the mob." At last Pilate gives way and pronounces
sentence of death. "With the words of satisfied revenge, 'Now
there is an end to the Galilean,'" the scene closes.

Led towards Golgotha, "wearily dragging the cross and often
collapsing, the Lord is ever and again hauled forward by the
four tormentors." Then, off stage, the hammer blows resound, as
the nails are driven into the hands and feet of Jesus. When the
curtain rises Jesus is seen lying on the ground nailed to the cross.
After the cross is raised, he dies. "The blinded people and
priests, their hatred not yet slaked, withdraw." The priests return
and ask for the body, "to have it thrown in a dishonorable grave."
With "curses and imprecations on their lips," they then go home.
The anti-Semitic director of this play later found that the story
of the Passion in the New Testament plainly needed corrections.

In the year 1910, Msgr. Dr. Frühwirth, the papal nuncio, at-
tended the play. He made a report about it to the Pope:

I followed the action of the play with inner joy and
hearty satisfaction. . . .I can only express the sum

of my impressions in the single wish, that God may
bless the Oberammergau passion play and preserve it
for ever, in his honor. . . .

And yet they pray:

Glory to God in the highest, and on earth peace

and

Forgive us our debts, as we also have forgiven our
debtors. Amen.

The years of Jewish persecutions are past. For long centuries
Jewish circles have devoted Easter week, with Good Friday as
a reminder of the murder of Jesus, to commemorating pogroms.
In 1957, a few years after Hitler's fall, a "Week of Brotherhood" was celebrated under the auspices of Christian Jewish
collaboration. How it was really kept in a Lutheran parish in
North Germany is shown by the following incident.

Shortly before Easter week, a loaned film, "The Cross of
Golgotha," was shown to the young people of confirmation age
and to members of the congregation. In effective and violent anti-
Semitic agitation, it even excelled the Oberammergau play. Among
other instances, Judas Iscariot was shown with repulsive and
pronounced Jewish features. Yelling mobs of Jews, shown with
distinct facial features, whipped children and adults alike into a
frenzy of anti-Semitic feeling without the use of words. In short,
the film presented in the church itself is a sad illustration on part
of the leaders of the evangelical church as to the meaning and
spirit of the "Week of Brotherhood."

The Ecumenical Council's declaration, late though it is and
powerless as it is to undo the injustice perpetrated upon millions
and millions of Jews unjustly accused of murder, is a welcome
first step. If, as is hoped, it will eventually serve to restore to the
Jews their right to walk among men with their heads held high,
their stigma removed, it will remove a worse stigma from the
face of Christianity.

12. THE INVENTED GOD

Nietzsche wrote in his book *On the Use and Abuse of History for Life:* "In the whole Western world, religion has been a warring chaos throughout the past and it still remains so." With this observation, he touched on a process taking place before the eyes of all in his time and in ours. If religion could be treated as a case pending in court, one would only need to wait till the evidence was submitted and the judgment delivered. But one cannot merely observe and wait until the evolution of religious forms develops order out of the chaos compounded of the main bodies of religion with their numerous splinter groups and hundreds of other cults and beliefs intertwining them. It would be fruitless to wait for a settlement of the religious issue; no single life would be long enough to suffice, nor would the span of the whole human race, because it is most unlikely that mankind will ever unite in one single way of regarding life and the universe.

In this fundamental spiritual question, mankind may never reach a generally acceptable solution to the problem. Emphasizing the full respect due to every true believer and his religion, we may take a position relative to the concealed or open conflict amid the present multiplicity of religions and attempt to give a factual account of this historical development in order to point out ways to a solution answering to the yearnings of a great part of mankind.

The general conception of religion is that the universe, the earth, and the race of man were created by a god, or, in polytheism, by the principal god. First, he brought order into the universe, which had previously consisted of absolute void or of chaos. Thereupon, he made man in his own image, to fashion a living being that should fulfill the purpose of creation by render-

ing him thanks and honor for his mighty work. Thus intention
and deed climaxed in the creation of man for the honor and glory
of the god. That is the essense of the three great revealed religions
proclaimed by Moses, Jesus, and Mohammed.

This explains the existence of the universe, but not the existence
of the god. His being is a matter of "faith," not susceptible of
proof. For the believer it is axiomatic, requiring no demonstration.
Yet pious thinkers have undertaken the attempt. The French
theist and philosopher Descartes (1596–1650), whose views have
permanently influenced the Western religious world, considered
the existence of God demonstrable. Starting from the statement
"I think, therefore I am" *(cogito ergo sum),* he supposed that
there is a god. From this he concluded that such a thought could
only derive from a god himself and that he had thus proved the
existence of a god.

The German philosopher Kant (1724–1804) treated the same
problem in his *Critique of Pure Reason,* but he concluded that
the existence of a god could not be proved. He defined god as a
mere idea which eventually flowed into the concept of a personal
god. His reflections led him to declare that man is guilty of a
fallacy in so far as he wishes to explain the phenomena of nature,
even those of a spiritual kind, by the concept of a god. He
described any such demonstration as "impure reason."

Since there is no prospect of being able to prove the existence
of a god by incontrovertible facts, nothing remains but to "believe"
in him. From this impossibility it follows irrefutably that God is
a creation of the human mind. Man craves for a satisfying explanation of the events of nature that baffle his understanding;
hence he evolves an explanatory god and supposes that as the
subject of a faith deeply felt this god must exist.

For all his brooding over the riddle of the universe, over the
meaning and purpose of existence, man finds a way to ultimate
truth in the will to believe in a god, a will that gives him happiness
and relieves him once and for all of further thoughts about
"Whence come I?" and "Whither go I?" And that holds even
though this edifice of the imagination rests on a highly uncertain
and improbable foundation. This gives the universe, including
man, a supernatural origin, ruling all natural explanation out of

court. This withdraws any attempt to arrive at a rational explanation. On this point all theistic religions are essentially the same.

In the New Testament, the author of the epistle to the Hebrews followed this line of thought when he said,

> Now faith is the assurance of things hoped for, the conviction of things not seen.
>
> (Hebrews 11:1)

This attitude raises religious bars halting the inborn urge to discover the truth about nature and preventing natural explanations about things which sooner or later could be ascertained. Ignorant, religious-minded mankind can never get a proper insight into events proceeding according to the laws of causal sequence.

One may well content oneself with the humble intuition that it is not mankind's task to bring light into the darkness of the ultimate foundations of the universe. Man should rather regard the universe with awe, admitting that it excels the power of his understanding and that ultimates are beyond the limits of human inquiry.

But man cannot suppress the echo which this majestic mystery awakens in himself. Somehow he apprehends by intuition a bond between the nature around him and that lying within him. Does he perhaps not also contain within himself some small fraction of that mighty power which moves everything around him? Is not the great unknown that shakes the earth and ripens the fruit at work within himself too? Why is he frightened by the roll of thunder, why seized with a deep joy at the warmth of the sunbeam and the refreshing rain on the thirsty soil? Is there a secret link between him and the forces which do all this? If so, he is clearly not divorced from all that happens around him; he is truly a part of nature. He is no outcast exiled from all this; he feels the great unknown at work within himself as well.

And now he begins to explore in order to understand the nature of the power that molds life around him and in him. Primitive people try to find an intelligible principle to explain the universe, to give a common denominator for the powers that move it. The intellectual level of the average man has not been high enough to attain to this; only few men are endowed with the special gifts of mind to do that; they give adequate voice to the hazy feelings and perceptions of the masses. The masses think that the motion of natural objects derives from spirits and gods that dwell concealed within these objects and direct the universe, including human beings, whom they also created.

This notion explains everything and so it must be right. A supernatural power, a god, stands over everything that exists; it also cares for us. We belong to this god, as he to us, and to the whole great drama of nature. Since we depend on him and we feel the power of this god and know that it is in us, he can only think as we ourselves do, for we derive from and are a part of him. Even though in his outer being and natural form he remains unknown to us because he resides beyond the earth, he must nevertheless rule as human beings in a human manner.

This god teaches us and cares for us as a father teaches and cares for his children. Even though we cannot see him face to face, yet as a good father he sends us blessings in the shape of seed and fruit, of sun, peace, and happiness. We must firmly believe in him, for he sees and knows everything. Should we doubt him or even think that he does not exist, he will strike us with the great store of evils that he has—and justly so. He slays the unbelievers with his lightning; he drowns whole human settlements with vast deluges because of their doubts, and he deals fearful and deadly blows of punishment in devastating earthquakes.

In this manner primitive man sees the works and ways of the god. This attitude is the basis of all religions. For one of the main bases of religion is the postulating of a supernatural being and turning it into a human shape, thereby making it familiar and intelligible and useful for a higher purpose.

The god, then, becomes the highest power and authority in bringing order to the human community. What was originally only an indefinite feeling of a relationship with some mysterious, extramundane power is now transformed into a certitude of faith on which to build a legal code to control the people with a divinely constituted authority in state and church. Henceforth, civil and church law allow no one to doubt the will of the god, for ruler and priest fancy that by revelation this god chose and elected them to see that this will be obeyed.

The only way belief in the supernatural can be established is through revelation, or self-manifestation, of this power, this god, or (to put it plainly) whatever the believer conceives it to be. And religion is no more able or willing to explain revelation in a natural manner than it is to explain the existence of a god. It must resort to miracles contravening natural law to connect man with a god. One of the miracles of this sort occurred at Sinai when the god spoke with Moses and, according to the Biblical notion, gave him the law in the Pentateuch or the Torah, this gift being the greatest of all divine miracles.

Thus we arrive at the following conclusion. Man believes in a god through a divine self-revelation. This rests on a miracle. The spiritual contents thus produced is the dogma of revealed religion, the only valid and lawful confession of faith, and it exerts a binding force on all believers. If anyone doubts that this code of law was derived directly from the god himself and communicated to his chosen, he is counted as an enemy of religion and a traitor to the will and law of the god. The communication to the chosen may be the ten commandments to Moses, the New Testament to the followers of Jesus as the son of God, or the Koran to Mohammed.

For the believer, the truths of revelation are received in supersensible ways, and they cannot and should not be accessible to reason. For the believer, revelation is more than reason, it is superior to it. Consequently revelation attained in such an extraordinary and abnormal fashion occupies the supreme place in the spiritual treasury of the faithful. It has afforded an actual perception of the god and proved his existence for the faithful. To believe in him is a duty. Thus a mystical experience, the god, and faith are transmuted into a definite common concept, that is to say, into a religion.

This posture of events is a self-evident certainty for all the devout, and it gives a permanent shape to the inarticulate sense of union with the universe. The only and indefeasible truth becomes the property of the creed as it emerges from a vague experience by virtue of a mysterious event. This creed not only solves the riddle of the universe in the simplest and most agreeable possible way to the exclusion of any later consideration, but, in addition, it creates a powerful religious consciousness. The god, as knowledge deeply felt, finds entry into the heart of the believer, elating him and making him joyful. The holy god within him makes him holy, too.

Only one truly devout, however, partakes of this inner experience, that is, one who is truly filled with knowledge of the god and whom the god has therefore endowed with the grace to believe in him. Mohammed thus expressed it in a sura of the Koran: "No soul can believe except by the will of God." And in *De Veritate*, Thomas Aquinas defined faith as

> the act of the intellect assenting to Divine Truth owing
> to the movement of the will, which is itself moved by
> the grace of God.

Thus the concept of religion widens from a vague hunch and belief in a god to an inward experience of religious awareness, a heart-felt devotion, and a divine act of grace.

Such is the story of the rise of divinity and of revealed religions. This, according to the religious view, completes the circle of all human reflection and knowledge. It is unnecessary to know more. Thought is folly if its subject is not the god.

To the Corinthians the apostle Paul wrote: "Has not God made foolish the wisdom of the world?" (I Corinthians 1:20)

One of the greatest fathers of the Christian Church and a co-founder of New Testament doctrine, Augustine of Hippo (354–430), discarded all knowledge so far as it does not rest in the god, with the verdict:

> Wretched is he who knoweth all but knoweth not thee,
> O God, but happy is he who knoweth thee though he
> know naught else besides.

The attitude of strict orthodox Jewry even today is to exclude secular learning from education. It only allows one to apply one's mind to Holy Scripture, the key to a successful life; for the god helps the faithful to succeed. Divine grace presupposes a boundless trust. To Solomon are ascribed these words:

> Trust in the Lord with all your heart, and do not rely on your own insight. In all your ways acknowledge him, and he will make straight your paths.
>
> (Proverbs 3:5–6)

And now this trust is exalted to the highest degree, as if a man did not have to live among men but only with and in his god, for

> It is better to take refuge in the Lord than to put confidence in man.
>
> (Psalm 118:8)

It is a counsel and a demand which bars the way to a trustworthy give-and-take among people, whereby the Jews cut themselves off from the gentile world around them. If one puts one's trust in a god, the heart of religious thought, one expects the god to deal with one as a man would. One trusts a friend. A friend stands by one who is in trouble. He helps one who is down and out. He comforts one who is in sorrow and affliction. And if he is a friend of friends, he becomes a savior and deliverer.

This deepening of religious feeling entails the unity and indivisibility of the concept of a god. Devoted friendship with one person cannot be shared with another. One cannot readily divide one's worship among several gods—the one averting evil, another dispensing happiness, a third giving rain in due season for a bountiful harvest, and others in addition. One can hardly place one's highest and ultimate confidence in a number of gods, for one would have to suppose that sharing in human nature they would be jealous of one another about the confidence and love of mortals. Likewise the people of every country in the world are subject to only one king, one ruler, one government.

Since men are allegedly created in the image of the god, inevitably the same order must obtain in heaven as on earth. Since the heavenly ruler corresponds to the earthly, there must be one ruler there as here; hence the impregnable article of faith—there is only one god. Yea, the god himself says so in a revelation to the prophet Isaiah, "I, I am the Lord, and besides me there is no savior." (Isaiah 43:11) The idea of three gods united in one god as in Christianity is difficult even for a Luther; he said,

> Besides Christ there is no God, and where Christ is
> there verily is the whole Godhead.

The idea of one god, the belief in one single god, is monotheism, which the Jews falsely assert they were the first to proclaim. This belief prompts a question: Why must the god, whose existence should be self-contained, be continually extolled before the faithful as being the one and only god? If we leave out of account altogether the almost unbroken period during which the Biblical people of Israel were polytheistic, there remains outside that period reason enough for wondering why monotheism is perennially on the defensive.

Why is the god repeatedly accorded praise for his mighty acts of creation and for his majestic qualities in prayers and hymns today in all three monotheistic religions just as was done in the book of Job? Why this constant stress on his uniqueness which excludes the existence of other gods? Why must the faithful reiterate in season and out the deeds that the god can bring to pass in his omnipotence? Thus Luther says to this purpose:

> How strange and wonderful it is that corn grows out of
> the earth. Who knows this art or has this power? God
> has, and he can do such unnatural things that from
> them we can imagine what a wonderful God he is and
> how mighty the power he has. . . . He could make gold
> out of a leather pocket, corn out of mere dust on the
> ground, and a cellar full of wine out of air for those
> who trust him. . . . He could give us light without sun
> or stars, or bread without plowing and tilling and other
> work. But he does not so will.

There are doubters and they must have instruction; for they often find the facts in their earthly contexts ill suited to strengthen their belief that a god is their friend and cares for them.

This means that the god needs many spokesmen to raise loud voices, like the prophets and priests. But why are champions and heralds necessary for a god who exists, and has from all eternity, and never passes away, who supposedly is the sole and almighty preserver of the universe, including mankind, and guides the destinies of men from the cradle to the grave?

In virtue of the god's omnipotence and oneness no man should be able to doubt his existence or even experience the thought that there is no god. If there is a god, this god is for every man. Then this god must by nature be in every human individual, belonging to man as seeing belongs to the eye and hearing belongs to the ear. It is not necessary to teach a child how to hear and see. This faculty lies within him and is exercised without our having to do anything about it. Thus the everlasting god who made man in his own physical and spiritual image would have to be in mankind and in every individual man; and each would have to know and feel this god in his heart without the need of any teacher or intermediary whatsoever.

But then we could not accept as true the doctrine we are taught that only he believes in the god who is endowed by his grace to know him. If this were so, there would have to be a second creator who made the men who lack the capacity to believe in the god, but that would be contrary to the doctrine of the singleness and omnipotence of the god.

There is thus a real distinction between the god that is supposed to exist from the beginning and to be the first cause and life principle of each individual, needing no manner of further praise or explanation, and the god of the religions that trouble themselves no end with expounding their god to their faithful, threatening them with severe punishments if they do not follow the prescribed manner of worshiping him. Consequently we are faced with this question: If there is a great and eternal god, why do the religions present this god as being different from their own? Perhaps there are two.

There is a vast number of religions, faiths, cults, and sects upon the earth. There are hundreds of different forms, and the majority hardly even know, let alone worship, the god of the three theistic religions as the Old Testament, the New Testament, and the Koran teach him. Furthermore, how can this only and eternal god conceivably degrade himself into a bone of contention among those who believe in him? Jews, Christians, and Moslems sacrifice themselves in wars of religion, crusades, inquisitions, and religious persecutions, not for the sake of conquering land or avenging some injustice they have suffered, but simply because the single and eternal god revealed himself in three different forms to Moses, Jesus, and Mohammed. Thus Christianity and Islam think they must extirpate each other because of their differing interpretations of their common god. And when they persecute, murder, and burn Jews, they both do so in the name of the god which the Christians got as god the Father and the Moslems as Allah from the Jews. Each protects the same god against the others with fire and sword. And the god lets this happen; he is even the occasion for it. God is silent.

A devout poet gave expression to this thought after the terrible pogroms of the thirteenth century in Franconia in which several thousand Jewish lives were sacrificed. He said: "Who is like unto thee among the dumb, O God: thou seest and thou art silent!"

In the Old Testament, Solomon questions the existence of the god even more sharply than this sorrowing poet. He said:

> Again I saw all the oppressions that are practiced under the sun. And behold, the tears of the oppressed, and they had no one to comfort them! On the side of their oppressors there was power, and there was no one to comfort them.
>
> (Ecclesiastes 4:1)

For what man most expects from his god is help in time of peril and the satisfaction of his most pressing human needs. The most faithful people become disloyal without this material basis or at least without the hope that their modest wants will soon be satisfied. When the post-Biblical Jews managed to hold out against an endless martyrdom thanks to prolonged tutelage under priests and scribes and to the prospect of the coming of a Messiah, that is indeed an achievement which demands respect both for their spiritual leadership and for their suffering population; and this is independent of the question whether it has brought any advantage whatever to Jewry or to mankind as a whole.

Many hundreds of thousands of times in the course of the tragic

history of Jewry the mouths of those dying as martyrs, beaten to
death, or bound on a burning pyre, have uttered a last terrible cry
which has faded away with a moving confession of faith in this
unique god, to whom they have held fast even unto death. A god
of whom Prometheus says in a lyric by Goethe:

> I honor you? Wherefore?
> Have you ever soothed the sorrows
> Of the burdened?
> Have you ever stayed the tears
> Of the distressed?

The righteousness the god gives to men ranks as the foundation
of truth and morality, for the god ranks as the ideal of truth, justice, and the love one is to show to one's neighbor. According to
the prophet Isaiah, the god said of himself: "Seek me. . . . I the
Lord speak the truth, I declare what is right." (Isaiah 45:19) The
psalmist also preached: "The Lord works vindication and justice
for all who are oppressed." (Psalm 103:6)

In numerous passages the Old Testament vouches for this concept of the god's righteousness, and this the New Testament then
repeats in the theory that the god is the supreme judge rewarding
the good and punishing the bad; he is the model for the execution
of righteousness on earth. But things on earth have a different
complexion, as Solomon had already asserted. In his complete
bewilderment at the injustice to which the innocent are exposed
without protection, he came to the conclusion:

> I thought the dead who are already dead more for-
> tunate than the living who are still alive; but better than
> both is he who has not yet been and has not seen the
> evil deeds that are done under the sun.
>
> (Ecclesiastes 4:2–3)

The devout must regard suffering as a test and punishment ordained by God, even if a Thirty Years' War is to decide with
powder and shot whether it is true that God appointed a vicar
on earth and assembled saints around his throne. Divine providence, which directs everything for the greatest good of man, sends

on earth two world wars as well, which have called forth more evil than all the previous wars of history put together.

But, as the confession of faith of the religions tells us, God knows how everything will end before it has even begun. Wars do not come to an end before he wants them to. It was therefore to no purpose that the Holy Father in Rome said in his peace manifesto of 1915:

> Ceaselessly I send the most fervent prayers to heaven
> to implore God for mercy and for an end to the ghastly
> horrors of war;

for the god had different plans and paid no attention to the prayers of his vicar on earth, who was ignorant of the Almighty's well-considered punishments ordained for the best interests of mankind. The just god regarded it as necessary to let the first world war rage for another three years and later the second world war for five and a half years.

The devotee, however, does not despair. The will of the god stands high above all human reason. No sacrifice is too great when it is a matter of obeying his commands. And since we do not know the wise deliberations of the god, we must even thank him for what we feel to be evil. Comfort and hope in every eventuality of life only befalls those believers who throw themselves completely on the Lord.

A Jewish scribe who later suffered a martyr's death himself at Nuremberg, wrote thus about the massacre of the Jews in the thirteenth century at Sinzig:

> O Lord, how much good thou hast in store for those
> who walk in thy ways and sacrifice themselves on the
> altar of thy honor.

That is the attitude which the god expects from his believers. The funeral pile is something good if one must mount it to God's honor; death is joyful if it is accepted for the will of God, for the Lord is all-merciful and wholly good. One is to thank him for evil and laud him for his goodness, even if men in their ignorance do not know why the god punishes them. *It is the will of the god.*

Even today clergymen officiating at funerals close their words of consolation at the graveside with these words, "The Lord gave, and the Lord has taken away; blessed be the name of the Lord." (Job 1:21) For the believer, praise is due to the god even for the death of the most dearly loved one; in his goodness he has thus disposed matters and turned all punishment into joy. The psalmist says, "May those who sow in tears reap with shouts of joy." (Psalm 126:5) In the book of Job, Eliphaz the Temanite says, "Behold, happy is the man whom God reproves; therefore despise not the chastening of the Almighty." (Job 5:17) All hardship comes from the god. He sends it to men as a proof of his love, "The Lord disciplines him whom he loves." (Hebrews 12:6)

All the holy books of the three monotheistic religions proclaim the god's love toward men. He is also the author of human love, which according to the Protestant conception is poured into the heart by the Holy Ghost. One of the most beautiful passages in the Christian scripture is the thirteenth chapter of the first epistle to the Corinthians, the song of songs to love. It ends with the avowal that love is greater even than faith. But the learned find these sentiments too simple; they cannot allow the love of the god to be put into such a simple human category. They explain love as the principle of divine creation. On this head the Protestant *Realenzyklopaedie,* edited by Herzog (1902), says among other things the following:

> God created the world in order to have outside himself yet for himself a realm for love which his love shall rule absolutely and transfigure into a creaturely image of his everlasting life of love. He did this not because he could not be without such a world or could not be happy without it or could not be sufficient unto himself, but because his wisdom knew the possibility of existence outside himself. This possibility made the idea of a world ever present with him. Thus his love, the joy of life, realized the idea in accordance with his pleasure.

Now we know it, but does the god also know it?

On the other hand, faith also presupposes love of man towards

God. As early as the Ten Commandments he promised to be merciful to those who love him, and, as he added, keep his commandments. He later widened his covenant, promising his mercy "to a thousand generations." This leaves the door ajar for some hope of good. But despite the uttermost love men have given to the god, he has given them only very rare proofs of his mercy and love in a thousand generations, and this is especially striking in the light of the fact that he himself put evil in the world as the prophet Isaiah affirmed with the words: "I make weal and create woe, I am the Lord, who do all these things." (Isaiah 45:7)

Perhaps this is what Luther meant when he said that the world was created through an oversight on God's part, for if the god had thought about heavy artillery he would not have created the world. Since Luther's time this field has made great progress, culminating in the hydrogen bomb. This seems to have escaped the god's notice, for all his omniscience and universal providence.

But the Almighty knows mankind and its boundless love toward him. He knows what he can expect from men without them giving up their constant trust and love. On the Day of Atonement pious Jews still pray: "Save us! How splendid is our lot, how lovely is our portion, and how fair is our inheritance."

Truly, in the face of the destiny of the Jews, the magnificence of this is astonishing. Here love and trust reach their ultimate. These words of prayer attain the zenith of devotion to the Highest. They know nothing of Jewish persecutions, or of a wrathful god who at the expulsion from Paradise cursed the ground so that from its harvest men should henceforth nourish themselves with toil and grief. They gladly eat their bread in the sweat of their faces as the Lord commanded them after Adam ate of the forbidden fruit. For them the be-all and end-all of their faith is—God is love.

If this faith were the common property of all men, how peaceful and how happy life would be in its simplicity. How much would be achieved if only the three religions were united in holding to this creed of love, if love for the god and his love for men would only allow us to live to see the beginnings of a time in which we could see the first steps taken on the road to the ideal of "love your neighbor as yourself."

Tensions mounted by the year until they culminated in the human slaughters of the twentieth century, so that we are further than ever from the fulfilment of the religious imperative of Judaism and Christianity. Protestant and Catholic peoples wage war with each other, and this ends by setting the whole world ablaze. Instead of words and deeds of love there is the crash of bombs and the fall of humanity into unimaginable horror.

And the religions are silent. God is silent.

13. WORLD VIEW OR PHILOSOPHY OF LIFE AND MORTALITY

The question whether mankind has always believed in a god and seen its savior in him is raised by the appalling misery of two world wars, unprecedented as they are in the history of the race. Is it only the belief in a god that explains the awe man feels in the presence of the universe? And have the ethical views of reflective people down the ages really corresponded with those of Judaism, Christianity, and Islam? At the very time when Israel was creating monotheism in Palestine, Greek students of nature and philosophy in the adjoining Mediterranean region were seeking to explain the riddles of the universe in their own naturalistic way. Beginning with the investigation of causality in nature they soon arrived at remarkable results, although the Old Testament and the Talmud had not been finished and the New Testament and the Koran had not even been thought of.

In the sixth century B.C., Anaximander broke away from all the traditional legends about creation and explained that all things had developed out of a primeval matter and are in a state of continual flux. He was also the first to venture the assertion that men were not created by the gods but evolved out of an animal ancestry, a theory one could not declare for several thousand years without risking one's neck but which has become the cornerstone of modern science. Anaximander's contemporary, Xenophanes, sharply condemned the anthropomorphic gods of the Greeks; he said they were the downfall of his country. He argued against this Greek view of the gods with the brilliant comparisons already quoted in another place. To him belong the philosopher's perception and modesty when he said:

There never was nor ever will be a man who has certain knowledge about the gods and about all the things
I speak of. Even if he should chance to say the complete truth, yet he himself would not know that it is.
For the quality of appearance clings to everything.

In the sixth century B.C., at the very time when the Biblical
authors of the books of the prophets were proclaiming their faith
in a god, Heraclitus declared:

The order of the universe, one and the same for all
creatures, was not created by any god or man, but has
always been, is, and will abide forever.

In spite of their lack of scientific aids, the Greek thinkers tried
to create a picture of the universe that was more consonant with
the observed processes of nature than were the fantastic conceits
of popular superstition. Even the philosophers, who were un-
willing to dispense with ideas of divinity, opposed the notion of
the crowd which always sees its gods as mere human images
instead of conceiving of divinity as a natural principle. About
2,400 years ago the Greek Anaxagoras was led by his own observations to conclude that everything in existence is composed of
similar elements in various combinations. He thus outstripped all
the ideas of creation in the Old Testament by several thousand
years and became the precursor of modern chemistry. His view
reads:

The Greeks do not understand the meaning of coming
into being and passing away, for nothing comes into
being or passes away; there is only mingling and sepa-
ration of things (elements) that are in existence.

He also assumed that other worlds than our own might be inhabited by men, just as modern astronomers have again begun
to surmise. He discovered that the moon does not shine with
its own light but gets its light from the sun, though religious
instructors still teach the children that a god put the sun and
the moon in the sky as the two great lights. They also teach them
that a god set the rainbow in the clouds as a sign that he will

never again visit man with a deluge, but Anaxagoras is almost correct when he says "we call a rainbow the reflection of the sun in the clouds."

The idea of "Biblical times" arouses in us memories of the legends of the creation of the world by a god, of Adam and Eve the first human pair, of the serpent which talked with them and with the god in Paradise, of the story of Noah's ark, and of many other mythical themes. It occurs to only a few people that these oriental fables were finding their way into the Bible at the very time when thinkers like the great men just mentioned lived and worked in neighboring Greece. The founders of the religion of God and the wise men of Greece were closely linked in time and place; but they were so far apart in their intellectual attitudes toward the world that it has taken almost twenty-five hundred years for humanity to judge rationally between them. Not until our time did the ancient Greek view of the world begin to burst the bonds of religion and superstition and catch on as the valid account of the universe among civilized men. It is modern science which carries on the torch of ancient Greek science and philosophy and at the same time justifies them.

At the very time when Jewish monotheism was taking shape lived the greatest investigator of nature in antiquity—Democritus. Along with his contemporary Leucippus he founded the atomic theory, the ultimate known unity at the root of all nature. At the very moment, so to speak, when the cornerstone of monotheism was being laid in Palestine to serve for the three edifices of Judaism, Christianity, and Islam, the philosophers of Greece were conferring on the earth (on which this act of faith was being carried out) a ferment which would work slowly for two thousand years and then increasingly threaten and sap the foundations of the three religions.

Democritus was born several thousand years too soon, but he is coming into his own. The natural science of this great thinker is teaching the twentieth century. Using his science as the foundation for his ethics, he erected his ethical system firmly on this earth. It is not reward and punishment in the next world that is to lead men toward the good and make them avoid evil. Soberly and clearly, he taught that virtue consists not in refraining from wickedness but in having no desire for committing it. Men are to do their duty not from external coercion but from inner conviction. His own words run: "Refrain from evil conduct not from fear but from a sense of duty." The fear of a god is a poor motive for good conduct compared with the thoughts of Democritus on this matter.

No reflection is so daring that he would stop short of it in his drive for truth. He wanted to discern the nature of things so that he could form a right conception of the universe and derive from it a solid moral foundation for the community of man. One of his sayings runs: "I would much rather discover one single natural cause than be the king of Persia." He recognized the structure of the world in atoms thought of as in continual motion, and his keen intellect attained the notion of countless systems of worlds. Thus he was the first to divest the earth of the central position demanded for it by religion and at the same time he dethroned the myth of divine creation with man as its crown and purpose. Not until two thousand years later, when Copernicus restated his supposition, did it finally become the basis of the modern idea of the world.

Far removed from the conceptions accepted by the faiths in a god or gods, ancient Greece arrived at solutions which have nothing in common with those of Moses, the prophets, the psalmists, and the evangelists. The Greeks yearned for knowledge and for a method about the universe, and in contrast to the founders of religions they kept their feet on the ground. The devout took flight far above the earth into the uncharted spheres of the supernatural and toward a god above the world; and the farther afield their vague feelings about the world led them, the more clearly and realistically did the Greek philosophers recognize that nature is the only road to knowledge and that the aim of knowledge is to discover the laws of nature. In the midst of the controversies of the day and amid a welter of popular superstition which forced the cup of hemlock into the hands of a Socrates because he was guilty, as the charge ran, of "not recognizing the Gods which the city recognizes," these philosophers leveled many pungent criticisms at the prevailing superstitions.

The Greek intellect was bent on freeing man from superstition and from conceptions of heavenly salvation beyond man's control. The Greek philosophers held that man could be hearty and happy only if he was liberated from fear of the gods. They sought to break the fetters of a religious code of morals which claimed to be rooted in the supernatural. The philosopher Epicurus was the chief representative of this doctrine. Nietzsche said of him:

> Many still think that the triumph of Christianity over Greek philosophy proves the superior truth of the former, when really only the coarser and more barbarous won out over the more sensitively spiritual and intellectual. The claim of superior truth falls flat when we note that the growing sciences adopt Epicurus' philosophy point by point and reject Christianity point by point.

Epicurus rejected the pretensions of religions, the intervention of divinity in the universal course of nature. He saw in this impersonal course of nature the basis of all morality making for the happiness of the individual and of the family of man. He explained: "It is absurd to pray to the Gods for what we ourselves are in a position to provide."

Admittedly he did not deny the existence of divine beings, thus making a concession to popular superstition, but he removed their dwelling place out of heaven to new worlds of space which he especially contrived for putting the gods outside the sphere of human relationships. They exist for their own happiness but have no concern with man, a solution which testifies at once to his superior wit and to his gentle mind.

Up to the time of Plato, the majority of Greek philosophers rejected the gods as a basis of moral laws governing the relationships among men; they started with observations of nature in which they achieved remarkably mature insight. After Plato, the Stoics reached their zenith; they defined the highest virtue as being true to oneself. That means knowing oneself, living conformably to nature, and pitting one's will to live and one's inner resources against the vicissitudes of life.

Seneca taught men to put trust in themselves, not in a god. He was a Roman philosopher who lived at the beginning of our era, and, having been educated in the spirit of Greek Stoicism, he was one of its significant representatives. For him and for the Stoic school there is no divine providence guiding the destinies of men and of the world. In their philosophy, God and nature are identical. The soul is not given by the gods but is an attribute of the living body, just as modern science teaches today. There is no providence, only a natural course of events arising out of an inner necessity. Seneca said:

> You ask me why the good people suffer so many evils
> if a providence rules the world. I could answer you
> more intelligently if you demonstrated that a providence
> rules the world and that this divinity takes an interest
> in us human beings.

Emancipated from any divine intervention, Seneca saw the duty of man to consist in obtaining the highest good possible for himself—invincible strength of character against all evils which life can bring, a loving comradeship with fellow men, and no undue or morbid anxiety about one's health. With such an attitude toward the natural needs of life, man will accept with self-possession the fate which derives not from a god but is the natural and inevitable consequence of the existing nexus of relations and circumstances, and he will steel his heart for the struggle with destiny. He held the lofty opinion: "What matters is not *what* happens to us but *how* we take it," and also that man should not regard adversities as divine punishments justly deserved.

He rejected the notion that a divinity dwelling somewhere off in space rewards and punishes man. Every man is the captain of his fate, if he only so desires. Stoic doctrine proclaims the sublimest wisdom of life, which seeks and attains the goal of man's inner freedom. Marcus Aurelius, the Stoic Emperor, who throughout his period on the throne remained a man of understanding and perception, said in his surviving "Reflections":

> The aim of an intelligent being, however, is to follow
> the oldest polity and the most venerable of constitu-
> tions, that is to say, the cosmos.

We realize how rotten thinking has become when in the course of history men can resolve their conflicts only by repeatedly resorting to arms on an ever increasingly destructive scale until nations mutually exterminate each other. Whither have three thousand years of teaching the love of God led? What responsibility have the god religions and especially the Christian religion taken upon themselves? For since the opening of the Christian era the Christian teaching has been largely responsible for the moral education of the Western World.

The wise men of Greece did not base their morality on a god or gods; they made no exaggerated moral demands like "you shall love your neighbor as yourself," or "if any one strikes you on the right cheek, turn to him the other also." They avoided such extravagances and in their moral teaching demanded only what any man of good will can achieve. These pioneers of real humanity reached a moral height which will remain a model for the whole future. Their way is not a god's way but is man's way, and in the past hardly any people has tried to follow it. Goethe remarked on this point: "When we confront antiquity, regard it with the purpose of educating ourselves by it, we come to feel that only then do we become men."

In that statement Goethe made a value judgment in favor of antiquity and against his own century. He also did not recognize the dualism of the religions, for he did not regard God and the universe, body and soul, mind and matter, as two different orders of being. For him the concept of a god and the concept of the universe are one and the same, there being no god over and above the natural order.

A century before Goethe, this doctrine was expressed by Spinoza, a philosopher who was expelled from the Jewish community at Amsterdam and laid under anathema as an apostate. He coined the phrase "Deus sive natura"—nature itself is God. The existence of the god ceases for the pantheists as also for Goethe. The universe is the basis of being. The concept of a god has no other bearing on mankind than does the cosmos. Trust in a god, fear of a god, and faith in a god all vanish as they are transformed into the recognition of the eternal laws of the universe which operate in it and in men, who are regarded as being parts thereof.

This confers on men a higher value than the revealed religions do with their notion that men are born with sin. There is no hereafter and no soul independent of the body which can be rewarded or punished after death. Morality, which had been founded on a belief in an extraterrestrial god, is now lodged solely in human life. The earthbound harmony which man must create for himself spells a harmony with his environment. An essential law for communal life is contained in the saying of Hillel, the Babylonian Talmud scholar, who lived at the beginning of our era: "That which is hateful to you, do it not to your neighbor."

To fulfil one's duties to one's fellow men in one's own interests, to live in harmony with them, becomes the moral yardstick for all conduct. Reward means personal well-being and the thoughtful esteem of one's fellow men. Punishment is misery and the contempt of the world around.

It is only a short step from this idea of the unity of the god and nature to the explanation and knowledge of the world propounded by Greek philosophy. This philosophical insight tells us that the moral duty of man rests on the observation of Protagoras—man is the measure of all things. While wandering along the path of his cultural development, Goethe was as little able as Heraclitus and Democritus were to move his own age to accept his view of the universe and the view of life it entailed. He, too, remained among the religious a lone pioneer on his solitary quest. His generation believed in God more than ever.

The recipe for faith was reserved for his contemporary, the philosopher Hegel, who said of his faith:

> What I believe I also know and am sure it is true. In religion one believes in God and in the doctrines which illuminate his nature more fully. To know means to have an object before one's consciousness and to be certain of it. And to believe is to do exactly the same thing.

In other words, since he believed in the idea of the existence of God, he also knew that this god exists. This ingenious solution is similar to that of Descartes mentioned above, who regarded the existence of God as proved because he could think of him, and this thought he could conceive only if God himself implanted it in his head. The old conflict between faith and knowledge which the Hegelian philosophy resolved out of hand with the above formula is now dead and buried. The view of Kant stands foursquare: "One has to root out knowledge before one has room for faith."

Modern science axiomatically takes the natural basis of being for granted, including the processes of mind and consciousness. Resurrected in the modern scientific outlook on the world, the thoughts of the Greek philosophers are gradually beginning to assume their proper place in the salvation of humanity. In his *Italian Journey,* Goethe said:

> I recently found in a pitiful sort of apostolical Capuchin declamation . . . the nonsensical words: "Everything which has life has it by virtue of something outside of itself," or something like that. Only a missionary among heathens could jot down anything as silly as that, and when he was revising it no genius plucked at his sleeve. This Capuchin statement has no glimmering of even the most elementary truths of nature. . . .

The knowledge one naturally grasps and apprehends about the universe, of which Goethe felt and knew himself to be a part, rebels at those evasions of thought that people increasingly accept as truth, refusing honestly to face ultimate questions.

In discussing the aberration known as supernatural religion, Friedrich Schiller says:

> The major portion of mankind is content if it can avoid the painful trouble of thinking, and so it gladly resigns to others the guardianship of its ideas and grasps with hungry faith the formulas which the government or the priests keep ready for it.

India, like Greece, and at an even earlier date, found it ridiculous to suppose that the gods uphold morality. The sages of that country evolved values which indisputably rank as the very best for giving insight into the world and aiding in the cultivation of life. The Indian thinkers elaborated moral laws on a loftier plane because they did not have to demolish edifices of cluttery supernatural beliefs before setting to work.

If one occupied oneself with ultimate questions of being in ancient India one did not run against any barriers from belief in a hereafter. The outlook on the universe and consequently on the basis of ethics and morals lay well within the limits of human knowledge. That country found a direct and natural approach to the universe and to man's integration with it; furthermore, it did so without any digression or appeal to invented supernatural powers. To be sure, it was familiar with gods of nature that called up wind, lightning, and such natural manifestations, but these gods in turn were begotten of the universe and not of a god. Thus they were no more than names for the forces of visible nature, to whom consecration and sacrifice were offered. They were not the prime movers; still in them were operative the functions accorded them severally by the nature of the universe.

People were so closely linked with nature that they did not dedicate a newly born child to a god or pray to him to protect it. The newly born child carrying on the race received from its own father in the presence of its mother, without any priestly assistance, the following prayer for its life, as the words have come down to us in an old Sanskrit text: "I give you a portion of the earth, a portion of the air, and a portion of the heavens." Henceforth the forces of the universe from which they had drawn their own being were to work in their child also. The little citizen of the earth needed only to be dedicated into life as a confirmation that he belonged to the universe like his parents, who conceived of all power and law as residing in the earth, the air, and the heavens.

No such wisdom surrounds a child which according to religious belief is born of original sin and must be baptized so that a god may forgive its sins and insure it resurrection from death. The basis of Indian thought is this: the universe is indifferent to all creatures including man. Such was the opinion of a race which was alive three thousand years before our era. That is close to the modern concept of the world but poles apart from a period which began with the Bible nearly two thousand years later, on which a system of ethics was constructed which still claims to have evolved morally effective doctrines. The watchword of India was not respect for God but respect for man. An ancient Brahmin teaching says:

> To do no harm is the chief of all duties, as the commandment of our ancestors runs; we should complete only that work which can be achieved without giving offence. . . . To harm no living creature—that is the principle which speaks home to us in all circumstances. . . .

Another ancient text speaks of the wholesome and benevolent duty toward all creatures, "which ranks as a very ancient one among men." It says further: "Honest and upright conduct, or as honest and upright as possible, toward creatures—that is the highest duty."

What an extraordinary understanding of human beings is expressed in these sayings! Here is no talk about requital or of life in a kingdom of heaven, nothing about fear of divine punishment or about a great righteousness and love dwelling somewhere outside the earth. Man is soberly reminded of his duty to others, namely, to do all he can to keep from troubling and harming them. Nothing further is needed. That thought, simply expressed and clear to everyone, proclaims moral behavior toward one's fellow men as the highest duty.

Man shall be honest and upright or "as honest and upright as possible," for the old Indian philosopher knew well the temptations men so easily succumb to. Under the circumstances he was content if a man struggles to be honest and upright even if he does not always succeed. Indian wisdom really amounts to nothing more than service to man. The great and sublime message that the philosopher has to pass on to his student is this: "There is nothing higher than man."

Rooted in nature, Indian thought teaches that moral sanctions like everything else originate in the universe. The opposite principle holds in the religions based on a god, for in them the origin of morality is wholly divorced from nature and the physical world. Morality being quite independent of the body inheres in a soul created by a god especially for each individual person and is received supernaturally as an act of that god's grace.

According to the idea of faith, the creation of the universe itself was a process that took place outside the natural order of things. The universe was not always there, in contradistinction to the opinions of the Indians and of modern science; instead a god took matter out of nothing and shaped it into the world. But of the origin of this god, the pious believer can only say that he somehow feels in his religious bones that this god exists as the scheme of supernatural religion demands. The Christian Church Father Augustine says in this regard:

> Blessed God! Thou has not made heaven and earth out of thyself, else they would be like unto thee. But as there was nothing outside of thyself, whereof thou couldst make them, thou has certainly made them out of nothing.

Long before the two religions based on a god explained that creation was made of nothing, an achievement adduced to stress the omnipotence of the god, the Greek and Indian scholars had concluded that nothing can come out of nothing. In the sixth century B.C., Parmenides asked:

> How can that which exists ever be destroyed or how come into being? I shall not let you say or think that it came from what is not, because one can not say or think that something is nothing.

Ancient India asserted:

> Nothing ever turns into something, and something never becomes nothing. Know then that the power operative in the processes of the universe is imperishable.

It is easy to teach men the concept of the universe and of its orderliness from such intuitions that are almost four thousand years old. This old notion does not come into conflict with the views of contemporary science, as the best ancient and modern minds have fundamentally the same ideas about the universe. On the other hand, it is very hard to teach the young people of our day that the Genesis legends of creation are true and that a god rewards and punishes people in a hereafter; it is exceedingly hard for anyone honestly to ask young people to believe that if they do not follow the priestly teachings, their souls will roast endlessly in a hell after death. This is hard because in advanced classes they learn what modern science has to tell about the universe.

This contradiction between the imperatives of faith and of knowledge is the tragedy of our younger generation. For orthodox Christian, Jewish, and also Mohammedan children learn as an article of faith, today as in the remote past, that God created heaven and earth, sun and stars, beasts and men within six days or in a brief time. Religions give their faithful no chance to get out of the dilemma posed by the fact that the findings of physics, biology, and astronomy are irreconcilable with the articles of dogma. Consequently people doubt traditional religious teaching, doubt the existence of God, doubt the reliability of those who teach these things—and the confessional cannot allay these doubts. For what is the world actually like?

It is said that God created the earth in one day. We know that the creation of the universe is a perpetual process. New stars are continually forming out of the consolidation of cosmic dust, the so-called interstellar matter scattered through the universe in the space between the heavenly bodies. This scientific hypothesis is the subject of extensive researches to show whether this can be proved like Einstein's theory. Research suggests that the transformation of one gram of uranium into one cubic centimeter of helium requires some ten million years. Analysis has also shown that helium is the chief ingredient of the solar atmosphere, which the god is likewise said to have made in a single day.

When the God asks Job, "Have you comprehended the expanse of the earth?" (Job 38:18) and also asks who determined its measurements (Job 38:5), Job should have given the following answer: the earth's equatorial diameter comes to 7,926 miles. There are stars with diameters of some ninety million miles, and our sun is so big that it has room to contain one million three hundred thousand earths.

When God asks Job, "Where is the way to the dwelling of light?" (Job 38:19), which God allegedly made and placed in the heavens in one day, this would be the answer: the sun is some 92 million miles from the earth. Of the total energy radiated from the sun, the earth intercepts one part in two billion; and yet 63 per cent of this intercepted energy amounts to three septillion candle power, a number written by three with twenty-four zeros following.

According to Genesis, God set the sun, moon, and all the stars in the firmament of the heavens. The sun is 332,000 times heavier than the earth. For every pound of earth there are 166 tons of the sun. The star Plaskett is 140 times heavier than the sun; that is to say, for every pound of earth there are 13,240 tons of the star Plaskett. The number of stars according to the estimate of modern astronomers is some eight hundred thousand million. To count this many stars out loud at a steady normal clip would take a man seven hundred years, keeping at it day and night. In other words, one would have had to begin counting two hundred years before the discovery of America to be done by the year two thousand. If one thinks of such a comparison as one looks at the stars in the night sky, one gradually gets a presentiment of the immeasurable universe of which we form a puny part.

In the Biblical account, God made the first man, Adam, out of a lump of clay and then breathed life into him through the nose; with his divine breath he gave man a soul. There is the further story that God made the first woman out of one of Adam's ribs. In contrast to these tales, modern anthropology and anatomy teach us that men evolved in the course of millions of years from the unicellular amoeba, through the series of lower and higher animals and through the last stage of the latter, the mammals.

Science never halts permanently but always moves on, making new discoveries. And every new piece of fundamental knowledge is a nail in the coffin of the godhead. In our century an Englishman, Rutherford, succeeded in smashing atoms, the building blocks of the universe. He thus cleared the way for new and immense power, atomic energy. As usual, this energy was first employed to destroy people instead of making them happy. Thus in August, 1945, at the end of the second World War, one single atomic bomb killed 78,000 people and wounded 324,000 in a few minutes in Hiroshima. This Japanese city was totally destroyed and only 20,000 survivors came through unscathed.

The people of Europe have been going to school to Christianity for almost two thousand years. In order to do good and avoid evil they do not take the direct road from man to man, but they make a detour by way of a supposedly superior being: God, his son, and the Holy Ghost. They must worship and believe in this trinity to obtain grace from it to be able to act decently.

The Church believes that ethical and moral behavior is impossible without this basis in faith and religion. Thus anybody who objects to making this deliberate detour for the practice of his obvious duties as a man is publicly put in the dock before his contemporaries and branded as an atheistic, materialistic villain. It is just as if for thousands of years, and even now, no communities or nations had ever preached and practiced the highest humanity even though they did not know or recognize the god of Christianity.

Nevertheless, throughout the western world the Church is still to be accepted as the only real prerequisite of good conduct and happiness, of which, however, the history of the West has little enough to report. Indeed, the whole world has been made an innocent sacrifice to this Western Christian "civilization" in our present twentieth century. Progressive circles in the Church do not blind themselves to this sad knowledge. We are beginning to realize that the primitive thoughts and life obtaining in hoary antiquity simply cannot fit in with modern times.

The experience of this century teaches a warning lesson that future generations must not forget, for the end of the Second World War should eliminate for good and all the impetus that started it. This impetus is the mentality contained in the doctrine of an overstrained stream of superterrestrial bliss after death; the burden of this doctrine crashed the foundations of the human aggregate in the most frightful explosion in the history of the world. The unambiguously drumming speech of heavy artillery, block-buster bombs, and rockets with atomic warheads reduces the ethical teaching of teleological illusions to sheer absurdity.

This senseless destruction of millions of lives and of irrecoverable cultural treasures in the course of two world wars, the ethical depravity witnessed in the appalling holocausts of the twentieth century, must somehow be related to the ethical education Western man has drawn from his religion. For the poisoned springs of false basic assumptions seem to bring forth poisoned results.

Moreover, the view that the earth is a vale of tears can only be desired and propagated by those who want to perpetrate evil and profit by it with impunity. Such doctrines as these are devised by the few to do wrong to the many, and they can never produce ethical results but only continual strife and want. Our generation should eventually learn a lesson from the experience it has bought with many tears and thus be able to understand that it is wrong to apply a twofold standard. Other generations, too, discovered this in the past, but they thought it was a fixed and immutable ordinance of heaven.

Trying to show to a humanity lashed by a tempest of unsubdued passions the light of morality through a divine lens focusing in an illusory hereafter, and hoping thereby to make humanity morally better, is to labor in vain. For though the sun is relatively near the earth, it cannot pierce through the thick mists which roll over the earth from the slue of greed. The chasm between a loving god and his son taking upon himself the sins of the world on the one hand, and the course of events on earth for which they are allegedly responsible on the other, is too vast for mankind to derive the slightest moral improvement from such a salvation scheme. And yet those preaching this salvation argue that mankind could not live without believing in God, and that without religion civil order could not endure. It is of course perfectly obvious that the majority of people in the world are completely unacquainted with the divine world of the Bible and that this "unbelieving" majority, now as in the past, maintains civil order and achieves genuinely humane living not through one rigid mode but through various modes of social organization.

The consequence of this emphasis upon the hereafter for our civilization can only be a moral vacuum displayed in its most wretched form by the events of our times. The needs of life determined by our natural drives and instincts, our cosmic heritage, are not humanely fulfilled. Even if they ever did exercise any control, the promise of rewards in heaven and the threat of punishment in hell, the stock-in-trade coercives of Christian education, have become quite ineffectual.

Every period uses God for its own purpose. Whether it is a summons from Church and princes to a crusade in the name of the god in order to spread the faith by delivering Jews, Moors, and heretics alive to the flames of the Inquisition, or whether the colonizer is bringing eternal happiness with fire and sword to the dark continent in spite of the resistance of the Negroes, the central motive behind this struggle between man and man is always the greater glory of God. God has ever been with those who despoiled the infidel Turks of their lands, cities, and people, deprived Jews, Moors, and heretics of their property, and drove Negroes off their territories and deprived them of their mineral wealth.

But until the twentieth century only isolated regions and sections of mankind had been sacrificed to religion; the moral void manifested on this scale had not yet broken out in a universal conflagration. Finally our century reached the climax of a disaster which burst in raging madness over the whole globe. The First World War gave the signal for this. What did mankind learn from that war? To apply a panacea for regulating the relations among states, i.e., a League of Nations without any teeth in it. Accordingly, there shortly followed a second world-wide slaughter, the greatest accumulation of crime ever achieved. And what came next? The institution of a world organization to hold aggressors in check, to distribute the wealth of the world more justly, and to effect similar praiseworthy measures for the good of the whole.

Though the arrangement just mentioned may some day turn out to be very effective, so far it has only been a poultice on a very sick body. Suffering humanity must itself intervene; its leading men and women must make a diagnosis of the disease and assume responsibility for its cure. Men must not leave matters in the hands of political leaders who still seek the salvation of man in a blessed hereafter, even though they as Christians give expression to the loftiest moral sentiments.

We do not want to call in question the fact that there have been and still are noble men and women who see the sole source of their moral conduct in the message of the Old and New Testaments and who behave accordingly. Often they are people living in secure hereditary wealth, unacquainted with the wretchedness of need and self-denial. When they are called to high offices in church and state, the height of their moral concepts corresponds with the dignity of their external rank. But in them there is little reflection on the sufferings of humanity. In every circumstance they are exalted far above the life of the disappointed and disillusioned mass of mankind. So the norm of the morally possible cannot be deduced from the few fortunate ones on top or from the idealists and dreamers, but only from the average of the many millions struggling for the right to live. We cannot, therefore, do away with moral evil by appealing to a god and a savior or to a heaven hereafter promised by them; nor can we do away with it by harkening to the evangelist who counsels us not to be anxious about food and clothing but to seek first the kingdom of God instead.

No. Mankind must stand on the sober facts of the earth and of life with a stalwart constancy of purpose. At the very heart of his being lies the duty of man to rely on himself and on men, not on God. Only if men respect the rights of all to live will they dwell together in peace. Only the respect for the rights of others makes for a worthy life.

The task of nations and their institutions is to apply these principles in everyday living. This is the law of life inherent in self-interest and in the demands for security, needing no supernatural props whatever. The morality of the anonymous masses derives spontaneously and unconsciously from this craving to live. For the supreme law of every man alive is to keep on living. This self-interest and these self-regarding impulses are intelligible and justified; fundamentally they regulate all relationships between man and man. When these interests are adequately considered and provided for, harmonious life on all levels will ensue, filling the moral vacuum created by religious illusions.

A man who has steady work and can amply satisfy his needs by his own efforts, who does not have to worry about sickness and old age eating up his savings, and who is content in his profession and happy in his surroundings instinctively supports law and order, the bases of all morality. With his goal and purpose clear before him, he goes merrily on his way which leads neither to a morbid utopia nor to otherworldly illusions.

To be sure, he will have his disappointments and sorrows, nor will death pass him by. But he does not seek or need an otherworldly comforter. All the buffetings of fate, far or near, serve to convince him ever anew that there is no god of mercy. Relying on himself and on his circle of friends he finds ever and again the strength and repose to endure the harshest blows and to go on shaping his life with the support of his own. So man is the master builder.

Man's purpose is to make the best of life on earth, not to gaze yearningly beyond the grave for a fancied paradise in a fairyland heaven. His thoughts and aspirations have limits imposed by nature and by his urge to survive, the most fundamental drive in every human being. When men become fountains of kindly, generous, and mutually forbearing conduct, peace and happiness will flourish on earth. This practical morality deriving from the heart of life requires neither rigid ethical rules nor doctrinaire moral laws, and least of all an appeal to a god of mercy and a savior. Mutual helpfulness will become the ordering principle and the lodestar in the community of man.

Those who see a connection between forms of belief and modes of behavior will derive from this knowledge the hope that sanctified superstitions will give way to knowledge on which alone can and must be built the mansions in which liberated humanity of the future may dwell.

It therefore behooves us to cooperate in living together peaceably according to the universal principles of nature. Only in this purely natural order will man find the basis for ethics and morals.

14. RESPONSIBILITY AND MORALITY

Since the advent of Jesus, man's will has received constant and pointed stress; otherwise the god could not serve as the highest principle of morality. This is a crack in the chief pillar of the confession of faith. It is only feebly covered over, it continually shows through and is not susceptible of any cure. Religions suffer as a result of it, and civilization suffers with them. Even such a god-fearing man as the evangelical theologian Rudolf Kittel does not blind himself to this fact when he says:

> Man . . . has made little or no progress in the things which constitute life, the cultivation of the soul, and the purification and ennobling of morals. Even religion has not yet brought about the ideal morality. This is partly because it has several times unfortunately missed its opportunity at decisive periods and partly because it seems to be one of the contradictions of history that it never obtained unlimited mastery over the forces that strove against it.

If Kittel suggests that religion has not yet produced the ideal morality, this implies the supposition that it is, in general, on the right road and has already gone a considerable part of the way toward the goal of this moral ideal in the course of the two thousand years during which it has had the leadership of Western mankind. History tells a different story.

The basis of morality, then, is righteousness, and this righteousness is found wanting especially when, as in our times, technological progress far outstrips general culture, and when the achievements of science are largely in the hands of power and greed. These facts give our generation emphatic proof that faith and morals, religion and ethics, have not been linked for the advantage of humanity and that the visible results achieved may be recognized as anything but an advance in civilization. And that is the very mildest one can say about it.

The English philosopher Shaftesbury separates morality from religion in his *Enquiry Concerning Virtue*. Since a religious man can lead an immoral life and a freethinker can lead a moral one, it follows that the moral element is based on the nature of man and is independent of any religion. Two thousand five hundred years before our era, the great Chinese sage Confucius came to the same conclusion with these words: "Where the right spirit of morality is lacking there all forms of religion are of no avail."

The religious motives of reward and punishment which aim to bring about moral conduct through hope and fear are not to be derived from the natural laws of life. Good conduct requires the insight to shun the bad in one's own interests, as the consequences of wrong doing will recoil on their authors. Good conduct is preferable to bad because it is much more likely to evoke pleasant responses from one's fellow men than evil deeds are. The principle of reciprocity alone can ensure the welfare of human society. These are the all important "ABC's" mankind is very slow to learn but is gradually beginning to grasp in the course of its own hard but instructive experiences.

Heaven and hell as incentives have given way to social approval and disapproval. This means that regard for family, country, and humanity lead to a life of freedom, justice, and happiness—paradise on earth. Crime against fellow men spells legal penalties, ostracism, and misery—hell transferred to earth. Threatening souls with punishment and promising them rewards in a hereafter have been useless in bringing about a sensible social order. Our world and time are the arena of life. What follows death we can easily tell if we open a grave. Whether the dead can arise again after their bones have fallen apart is a question the priest and scientist alike can examine.

Men will never reach the ideal of righteousness, for ideals are unattainable. But they can gradually develop a communal life which will lighten the drudgeries of the masses, thereby making their lives more worth living. Bringing about the good life depends upon man alone.

Religions have been unable to prevent injustice and wars. The ambitious attempt to promote and preserve a life of order by supernatural means has miscarried. If history has not yet declared this judgment, it will in the years to come. It will respect the noble intentions of the founders of religions but at the same time it will pronounce them utterly impracticable. Religion can indeed bear good fruit in the hearts of those who are truly devout and who model their lives on the patterns of the founders of religion and live in accordance with their moral codes. But how many does that include among the 1,360 millions of Christians, Mohammedans, and Jews, and what means is there to lead them to it? The morality based on a future life has not sufficed. The judgment of the seventeenth-century Dutch Bishop Cornelius Jansen runs:

> The intention of abhorring evil and doing good merely in order to attain heavenly glory is not right and does not please God.

As long as education is based on the theory of superterrestrial reward and punishment, the fear of punishment after death is one of the mainsprings of action for believers. An educational system orientated only toward a god entails a perilous vacuum for nonbelievers. They must then rely on themselves individually for guidance, and that is not wholly desirable because the best results are obtained when the educational impact of a total culture imparts and supports one's moral insight.

At all events, with them the central moral problem is not fear of punishment as it is with believers. The words of the psalms, "Let all the earth fear the Lord, let all the inhabitants of the world stand in awe of him." (Psalm 33:8) finally break into a crescendo of terror, "My flesh trembles for fear of thee, and I am afraid of thy judgments." (Psalm 119:120)

They must know that the God punishes not only justly but also vengefully. He himself says that when you do not obey his commandments, "I will bring a sword upon you, that shall execute vengeance" (Leviticus 26:25) and "in anger and wrath I

will execute vengeance upon the nations that did not obey."
(Micah 5:15) The lengthy chapters 26 of Leviticus and 28 of
Deuteronomy pronounce curses, imprecations, and almost inconceivable punishments in such abundance and of such vehemence
that they must have put every believer into lifelong terror even
without the concluding threat:

> As the Lord took delight in doing you good and mul-
> tiplying you, so the Lord will take delight in bringing
> ruin upon you and destroying you.
>
> (Deuteronomy 28:63)

The idea of revenge is not alien to Christendom either, as the
passage in the epistle to the Romans shows where Paul draws
upon the Pentateuch:

> Never avenge yourselves, but leave it to the wrath of
> God; for it is written, "Vengeance is mine, I will repay,
> says the Lord." (Romans 12:19)

The Koran contains the same sentiments. Mohammed says in it:

> God forgiveth what is already done, but he will take
> his vengeance on the one who doeth it again, for God
> is almighty and full of vengeance.

At the time when the Bible was taking shape, the sages of India
were using totally different methods to teach men good conduct;
they used noble human beings to exemplify good modes of living.
An ancient Chinese treatise on ethics says:

> Loving the good without hope of reward and hating the
> bad without fear of punishment are qualities found in
> only one kind of men. Therefore men who are noble
> lay on themselves the responsibility of going the right
> way, thereby setting an example for others.

We know that amid the moral vacuum obtaining today, men
discount the value of noble lives as models and instead hold self-
interest decisive for good conduct. But recognizing the principle
laid down by Confucius achieves more than all the threats and
promises of a future life. Supernatural religions by their very

make-up cannot accept human behavior as based on nature—
a view entirely compatible with right and morality—because doing
so would dethrone every godhead. The education of humanity can
only be based on human nature, never on a divine orientation.
Goethe puts it in the following words:

> If God had been concerned with having men live and
> act in accordance with truth, he would have had to
> arrange things differently.

Christianity has been dominant in the Occident for nearly two
thousand years and during this time it has been teaching Western
man that the world is a vale of sorrows and that real life begins
only in a hereafter; it has thereby hindered him from bettering
his general living conditions and robbed him of incentives to
improve his lot. Belief in a future world paralyzes the strength of
those who in the face of boundless wretchedness on earth put
their entire hope for happiness in a heaven hereafter blessed with
the presence of God; worse still, it also provides excellent ex-
cuses for those in positions of power and influence to keep from
doing anything to make life better for the masses. Indeed, this
theory of a hereafter that will make up for the wrongs and
hardships people suffer on earth appeals all the more to the
powerful propertied classes, because it enables them freely to
enjoy their delights on earth, which are really more important
to them anyway than the notion of a compensating hereafter is.

It all depends on what angle we approach this question of
happiness. The majority of people in the Western world regard
morality as linked with God and a hereafter. This doctrine promises to give them in a paradise or kingdom of heaven the happiness
they missed on earth. The Church has continually used its immense
power to inculcate the view that God would make things right,
after death; so much so that men under this influence have not
been able to take their destinies in their own hands and on their
own initiative create a better way of life. But some day the
elemental force of events will open the eyes of the people and
of the Church.

When the ground begins to quake under men's feet, the labors of their fathers to crumble into dust, when they have to struggle for the ultimate essential—for bare life, when they are hungry, defenseless, persecuted fugitives, when out of the clouds bombs rain down upon them, and the horrible fantasies of hell are turned into hideous reality on earth, then and perhaps only then will men know that there can never be any adequate future recompense for these frightful experiences. An old Chinese proverb says: "When everything people owned has been blotted from the face of the earth, then one can begin to talk sense with them."

When God, who is all-merciful, all-wise, almighty, and above all the universal providence, knows of this misery and lets it continue, when he fails to shield humanity from this horror, then happiness after death loses the meaning it had for generations of the faithful. Nobody has sinned so grievously either against God or against man as to deserve such a visitation from God. Men no longer recognize the truth of the words of the Bible when it says: "With the Lord on my side I do not fear. What can man do to me?" (Psalm 118:6) They had put their hope in God; now they know what fear means and what men can do by venting fire and death out of heaven.

All this awakens the realization that it is not up to God but up to man to help himself when in trouble. He realizes that he must rely upon himself to overcome the mortal dangers threatening himself, his wife, and his child. He is not to wait for justice and recompense from God after death, after he is separated from his family in the grave, but instead he must work to produce justice for them and with them as long as he lives.

Then he is fulfilling his duty as a man. With a high sense of responsibility, he regards it as an act of true morality to resist injustice on earth and thus to bring a stone, albeit a small one, for the construction of that edifice in which alone justice and morality can find a dwelling place for coming generations.

Through his own efforts, man becomes serenely independent of destiny and of interference from supernatural powers. He builds up for himself an inner strength against hostile fate, which gets ever stronger the more fate buffets it and does not await redemption in a future world. He has confidence in himself and not in God, for no god came to his side in time of need. It is here on earth that man needs help; here he has prayed, here he has waited and hoped; now the horror of our times has shaken his reliance on supernatural illusions.

Mankind may see the crimson dawn of a new ideal of brotherhood made by the strength of men who are their own saviors and need no other help than that of men. Though might still goes before right—it takes time for a new order to develop—man stands firm, he knows that his salvation lies in the new ideal of mutual cooperation. Whatever may befall him, one thing no mortal hand can ever take from him: serenity of soul, his worth as a man, and his inner resolution. That stands firm over all injustice, over all the daily round of misery. In him the words of the Stoic philosopher Seneca are at work: "It is thanks to the free republic of humanity that there is a man who is unconquerable and proof against fate."

Anyone so emancipated can easily see that religion does not enforce morality and does not ensure the future of humanity. Ethical laws coming from without and making responsibility depend on supernatural powers cannot lead men to the good. Morality grows out of group life and behavior and is completely under the control of the laws and forces of the universe. In him the universe lives, thinks, and feels. Nature moves all things impersonally and brings men and suns into being and lets them pass away without aim or purpose

Uncreated, the universe is an eternal and self-existent system of order operating impersonally in and through itself. The laws and forces of the universe enable man to do good or evil according to his lights, his cultural conditioning, and his sense of responsibility to himself and to his fellow men. The firmer a man's character is, the more he relies upon his own strength; the stronger he feels the nexus to be between himself and his environment, the more noble his moral conduct becomes and the happier the response of others toward himself.

The root of moral actions lies in man alone and he himself determines his own moral worth. There is no difference between the laws of the cosmos and those which condition morality in man. They are operative in healthy men and need no supernatural power to account for them. As Kant says:

> Two things fill the mind with ever new and growing wonder the oftener and the longer we reflect upon them: the starry heavens above and the moral law within.

15. ERROR AND TRUTH

How pleasant life would be without care and want. So, the Bible tells us, it was at the beginning before Adam and Eve ate of the forbidden fruit, thereby bringing want and woe into the world. Ever since then we have been trying to regain that lost paradise.

Had Adam and Eve not transgressed, then, according to Judeo-Christian theology, everybody would have enjoyed eternal happiness. All of life's problems would have been solved, and everyone could have given himself over to full, undiluted enjoyment. Man would have known nothing of misery and sorrow and nothing of the meaning of help and consolation. These experiences would have escaped him, since without death he would have lived forever. Happiness would have been a part of life, as are the air and sunlight or the heart's blood pulsing through the veins. At harmony with himself and with the world, he would have felt at one with nature.

Thus man would have belonged to the universe and like it would have remained forever. Length of life would have been no problem to one who lived forever. Before Adam sinned, no evil had marred his unending happiness. Enmity had remained unknown to one instinctively possessed of the highest morality. Providing for the needs of life had occasioned no aches and pains. Everything had belonged to everybody, preventing all envy and greed. In the absence of all evil, no occasion for pardon could ever have arisen. The good had been a function of life in exactly the same measure as is the beating of the heart. Both had gone on automatically without any act of will. Morality had been as inseparable from the process of life as breathing and blood circulation.

The conditions of life must have been like that before the fall in paradise. The words and the sense of the Old Testament can mean nothing else. Under those conditions, therefore, man could have known no god of mercy and no redeemer, since he had no need or room for any. Ideas like compassion, forgiveness of sins, divine protection, liberation from evil, or whatever else one may call the religious acts of salvation which depend upon a god—these would have all been utterly meaningless.

In the same way, the sinless people in paradise, as they are conceived in the beliefs of Jews and Christians, could have known nothing of divine providence, as they had no need for it. Free of all those blows of fate and of all that earthly want in which, according to the Old Testament and the Gospel, Adam first involved us, man could have known nothing of god or Christ, of Mary or archangels, saints, churches, priests, religions, sacraments, or divine services. They would have been beyond every thought of man.

While men possessed eternal life and bliss, they could not have felt or thought about any physical or spiritual shortcomings, nor could they have evolved any notion of a supernatural being to help them, or of rites and ceremonies and places of worship to appeal to it with.

Let us go a step further and assume that the Biblical accounts of creation whereby Adam was created out of clay and the breath of God, and Eve out of Adam's rib, are not fairy tales. With it God would have completed his function for mankind. For man cannot expect to ask more than to have eternal life and bliss. And so with the act of creation God's task was accomplished.

Now we understand why something had to take place in order to make God and providence, church and priests, faith and religions, an absolute necessity for mankind. Adam had to become the great sinner. It was impossible for him to resist eating that apple so heavy with destiny. Had he known the consequences, he would have summoned up strength to resist the serpent's cunning and the woman's temptation. Then humanity would have always remained in its primeval happiness.

But the sin of Adam is only an invented pretext. If the theologians had not happened on this motive for the necessity of religions, they would have thought up some other framework in order to attain their purpose. The well-contrived fable of the sin in paradise, however, remains the source for the human philosophy that a god must exist and that revelations he granted are needed to round out man's limited knowledge. This story of sin also explains man's need for Christian redemption and for his nurture in the church.

Thus a serpent diverted the whole current of life. A serpent made man lose forever his eternal life and happiness on earth. Now man must toil and eat his bread in the sweat of his brow and full of trouble. His fields, cursed by God, now yield thorns and thistles, and since then women have had pain in childbirth. And hence man is afflicted with evil and death, and life is the botch it is. Instead of glorious earthly bliss, we spend ourselves in yearning for lost happiness. Fear of death grips us, want and terror are man's perpetual companions. The theologians have reached their goal: only Yahweh, Jesus, and Allah, and their three religions, can save mankind from the conditions of sin and death.

Such demands made on belief by the various holy scriptures no longer raise an echo in modern men. They know the doctrine of evolution and are aware that the cosmos is infinite and eternal in space and time and that man is the product of millions of years of evolution out of the animal kingdom. They know that men themselves in the dawn of history invented the Biblical God, his son, the heavenly throne, the angels, the next world, and the terrors of hell for the resurrected, in order to control the relations between man and man.

One may wholeheartedly recognize the lofty spiritual achievement of antiquity even though, as history proves, the idea of a god and faith is almost useless today in making for moral excellence, for a just and free life. When the thinkers of Egypt, India, and Palestine used their creation myths to order the relations of man to man, they exhibited broad understanding and moral strength. The attempt to regulate the course of life by means of the gods bespeaks a deep insight into human character.

Thus out of the interplay of natural events and human fears and hopes, antiquity created those concepts of faith we still admire in their surviving documents. To them belongs also the Bible of the Jews. In it Moses imitated the Egyptian Pharaoh Amenhotep IV, who lived generations before the legislation of Sinai, though Moses fell short of Amenhotep in majesty of thought. For as his hymns show, the Egyptian already then regarded the sun as the one great creating and preserving power on earth, and modern science fully agrees with him. In contrast to this, the personal God of the Old Testament is petty. Faith in him does not recognize the sun as the principle of all life on earth, but recognizes a loving, revengeful, scourging God the Father remote from the world of nature and operating only through miracles. Changing from the worship of many gods to the worship of one unwittingly adumbrates the natural order and the unity of cosmic processes.

The Pharaoh's worship of the sun is sublime compared with the belief of Moses, just as the sun is real and near compared with the anthropomorphic God of the Bible. Christianity adopted this god from the Jews. It added the more incomprehensible son of God, a man born of woman but turned into a god. With him it evolved a belief in three gods that must nevertheless be regarded as one person. The third member of this trinity is the Holy Spirit—thought and grace; it dwells in God but at the same time is also an independent being to be poured upon man.

Thus Christ and the New Testament were superimposed upon the primitive gods and the Yahweh of the Jews, and they are supposed to be the supreme purpose of our culture. The fundamental thought is that the happy time of paradise is past and gone forever. To regain happiness man needs the help of God, of the savior, and of religion. The Almighty and the sacrifice of his son Jesus are necessary in order to free man from the guilt of Adam. Only because of this guilt, wretchedness abounds everywhere. There is no need to explain to the suffering that the earth does not offer them joy; this they know from daily anguish and want. The worse they fare, the more important their faith becomes to them.

The priest consoles them with words; for their endurance of earthly suffering he promises them a rich reward in the beyond. The suffering masses have little room for the thought that they might have some claim to a pleasant life upon earth. Their faith teaches the very opposite. It promises them eternal bliss in heaven; it convinces them that everything on earth is vanity. If they were told that our planet affords everything necessary for people to live in peace and happiness, their jaws would drop. Their priest disputes it, and he is the messenger of God's word and will.

Ignorant of their true place in nature, they fasten their gaze on God and heaven; their goal in life remains to strive after them, and to attain this end they accept in blind faith the promise of the life to come. The universe does not perplex them, for the Bible explains exactly how God created the world and all living creatures. And the devil will get all those who doubt what God revealed in his book and Jesus in the gospels, those who doubt that God made himself and everything out of nothing, established religion, and instituted priests to proclaim his will, he will get those who doubt that Jesus existed from all eternity but was nevertheless born of a virgin and that he alone is able to give men salvation after death—yes, if anybody denies or even doubts these demands of faith, he forfeits himself to the devil.

On Judgment Day all these sinners will be delivered up body and soul to Satan and his tortures in hell. So people beware of deviating from the path of true faith. For them the salvation of their souls and the coming joys of heaven hereafter outweigh anything and everything life on earth can give. "For what will it profit a man, if he gains the whole world and forfeits his life?" (Matthew 16:26)

Since the institution of the Jesus church, the heart of the fortress of faith has been guarded by this bulwark of hope in heavenly reward and terror of infernal punishment. But just as in modern war, wooden breastworks no longer halt an enemy attack, so these ancient ecclesiastical ramparts no longer prove effective. The chief enemy is modern science, for its telescopes, microscopes, and spectroscopes have made wide breaches in the strongholds of divine beliefs. In order to eliminate this contradiction between faith and knowledge, the church accepts in principle the findings of modern science but contends that the secrets of life and existence lie outside the pales of science.

Now theology imagines that it has won the game, since, in its opinion, this admitted lack of knowledge means that the final cause of the universe can only be the love of God, who created and preserves all existence. Since nobody can prove that God is not the first cause of the universe, God must be in charge of the eternal processes of the universe and of mankind and every individual in particular. Nobody should be led astray by the teachings of modern science into abandoning his faith in God; "For the wisdom of this world is folly with God." (I Corinthians 3:19) Ultimate knowledge lies only in God and Christ and belief in them brings salvation hereafter.

This is what children are to learn in church schools instead of the doubt-instilling science taught in secular schools. This makes it simpler for the leaders of the Church to convince the parents to send their children to parochial schools, where the teaching of religion still often follows a curriculum derived from the time of Charles V and the older Roman office.

Education under church auspices caters to the mentality of two classes. One is composed of the well-to-do minority of the upper middle and upper classes, the reliable props of crown and altar. Its members gladly let the priests take care of the content of the creeds, rejoicing that these creedal statements fit in so neatly with their own line of thought. The other is the overwhelming majority of people not belonging to the children of destiny. Members of this class cannot simply and submissively swallow the doctrine of happiness in a hereafter. Over and over they ask themselves about the relationship between their toilsome lot and the universe, between their fate and merciful God.

They are aware not only that the Jews have a single god and the Christians have one god made up of three gods, but also that a great number of Gods, saints, and religions are found in various parts and among various peoples of the earth. Humanity has never been united on the subject of the single god and of Jesus Christ as his son. The three monotheistic religions of Judaism, Christianity, and Islam are not only at loggerheads with each other, but externally they are in conflict with the hundred other gods, creeds, and religions, each one of which claims separately that it has a monopoly of the true god and is the sole purveyor of the genuine faith. Indeed, the Christians themselves are not united in the Christian faith under their god the father, Jesus, and the Holy Ghost. Besides the several main church bodies mutually sundered by their beliefs, there are subdivisions into numerous sects, representing various nuances of belief.

Being unable in the course of two thousand years to come to any agreement, Christians have manifold conceptions about their god and Christ and are divided into diverse camps regarding the religion based on these divinities. One glance at this remarkable situation is enough to raise doubts about the dogmas of the Christian faith. The phrases of the creed about God having created everything, about his son coming to save all mankind, and about his will being done in heaven and also on earth, arouse a certain mistrust, especially in the face of the above considerations. For the very first assumption of divine omnipotence remains unfulfilled: the people of this god the father and god the son have to date been unable in their religion to come up with a single dogma demonstrably true.

In the middle of the twentieth century there are only about one billion three hundred and sixty million Christians, Moslems, and Jews believing in the one god Yahweh out of a total world population of three billion one hundred and fifty million inhabitants. Therefore a clear majority of the world's population are wholly strangers to this god and to Jesus. How is this god to be the almighty creator of the eternal universe and of all life when he is not mighty enough to enlist even half the people of the earth under his banners?

But a man may hesitate to doubt God and Christ for the above reasons, because conceivably the almighty might have motives for this imperfection, motives he hides from the understanding of limited man. Moreover, a man may think that it is no vital matter whether all the people believe in God and the Savior, so long as they become worthy, as it were, of divine grace and love.

Also, a man may know the doctrine that the Lord is merciful, helping the poor and oppressed and protecting the devout in every need, and that Christ is love and delivers from all suffering. And yet, though he knows all about this doctrine, he can only reply with Faust, "I hear the message clearly but lack the faith to believe it."

For where is mercy, where protection, and where love? The alleged aim of religion is to nurture mankind in moral excellence in order to find the meaning of faith in love of neighbor, but this faith has been turned into its opposite. For huddled in fear and terror, this neighbor has received no help from a merciful almighty protector and God, neither he nor his family nor his people. So he doubts whether God and the Savior are really truth and goodness guiding all things toward righteousness.

When balanced against destiny, faith proves to be too light. Possessed of a serene conscience and a sense of right judgment newly won, the thoughtful man turns his back on the otherworldly images of belief and asks himself: can I find in the universe the meaning of life, can I satisfy my mind and understanding and still the turmoil of my heart by bringing it into peaceful harmony in the quiet and eternal light of the suns?

His attention turns to that which is nearest to him. He needs no proof to show that he owes his being to the inner companionship between man and wife, his parents. From the teaching of evolution he knows the separate events of the origin of human life. He knows that the development of the human embryo roughly parallels the evolutionary development of the race. For the womb of the mother foreshortens to nine months the evolutionary processes that nature took millions of years to achieve. No exception touches these laws of life, and no man has ever been made in any other way. This common mode of origin and growth unites all people of whatever race and color.

Growth is linked solely with the conditions for life presented by our globe. Only on our sunny soil can life develop in the mother's womb; only by the plants and animals of this earth can man maintain himself. Neither is possible in the icy chill of the earth's neighbor, the moon. This link with our planet is the second common factor uniting all mankind. But man knows that his earth is a celestial body which derives light and warmth from the sun and with them the potentiality of bringing life into being. The sun is in truth the preserver of every living being. It is the third principle uniting us all and to which all are alike subordinate.

Our sun with its planets and with their moons, this solar system of ours, is, however, not alone in the spaces of the universe. We know that untold millions of other similarly constructed solar systems form our Milky Way, visible in the night sky with its fork-like, far-stretched whitish glimmer. But there are in turn an unknown number of such galaxies which reveal themselves only to our finest instruments. Modern cosmic photography has already detected more than a billion of these galaxies. By means of spectroscopic analysis we have established their movements and the kind of materials they are composed of. Newton's law of gravity and especially Einstein's general theory of relativity apply to these movements, thus proving their conformity to law.

The universe comprises a vast number of milky ways. If by spectroscopic analysis we examine the composition of the nearer and farther galaxies and if we compare their composition with the elements of earth and of its living creatures including man, we discover that the elements of earth and of the galaxies so far investigated are surprisingly similar. These light points originating from remote galaxies reveal the same elements composing our earth and everything on it.

Man is the product of earth and sun, parts of the unity called solar system, which with myriads of others forms the Milky Way cluster, in turn only one of many like it scattered through the infinite reaches. He partakes of the same elements with this whole, vast, eternal universe. By way of countless sequential processes in nature constituting demonstrable evolution, man is a part of the earth, a child of the cosmos.

All men are equal in their inherent relationship with the universe, in their sublime union with the stars. This is the fourth common denominator joining each to all.

These similarities extend to the life course of man and star. As all men come into life and leave it by the same natural development, so the heavenly bodies follow parallel courses of natural development. Their diverse forms exhibit the several phases of growth and decay as we know from the photographs of astronomers. Stars have their analogues in the dawning embryo, morning birth, forenoon growth, high noon maturity, afternoon aging until their red dusk light dims out in the night of death.

Every star, too, is subject to this cyclical process of birth in glowing white light and development through the phases of its gradual cooling until its final demise in darkness. Our earth is no exception, although no man need worry about that either now or for long ages to come, as the final stages of our planet will be enacted in what is for us an unimaginably remote future. Meanwhile the sun will be gradually growing weaker with age in the course of billions of years, until this decline will evoke such climatic and organic changes that we can not imagine any men in our present form remaining on earth. But when at last cosmic death will overtake the earth in the remote future, all its organic life will have ceased—whether men, plants, or animals. No reason for anxiety, however, need arise on account of this natural course of events.

Death and dissolution is not in itself depressing; it is only the operation of a natural orderliness which is perpetually active throughout the cosmos. Our dead are never completely dissolved into nothingness, for their traces remain ever preserved in earth, water, or air—the three different molar aspects of existence; and in the same way the death of worlds is not complete annihilation. Their smallest particles in the same way always serve again for the reconstruction of the universe, just as the residual matter of the dead is again incorporated in the raw material of life. It is this cyclical process of nature that spells the real immortality of the universe and of men.

In this respect, too, we are subject to the same laws as the cosmic whole. The physicist observes the minute components of the organism, the atoms, and the elements which we know comprise the material unity of the universe; and he observes what is for now wisdom's marvelous ultimate insight, that the smallest particles of matter express themselves as electrical charges with movements corresponding to those which our astronomers have found valid for the stellar world. The stars in space and the smallest building blocks comprising earth and man move in courses set by the same eternal laws. It is hard to contemplate or imagine anything more majestic than the unity of man and nature with the subtle underlying law governing all motion alike. It has been man's immemorial desire to get an understanding of nature and of his place in it. Nothing can appease this ancient longing better than the knowledge that in origin and destiny he is an intimate part of nature, a child of the sun.

The universe encompasses earthly man within its orderly and natural cycle of being. He no longer has any need for supernatural notions or any god above the world for comprehending life and existence, when the vast eternal source of being courses through his mind and consciousness and when the very essence of the universe dwells in his heart. The universe could give no more joyful reply to the questions asked of it by man.

Whence, then, come the world and life? This question no man, no science, can answer. Ultimates are beyond comprehension. Science can not explain how matter, motion, and life came into being. It can give an account of the composition, development, and movement of the cosmic bodies, but not of the ultimate ground of their being or of man's life. Certainly it knows that the ovum fertilized by a sperm can grow into a new individual but it does not fully understand the biochemical forces and processes involved. The microcosm of life is so delicately organized that it would seem to be rash to suppose its forces and processes will ever yield to a purely mechanistic explanation. Analyzing the atom into smaller and smaller components does not promise fully to explain the processes of life.

We may be able to establish that the ultimate base of matter is of an electrical nature. But even if we could demonstrate that protons, electrons, neutrons, and the like are the ultimate entities of the universe and that these are positive and negative electricity with attraction and repulsion, we should still hardly have come a hair closer to the problem. For what is electricity?

Just as in the course of history we can never reach a last chapter because every conclusion is the beginning of a further development, so we shall never attain to the first cause of being. It is true that each new piece of scientific knowledge brings us relatively nearer to the goal, but it makes no absolute change in relation to the goal which lies infinitely beyond reach. Just as we can never reach an infinite goal, so we shall never attain to the ultimate cause of the universe; to do so we would have to comprehend the universe fully in its totality in space and time. We cannot expect a complete understanding from a partial investigation.

Science may discover ever so much, still every new discovery will always reveal new questions and problems. The universe is boundless in space and time and so only partially available to man limited in his reach. In the presence of the eternal stars and their mute appeal, all that man's knowledge can do is to fill him with awe and humility.

Even though we may never know the ultimate cause of life, the question still rises: How did life appear on the earth? In order to be able to form life, the whole universe including the earth as a component must possess the innate capacity of producing life.

Thus the potentiality for the formation of life can lie only in the materials which have always been available. It can always develop so far as the atmospheric, climatic, and other conditions allow this process. When the necessary conditions obtain, life forms itself out of the material at hand. It is idle to postulate either the intervention of a god situated outside nature or the arrival of life after journeying aeons through icy space from another star system where it developed. For life is not different from everything else in the cosmos—a phase of mutation of form.

Out of the inorganic, a living organism can develop, given certain conditions. Life lies locked within what we regard as inanimate matter, even though we do not yet fully know the aboriginal transition stages. Some day it will presumably be possible for science to detail these processes without getting much nearer to the ultimate cause that puts together the primordial life particles. How life arose on earth and what the first germ of life was like are questions eluding comprehensive answers but requiring no mysterious supernatural explanations whatsoever. Perhaps in days ahead man will discover the "missing link" between inorganic and organic compounds, for the results of the American scientists Miller and McNevin, who are active in this field, already mark a stage on the road. Both managed in their physicochemical experiments to obtain from salicic acid, methane, and other materials, protein constituents like amino acids and molecular constituents of chlorophyll.

On this subject Dr. Harald Steinert writes the following in his treatise *On the Tracks of Primordial Generation*:

These experiments complete a chain of arguments. For they prove that "organic" substances can be artificially formed out of inorganic components under conditions we may legitimately suppose to have prevailed on the terrestrial globe during the period when life was generated.

Nevertheless, knowledge about the natural laws of the driving force which brings forth life are still beyond our ken. For the present the only honest answer to the inquiry about the cause of life and the mode of its origin is still the simple one—"We do not know." This is the point at which religion introduces the loving god. We, on the other hand, content ourselves with the naturalistic insights men have won and for the rest humbly admit our lack of knowledge. Faith is not thus content. It claims to know precisely how everything happened. For faith, the original creator and prime mover is an eternal and almighty god.

Life and the universe are natural; God is supernatural and unnatural. The attempt to explain the natural by means of a postulated unnatural is hollow and self-contradictory. The existence of a god, assumed to be outside the universe, would be a much greater marvel than the process of life itself is, even though we cannot logically trace it back to its origins. The reality continually enacted before our eyes is not to be explained by an invention of faith lying wholly outside man's experience and urged on him to accept only because he does not yet fully know the right explanation.

Nor do we need a god for us to orient ourselves aright toward nature in other respects. Wood that looks dry, dark, and unimpressive in winter suddenly thrusts forth buds and leaves in spring. Then in a little while we get from it a rich harvest of fruit. Is that the work of a god? Do we not rather know that the warmth of the sun has made the sap rise up in the delicate capillary tubes until it reaches the highest tip of the tree and that it was these events which made possible the whole development culminating in the fruit? Should it not then be the work of nature itself which brought about this production of leaves, flowers, and fruits? Must a god first have created the sun and made it bright and warm, have made the sap mount in the tree, have personally put out each of the buds, until at last everything is as we know it to be?

No. For all this there is no need for the help of any supernatural being. Not thanks to a god but thanks to itself, nature in magnificent unconsciousness disposes everything according to impersonal laws and forces inherent in itself.

Thus human life, too, is integrated into the universe; for, as we have shown, we are flesh of its flesh and soul of its soul. It is not a god which arouses in us the sense of being alive, but it is the universe itself; and to know ourselves to be at one with that seems to us something greater than all notions of posthumous happiness in a beyond. Man comprehends this mysterious universe when he stands on a lofty mountain and watches the sun rising in all its beauty over hills and valleys, or on the seashore when he sees it sink into the deep, in fiery splendor; or when the green cathedral of the forest encompasses him, a lonely wanderer at the early hour of dawn, and the call of the lark accompanies him as he goes rejoicing through the fields of golden grain. This universe is part of him and he of it. To feel and to know himself to be a tiny part of this fair world spells inner happiness for him and makes his soul resound in full and glorious accord with the symphony of life.

The soul of an unbeliever, if soul it is, should not thrill with sublime emotion in contemplating the universe, for allegedly only belief in God endows the soul with this capacity; without this belief the soul can harbor only low thoughts.

Has not many an unbeliever refrained from deliberately harming anyone and in quiet unostentation done kind deeds and been blessed with tears by the poor and wretched whom he helped? Has he not despite all the teachings of the faith experienced this deep and majestic experience of life to the very last fibre of his consciousness?

The chain of life has been bound about him. The same elements are in him as in them. The stars in their courses and the smallest cells of life obey the same laws. Man is within the universe as the most minute of generators with a billionth fraction of a cosmic horsepower. Humanity, earth, planets, and suns belong in ever-mounting internal and external capacity to this engine, right up to the gigantic generator which is the Milky Way. The central source of power is the universe eternally in motion and producing the current of events in nature.

This galactic generator producing the universal electric power, so to speak, is set in motion by laws without bounds in space and time. Astronomers have determined the paths and periodicities of the celestial bodies and also the rotational period of our galaxy, this cosmic dynamo. Let us be silent a little while. Let us allow this current of the universe to fill our hearts, which are striving toward it. Whence our journey begins and what its name and nature, the answer we feel and know: the sole guide and guardian of our lives is the universe of nature.

To control every force, to grasp life in its innermost essence, to create it out of matter, are things that require the totality of the universe. For this cosmic by-product man, this organized minimal mite of the universe, this insignificant little particle of the mighty process of nature, to demand that it must have the answers to the ultimate problems of being is tantamount to demanding of the eye that it should also be able to hear, and is the same as wanting to learn how one may jump over one's own shadow.

Nature imposes limits: not to hanker after unnatural phantasies in a mythical heaven, but to take ourselves for what we are— children of the sun and of the earth which have begotten us, nurtured us, and preserved us.

For these alone form the foundation of our life. The universe produces the power of thought and feeling within us; and it assigns us our limitations both within us and around us.

Knowing this we can not be haughty toward others of like parentage, whom we have kept up with on the ladder of evolution purely by chance and without any effort on our part. We have no reason to be too conceited about our bodies. Mankind does not display in them the only masterpieces of nature. In fineness of organs of perception great groups of the animal kingdom excel us. The eye of the bird, the nose of the dog, the ear of the roe all have a keenness beyond the normal range of man's sensory equipment. In length of life, too, we are beaten by some lowly turtles. Still and all, man is not too mean a specimen among animals.

But man likes to boast of his spiritual side as something uniquely magnificent. He looks down on everything disdainfully as if he himself had created his own spirit. And how does he set about this? He cites Raphael's brush, Michelangelo's chisel, Shakespeare's pen, and Beethoven's music. In Marconi he invents wireless telegraphy, in Lilienthal he foreshadows the airplane, and in Einstein he conceives the atomic age. But this human spirit he is so proud of also burns the pictures of the old masters, smashes antique statues, organizes autos-da-fé, destroys homes, and annihilates cities and countries. Through the abuse of the tools of civilization, man extirpates peoples and massacres the world's male youth meant to carry on the race.

If once the beast is aroused within man, he becomes more bestial than ever any beast could be. The tiger slays the buffalo, the martin eats the hen, and the snake chokes the lamb, true enough, but this is only from hunger to preserve their lives. One tiger never devours another, nor a snake its fellow snake. Nature does not have much fighting between members of the same species. Even between differing classes of animals there is hardly any senseless murder.

What may we pride ourselves on? That spirit which generates greed and delivers humanity over to chaos without sense or reason as an earthquake does a peaceful city? The cosmos itself knows no such devastations as man prepares for his like.

Only men bring about chaos for their fellow men. Just as the processes of nature go on in an orderly way, so through self-knowledge and a sense of responsibility men, too, can manage to live together peacefully. The universe proceeds on an unconscious level, but man has forfeited this capacity by rising above the instinctive animal level; so he must consciously order his ways by means of his mind and spirit.

The near future, the second half of the twentieth century, must demonstrate whether humanity has learned the one all-important lesson, namely, that moral order cannot be established within the human race on the basis of a supermundane faith. Will not man finally begin to abandon this notion and will he not by practical actions begin to create for all the conditions of a worthy life on earth without any mysticism about a hereafter?

The new civil state will be tolerant in the broadest sense, even respecting religions, but it will no longer regard them as desirable or necessary for regulating the relations of man and man.

Ever since men have created ideas of the gods, all religions have been under an unfulfilled obligation to show evidence of their ability to give humanity firm moral and ethical guidance by believing in a world beyond, however ideally conceived. This cannot surprise anybody for whom the course of history has always been an object lesson in self-denial. Our period does not need to obtain such wisdom from books. Those who survived have learned it personally, and our loved ones who were killed experienced it to an even fuller measure. Three thousand years of error have taken a terrible toll.

Chance and fate, two words with a single fundamental meaning, are the products of our cosmic origin and membership, and they ever accompany man through life hand in hand with the necessities embedded in nature. Within this context occurs every event of our lives from the first day to the last; nothing takes place in our lives outside this framework. Childhood and upbringing, years of maturity and work, old age and infirmity make up the external milestones along the road of life; internal correspondences are the play of children, joy in life, family happiness, and knowledge and wisdom.

The journey does not follow an orderly plan. Nor do events follow our wants and wishes. Ever and again we are brought to a full stop by the unexpected and the unforeseen, be it joy or grief. We can never be wholly sure of our path. We cannot avoid fate and chance, for they always lurk round about us. At times by skill and observation we can harness them to our purposes, but frequently our attempts miscarry. Oftentimes we are but the playthings of history, tossed to and fro, cast hither and thither, sometimes coming to the top but generally going under. Such is life. It is well for those who do not rely on visionary, otherworldly help, but who take a vigorous hand in the haphazard ups and downs of life, to make it as meaningful as possible.

Here then begins "the whole duty of man." No purpose resides in chance and fate, for the universe as such has none. If we wanted to ascribe purpose to the universe, we would first have to discover why the cosmos exists, why the processes of development, of growth and decay, follow their never-ending course, and above all why there are human beings. The cosmos is self-subsistent and derives its meaning solely from itself by following the eternal laws inherent in itself; in like fashion man derives his meaning from qualities within himself. But whereas the universe performs its processes unconsciously, man performs his activities with some conscious understanding.

Among all beings, at least on our planet, man alone happened to develop the powers of mind by which he can give meaning to himself and to the human community. The cosmic forces in man may be abandoned to chaos or given order and form. By ordering them so as to give value and meaning to individual and group life, mankind achieves aim and purpose for itself. Active awareness of these things should lead only to the following: saying yes to life, recognizing and respecting the urge of all to live, making this urge the basis of individual and collective life, and realizing that the earth offers enough for all to live in peace and plenty if people restrain themselves and work.

The meaning and significance of life can never lie in perpetuating injustice, in providing a happy life for the minority at the expense of the majority, and in consoling this majority with the promise of happiness after death when all life, joy, feeling, memory, and happiness are snuffed out. To provide the greatest possible happiness for all people is the aim, purpose, and attainable goal of life. This we can achieve if we mutually work to fulfill all the claims to happiness to which men have a natural right.

INDEX

230